# Paper Walls

David S. Wyman

# Paper Walls

America and the Refugee Crisis 1938–1941

The University of Massachusetts Press   1968

to my mother and father

# Preface

When German anti-Semitism turned to widespread terror in 1938, the world and most persecuted Jews realized that flight offered the only hope. For three years that hope remained a possibility. Then the Nazis blocked the exits. If, in the crucial years from 1938 to 1941, the world had opened its doors to the victims of persecution, the history of Europe's Jews from 1942 to 1945 would have been significantly different. Instead, the barriers held firm and relatively few refugees found asylum.

Whatever chance existed for solving the refugee problem depended importantly on the leadership and example of the United States. President Roosevelt acknowledged as much in 1938 by convening a 32-nation conference at Evian, France, for the purpose of establishing an international organization to facilitate emigration from Germany. Yet the total response of the United States, though more liberal than that of most nations, fell tragically short of the need. The pages which follow trace the unfolding of that response from 1938, the year when pressure to leave Nazi Germany became intense, until the United States entered the war in December 1941.

This book is critical of American refugee policy. It could hardly be otherwise, for the American record was not generous, and government officials too often attempted to obstruct refugee immigration. But the purpose of this volume is not to censure narrow-minded individuals or organizations. Rather, the investigation has aimed from the beginning at two other goals: to obtain a full and accurate picture of American refugee policy in the years 1938 through 1941 and to try to understand the forces and pressures in American society which explain why that policy took the form it did.

Although the word refugee appears to present no semantic problem, it is useful to clarify the meaning of that term as used here. From the above-mentioned intergovernmental conference at Evian in 1938 emerged a workable definition: people "who must emigrate on account of their political opinions, religious beliefs, or racial origin." By including "persons who have not already left their country of origin" as well as those who had by then fled but were not permanently settled, the term also covered those who might have been called potential refugees: individuals who needed to emigrate if they were to avoid the wrath of the controlling powers.[1]

Once World War II broke on Europe, the word refugee took on much wider connotations. People fleeing from the paths of war, but not necessarily subject to political or religious persecution, became refugees. For example, as the German forces pushed through the Low Countries in the spring of 1940, millions of persons flooded south across France. The Nazis shifted other hundreds of thousands of people about Central Europe in an effort to concentrate ethnic Germans in the enlarged Fatherland. Important as these vast population displacements were, they are not within the bounds of this study. In it the narrower definition of refugees is used: those who needed to emigrate to avoid persecution because of their political views or religious background. The scope is further limited to refugees from the Nazi regime.

Use of the term Jew entails considerable ambiguity. Because the Hitler persecution was in large part aimed at the Jews, the refugee problem mainly involved Jews. However, confusion results when one tries to ascertain what the word Jew meant in that period. To the German government anyone with one or more grandparents of the Jewish faith was in effect a Jew. But actually the German legal definitions were very complex. People with three or four Jewish grandparents were termed Jews. Those with two Jewish grandparents were also Jews if members of the Jewish religious community or married to Jews. Any others with two Jewish grandparents, as well as those with one Jewish grandparent, were technically "non-Aryans." In theory, non-Aryans had fewer legal disabilities than full Jews. In practice, non-Aryans were hardly less oppressed.[2]

Many whom the Nazis classified as full Jews, and of course a much larger proportion of non-Aryans, were members of Christian denominations. Others were nonreligious. These people were not persecuted for their religion. Nor were many of them oppressed for their political opinions. The definition devised by the Evian Conference met this problem by adding the category "racial origin." In the 1930's and the early 1940's the concept of a Jewish race was widely accepted, not only by the Nazis, but also by some opponents of anti-Semitism, the United States government's Immigration and Naturalization Service, and much of the American public. The problem of the Jewish refugee consequently was often ascribed to racial persecution.[3]

Since the notion of a Jewish race has no validity, it might be more accurate to say that while many Jews were maltreated because of their religion, Jews as a whole suffered oppression on account of their religious background. That is, they were persecuted because among their forebears were members of the Jewish faith. On this basis, the term refugee as used here includes people who emigrated or needed to emigrate because of their political views, religious beliefs, or religious background.

ACKNOWLEDGMENTS

Anyone who works for a long time on the subject of refugees—any refugees—must labor under a heavy burden of sadness. For me this burden was lightened by the sensitive interest and the cordial cooperation invariably offered by those to whom I turned for help. Though this brief notation cannot discharge my debts to these people, it can record my gratitude for their thoughtfulness.

The considerate assistance of the staffs of the Franklin D. Roosevelt Library, the National Archives in Washington, D.C., and the Manuscript Division of the Library of Congress expedited my use of the sources under their care. I am heavily indebted to Miss Hester Grover, Archivist, and Mrs. Kathleen Hanstein, Archives Specialist, as well as to the organization they serve, the American Friends Service Committee. The cooperation of the American Jewish Committee was extended especially through the helpfulness of Harry J. Alderman, Director of the Blaustein Library. Miss Ardith Emmons, Curator of the Swarthmore College Peace Collection, found time to facilitate my search for materials as did the Rev. Alan Seaburg, then in charge of the Unitarian Universalist Service Committee Records at Tufts University. I am grateful to Mrs. Anna J. Marshall and to Clyde F. Wilmeth for their kindness during my visits to the offices of the National Council, Junior Order United American Mechanics. Professor J. Joseph Huthmacher and Georgetown University made the Robert F. Wagner Papers available.

For enduring my questions and suggesting fruitful sources and insights I want again to thank Mrs. Dorothy Detzer Denny, Kurt R. Grossmann, Philip Levy, Mrs. Marjorie P. Schauffler, and George L. Warren. Clarence E. Pickett, since deceased, contributed a morning from a full schedule. In addition to conferring with me, Mrs. Robert C. Dexter, Varian Fry, and Professor Henry M. Hart, Jr., generously opened their personal files. I am deeply grateful to Mrs. Laura Z. Hobson for the use of important private correspondence and for help and encouragement when they were most needed. Phillip and Lucille Marsh have listened and assisted far beyond the call of close friendship.

Professor Howard H. Quint contributed many more hours of expert editorial help than I had any right to ask. Professor Ernest R. May read the original manuscript and suggested valuable revisions. Professor Oscar Handlin offered perceptive advice at a few critical junctures.

I found the staff of the University of Massachusetts Press always considerate and highly competent. I benefited especially from the efforts of Paul M. Wright, Manuscript Editor.

Professor Frank Freidel has been an unfailing source of intellectual leadership, professional guidance, and personal encouragement. He, more than anyone else, is responsible for whatever of value may emerge from this study.

My deepest debt is to my wife. Her constant support and uncounted hours of work, together with the thoughtfulness of two very patient and understanding children, have made this book possible.

DAVID S. WYMAN

*Amherst, Massachusetts*
*March 1968*

# Contents

# Contents

*It is a fantastic commentary on the inhumanity of our times that for thousands and thousands of people a piece of paper with a stamp on it is the difference between life and death.*

DOROTHY THOMPSON, 1938

Part I
# The Setting

# Chapter 1

# The American Scene

Three major factors in American life in the late 1930's tended to generate public resistance to immigration of refugees: unemployment, nativistic nationalism, and anti-Semitism. Debate, generally centering on the first two elements, often carried overtones of the third. Indeed, separation of these three factors is nearly impossible. For example, nativistic nationalism included a general dislike of aliens which at times shaded over into anti-Semitism. Many people, no more than a generation removed from being immigrants themselves, responded to several years of economic insecurity by wholeheartedly accepting the nativist slogan "America for the Americans."

## UNEMPLOYMENT AND RESTRICTIONISM

In 1930, in the face of steadily rising unemployment, President Hoover requested that the State Department seek administrative means to curb immigration. Through reinterpretation of a provision in the Immigration Act of 1917 which excluded persons likely to become public charges, a method was found by which entry of aliens could be almost completely ended. Before the depression, this "likely to become a public charge" stipulation—often termed the LPC clause—presented virtually no obstacle to immigrants. American officials took it for granted that any healthy alien who had enough money to reach the United States would be able to earn a livelihood after arriving. Under the new interpretation the government assumed that, because of the depression, a newcomer would probably not be able to find employment. Consequently, in order to satisfy the LPC provision of the law, an intending immigrant had either to possess enough money to support himself without a job, or he had to produce affidavits showing that relatives or friends in the United States would provide for him if he found no work.[1]

Since under the law responsibility for examining prospective immigrants to determine whether they qualify for entry into the United States rests with consular officials abroad, the Hoover Administration instituted the new LPC policy by issuing fresh orders to the American consulates. According to a White House press release of September 8, 1930, the instructions directed that "if the consular officer believes that the applicant may probably be a public charge at any time, even during a considerable period subsequent to his arrival, he must refuse the visa." With consuls requiring proof of substantial financial support, the effect was immediate. In December the State Department reported that underissue of the immigration quotas for October and November had been 78 percent and 85 percent respectively.[2]

The Hoover Administration intended the new LPC policy to be an administrative stopgap until Congress could enact one of several plans for cutting the immigration quotas which had been assigned to foreign nations under the National Origins Immigration Act of 1924. In 1931 a bill for a 90 percent reduction in all quotas passed the House and would probably have succeeded in the Senate by a large majority had not the legislative session ended before it came to a vote. In December 1931 the Democrats, because of their gains in the 1930 elections, took control of the House of Representatives. Antirestrictionist Samuel Dickstein of New York, the new chairman of the Immigration Committee, succeeded in keeping further bills for drastic cuts in the quotas from reaching the floor of the House.[3]

The Roosevelt Administration continued the Hoover Administration's policy of keeping immigration down by means of the LPC interpretation. Yet, small increases were recorded from 1933 through 1936, and a larger rise occurred in 1937. In part, these increments resulted from a steadily increasing flow of refugees out of Germany. In response to the worsening of the position of Jews and others in the Reich, President Roosevelt by late 1935 had moved to have restrictions eased for entry of German refugees. The State Department directed its consuls to give people forced to leave Germany "the most considerate attention and the most generous and favorable treatment possible under the laws." But by May of 1936 persecuted Germans were still finding it difficult to obtain American visas because of inadequately staffed American consulates and very stringent financial means requirements. The Administration soon increased the working force at the crucial Stuttgart consulate. Then, in December 1936 and again in the following month, the consulates received instructions "to the effect that consular officers, in reviewing applications for immigration visas, should bear in mind that the law referred to the likelihood of the applicant becoming a public charge, and not to the possibility of it." Immigration totals soon reflected this easing of the LPC policy. While German immigration to the United States in fiscal 1936 had increased 20 percent over that of the previous year, fiscal 1937 showed a rise of 78 percent above 1936.[4]

Seeing the tide moving against them after two decades of successes, restrictionists were not pleased with this turn of events. And when, in the wake of the German-Austrian *Anschluss* of March 1938, President Roosevelt indicated that full use of the German and Austrian quotas would be made for those suffering the rapidly heightening Nazi persecution, claims that immigrants were taking American jobs intensified and spread. Unfortunately for the refugees, the great increase in Nazi oppression which occurred in 1938 coincided with the worst phases of the "Roosevelt Recession" which had begun late in the summer of 1937. Unemployment, on the decrease since early 1933 and down to 7.5 million, jumped rapidly in late 1937. Only by mid-spring of 1938 did an emergency appropriation of five billion dollars for public spending start the slow upswing. Through 1938 and much of 1939 unemployment stood at between eight and ten million. The economy did not again reach the level attained in mid-1937 before World War II. Against this background restrictionists had little difficulty making credible their allegation that every refugee who entered the United States and found employment put an American out of work.[5]

Veterans of the anti-immigration struggle of the 1920's and after seized the occasion to press for a total stoppage of admission of foreigners. People who had formerly paid little heed to the restrictionists' viewpoint were now ready for their message. In a milieu of insecurity born of nearly a decade of depression, urban lower- and lower-middle-class elements were especially prone to fear and resentment toward newcomers. Particularly in New York City, the main area of refugee penetration, strong feeling developed against the refugee as a job competitor.

The patriotic and fraternal Junior Order United American Mechanics, restrictionist since 1853, saw each new arrival as "an added threat to the ultimate solving of the economic situation in the United States." Pickets in New York City, protesting radio station WMCA's refusal to carry Father Charles E. Coughlin's addresses, appeared with such signs as "Refugees Get Jobs in This Country. Why Don't 100% Americans Get Jobs?" Even among groups particularly concerned about refugees, similar complaints arose. A jobless young man's letter to the editor of the *National Jewish Monthly* asked why, with so much being done for refugees, little was being accomplished for unemployed Jewish youth. And on Capitol Hill Democratic Senator Robert R. Reynolds of North Carolina, leading spokesman for the antialien forces in Congress, read into the record of a Senate Immigration Subcommittee hearing two and one-half pages of advertisements from New York newspapers by refugees seeking employment. Said Reynolds: "If that is not competition with our people, I do not know what is." [6]

Agitation against refugees because of their competition for work focused most strongly on department store hiring. In large eastern cities this was obviously a powerful point of departure for any anti-refugee campaign. Many large department stores were Jewish-owned, and some undoubtedly did make a special effort to place refugees. The Brooklyn *Tablet,* at that time a reactionary Catholic weekly, mentioned that "we have heard" that Jewish businesses were pledged to hire refugees, thus throwing Americans on relief. In Elizabeth, New Jersey, a leading American Legionnaire charged that a large Jewish-owned store removed American workers to give positions to refugees. The management agreed that it had hired refugees, but denied having discharged anyone. In New York City similar rumors circulated so widely that Macy's, Abraham and Straus, Stern Brothers, and other stores issued public denials. Bloomingdale's swore an affidavit that out of a working force of about 2,500 it had employed 11 possible refugees during the preceding three years. In Philadelphia the *Evening Bulletin*'s inquiries of department stores employing a total of 15,000 workers obtained the information that over a five-year period no more than 25 refugees had been hired. In Pittsburgh a Better Business Bureau investigation of five large stores found that out of over 10,000 employees only seven were refugees and none of them held more than seasonal work. Accusations that refugees had displaced American workers in factory jobs in Shelton, Connecticut, led to a probe by the state's Department of Labor. Investigation of six industrial plants turned up a total of one refugee workman.[7]

Refugee aid organizations in the United States, extremely sensitive to claims that refugees usurped American jobs, worked hard to place their charges in noncompetitive positions. Where feasible, job retraining was given to newcomers to prepare them for occupations in which labor surpluses were minimal.[8]

Those who favored admission of refugees argued vigorously that these newcomers did not deprive Americans of jobs. One line of reasoning was that, even with full use of the relevant quotas, the possible refugee influx was tiny in proportion to the population of the United States. Moreover, since at least half of these immigrants would not be wage earners, the refugees could hardly aggravate significantly the problem of eight to ten million unemployed.[9] Proponents of this argument thereby indirectly indicated that they did not advocate any modification of the quota system, at least in regard to entrance of adult aliens.

A second argument to counter the "refugees make unemployment" reasoning stressed the fact that the immigrants would be consumers. Especially since this migration was a family movement, one could expect that the newcomers would provide markets which would lead to the creation of at least as many jobs as their wage earners would occupy. One writer assailed the notion that added residents increase unemployment and that deportation of aliens would open up more jobs: "Carried to its logical conclusion, this line of reasoning would lead us to believe that that country is most prosperous which has the smallest population." James L. Houghteling, United States Commissioner of Immigration and Naturalization, responding to the Senate Immigration Committee's request for comment on a bill to end all immigration, cautioned that "a drastic reduction in immigration may well represent a decrease in consuming power which will injure industry and increase unemployment far more than proportionately to the present influx of employable aliens." In general, restrictionists did not seem to press very hard to refute the claim that refugees, as consumers, provided as many jobs as they occupied. An official of the Sons of the American Revolution, referring to the refugee immigrant, played intellectual possum: "They say he is a consumer. I do not see the logic of that." [10]

Going beyond the assertion that entry of fugitives from Nazism would not worsen American unemployment, supporters of a liberal refugee policy declared that this particular immigration movement could have a very positive effect on the economy. Pointing to the special skills and capital that many refugees had already put to use in developing new industries in the United States, advocates of refugee immigration maintained that, far from displacing American workers, many of the newcomers were providing more jobs for them. Shoes and other leather products, photographic supplies, and textile prints were included in the wide variety of specialty businesses which did re-settle in the United States. Supporters of the refugees insisted that these transplanted industries not only would be noncompetitive with American businesses, but would increase United States exports by bringing their international markets with them. Almost all of the immi-grant enterprises employed far more Americans than refugees. In 1939 the National Refugee Service, the largest refugee aid organization in the United States, initiated a survey of refugee enterprises. Findings showed that in the more than 300 businesses responding to the ques-tionnaire over 70 percent of the 3,700 employees were American citizens.[11]

Some observers maintained that expansion of the population by im-migration might well help lift the entire economy out of the doldrums. Dr. Bernhard Ostrolenk of the City College of New York declared that the depression was largely due to the decrease in population growth resulting from birth control and immigration restriction. Im-portant industries such as construction, geared to an increasing popu-lation, had declined, tending to initiate a slowdown in all business. Ostrolenk maintained that, far from causing unemployment, immigra-tion had instead been an important contributing factor in the general prosperity of the years before the First World War. Dr. Felix S. Cohen, Assistant Solicitor of the Department of the Interior, expressed similar views. Pointing to the large increase of jobs in the period of greatest immigration and to the unprecedented unemployment which followed the imposition of restriction, Cohen concluded that the nation's eco-nomic system depended on an expanding market. Responding to the argument that every immigrant worker took a job from an American, he asserted that the assumption that there was a fixed number of jobs was untenable. Otherwise the unemployment problem could be solved by killing or deporting 12 million people. Cohen declared that the economic consequences of such a loss of consumers would be market crashes, shutdowns, bankruptcies, and at least 12 million *new* people on the unemployed lists. By the same token, he held that immigration would not increase unemployment; instead, it might help to revive the economy.[12]

In the effort to counter antirefugee sentiment, these various answers to charges that refugees were taking American jobs were widely circulated in newspaper and magazine articles, on the radio, in speeches, and in pamphlets especially prepared for this purpose. *Refugee Facts,* a pamphlet issued under the imprint of the American Friends Service Committee, advanced most of the arguments. The refugee influx had been very small and, because of the quotas, it could never become a flood. Only about one third of the newcomers would seek work, but all would be consumers. Some, bringing business and other skills, would re-establish firms whose goods were formerly imported. These enterprises would provide some jobs for Americans. Refugees must not, and would not, displace American workers. A total of 250,000 copies of *Refugee Facts* was distributed, 100,000 being used to reach the entire Protestant clergy. Writers, editors, college presidents, public officials, and congressmen also received the pamphlet. It obtained coverage in more than 100 newspapers.[13]

The effectiveness of the vigorous efforts made to show that refugees did not deprive Americans of jobs cannot be accurately evaluated. Restrictionists in and out of Congress remained convinced of the persuasiveness of the unemployment argument and continued to use it as their major theme until 1941 when economic recovery had dulled its edge. Conceivably, attempts in Congress to diminish or halt immigration might have mustered enough support for success if claims that hordes of refugees were taking American jobs had gone unchallenged. As it turned out, opponents of immigration failed to win a reduction in the quotas. But the unemployment argument did play an effective role in blocking the few efforts which were made to widen the gates. Increasing the quotas for adults never was a possibility in the face of restrictionist strength. And even when a movement arose to amend the law in favor of 20,000 children, the unemployment argument was called on to help defeat the effort. The economic situation, however, was not the only force working against refugee immigration.

## NATIVISTIC NATIONALISM

Nativistic nationalism refers to an attitude held in this period by most patriotic and veterans' groups but by no means limited to members of these organizations. It included a pride in "100 percent Americanism," an emotion which carried as a corollary a strong strain of antialienism. The isolationism of the era provided a matrix which encouraged this point of view. This type of nationalism was an outgrowth of long-term nativist impulses which had solidified in the immigration restriction acts of the 1920's. Indeed, major aims of these "100 percenters" in the thirties and early forties were to cut off all immigration and to control rigidly, if not deport, all aliens. Nativistic nationalists were vocally represented in Congress by such figures as Representatives John Rankin (D.) of Mississippi and Martin Dies (D.) of Texas and Senators Robert Reynolds (D.) of North Carolina and Rufus Holman (R.) of Oregon.

The goal of eliminating foreigners from American society reflected two nativist anxieties: concern to preserve American resources for American citizens and fear of the alien as a threat to American culture in all its aspects. In phrases typical of nativist expression, Senator Reynolds summarized the first interest: "Why should we give up those blessings to those not so fortunate? . . . Let Europe take care of its own people. We cannot take care of our own, to say nothing of importing more to care for." Explaining the American Legion's restrictionist stand, National Commander Stephen F. Chadwick declared that the nation had welcomed immigrants while the frontier remained, but in 1939, with 13 million unemployed, the country's responsibility to its citizens required that the gates be shut.[14]

Insight into fear of foreigners as a cultural threat emerges from a picture of immigrant life drawn in 1938 by fundamentalist preacher and editor Gerald B. Winrod of Kansas, leader of the rabidly anti-Semitic Defenders of the Christian Faith. Winrod warned that

> the names appearing on the places of business, the condition of the shop windows, the babble of foreign tongues, the language used on the signs in public places, the filth of the streets, the

greasy lives of the people, the utter disregard for American standards of morality, the flagrant violation of the Christian Sabbath . . . the whole atmosphere of these great unassimilated sections of foreign population is such as to cause serious concern.

Not only inlanders, limited in their contacts with aliens, were apprehensive about foreign influences. From Philadelphia the Junior Order United American Mechanics editorially expressed similar anxiety: "Let us stop immigration completely for awhile and give our present alien population an opportunity to become Americanized before they foreignize us." On another occasion, the same voice had praised North Carolina "whose proud boast is that it has the highest percentage of Anglo-Saxon blood of any state in the union . . . a thoroughly Americanized community which has not yet experienced the influx of foreigners that other states have had to bear." [15]

A scholarly presentation of the threat posed by entry of foreigners appeared in May 1939, published by the New York State Chamber of Commerce. Dr. Harry H. Laughlin, superintendent of the Eugenics Record Office of the Carnegie Institution of Washington, D.C., offered his 267-page *Conquest by Immigration* as "a research on the essential long-time parallel between conquest following successful military invasion and enforced settlement on the one hand and legalized, peaceful immigration and settlement on the other." The text presented such traditional restrictionist arguments as high incidence among aliens of mental disease, criminality, and appearance on relief rolls. The assertion that immigrants take jobs from American citizens appeared. To ward off the foreign threat, Laughlin recommended that a "personality or character-test" be required of prospective immigrants, that the quotas be reduced by 60 percent, that the deportation laws be tightened, and that all immigration be halted in times of large unemployment. In a thinly veiled burst of anti-Semitism, Laughlin suggested total exclusion of persons of "alien races or organizations" whose members already in the country "tend to resist assimilation in the United States." The book closed with the assurance that "no living nation need permit its own conquest by unselected immigrants." [16]

The nativism of many "100 percent Americans" included an undercurrent of suspicion toward people who were connected with international organizations or who were concerned with the welfare of foreigners. Nativists doubted the patriotic loyalty of "internationalists" because their interests appeared to be mingled with those of foreigners. The following exchange between Senator Rufus Holman and Ralph Emerson of the CIO Maritime Unions occurred at a Senate subcommittee hearing:

Senator Holman: The C.I.O. is not an exclusive American organization; it is an international organization, is it not?

Mr. Emerson: It is composed of a large number of organizations which have international unions.

Senator Holman: In other words, you are speaking as an internationalist, not as an American.

Mr. Emerson: I am speaking as an American.

Senator Holman: I doubt it. Go ahead.[17]

In the same hearings Senator Holman expressed the distrust of the Labor Department and its Immigration and Naturalization Service which was widespread among nativistic nationalists. He suggested that the department's attitude was one of "holding the door wide open." To James L. Houghteling, Commissioner of the Immigration Service, Holman stated: "I am trying to enlist the services of you people on the American side." Behind the feeling that the Immigration Service was coddling aliens lay the nativists' belief that swarms of refugees were eluding the immigration inspectors or were entering by use of visitors' permits which were not limited by quota restrictions. Actually the State Department issued visitors' visas, while the Immigration Service was responsible for seeing that the sojourners departed at the proper time. Nativists charged that these visitors were not being forced to leave. Another complaint, current since the start of the Roosevelt Administration, was that the Immigration Service allowed deportable aliens to remain in the United States, choking relief rolls or holding American jobs.[18]

The main force of the attack on the Labor Department fell on Secretary Frances Perkins. Convinced that she and her chief assistants opposed deportation of undesirable aliens, close control of the borders, and enforcement of time limits on temporary visitors, nativists concluded that Miss Perkins was an internationalist who valued foreigners over Americans. J. H. Patten of Washington, D.C., and Belton, South Carolina, a long-time leader in numerous restrictionist organizations, even undertook considerable research purporting to show that Frances Perkins (she "retains her maiden name, after the Red Russian custom") was not born to her presumed father, Frederick W. Perkins, but "was a foundling on Perkins' doorstep, 12 Worcester Square, Boston in the foreign quarter." Most probably, Patten revealed, she was born Matilda Watski of Russian immigrant parents. In this preposterous fashion Patten explained Frances Perkins' alleged partiality toward foreigners.[19]

Opponents of immigration repeatedly sounded the alarm that great numbers of refugees were slipping into the United States. From New York City, Messmore Kendall, president general of the National Society of the Sons of the American Revolution, spoke about "the horde of illegal entrants or aliens who have seeped across our borders." In Washington the National Defense Committee of the Daughters of the American Revolution heard that the United States was flooded with refugees, many of them Communist agitators. Senator Robert Reynolds read into the *Congressional Record* a clipping from Father Charles E. Coughlin's *Social Justice* which relayed a report "about the New York barges that slide out to clandestine meetings with ships anchored off the 12-mile limit to bring in overall-clad refugees with 'W.P.A. shovels' in hand." Coughlin commented dryly that the report was hardly credible because such procedures were so unnecessary. Refugees, he said, were "pouring into this country by the thousands on every ship" simply by using visitors' visas.[20]

Confirmation that claims of a huge refugee influx were making themselves felt appeared in the *Annual Reports* of the Secretary of Labor. The 1939 report pointed out that in the preceding fiscal year there had been only a very small rise in the number of nonimmigrants (the category in which visitors are classed) entering the United States. For 1940 a *decrease* of over 25 percent was announced. Both reports emphasized that the figures were "clear evidence that sensational reports to the effect that floods of alien visitors are being admitted to this country on any sort of excuse are not based on cold facts nor on the accurate records of a responsible Government agency." A *Collier's* editorial in early 1940, using immigration statistics to refute talk about "vast tidal waves of human flotsam" from Europe, provided further evidence of the currency of stories about a deluge of refugees.[21]

Rumors that hordes of refugees were landing on American shores reinforced fears about job competition, fears already deeply ingrained by years of depression. These economic insecurities, in combination with traditional nativist anxieties about an alien cultural threat, whipped up strong currents which restrictionists were able to ride in their effort to close the gates completely. One further important aspect of life in the United States in this period reinforced the cause of those who fought against immigration of refugees.

## ANTI-SEMITISM

The years from 1938 through 1945 saw anti-Semitism in America reach a peak. Groups such as Father Charles E. Coughlin's Social Justice movement, William Dudley Pelley's Silver Shirts, the German-American Bund, and a host of others throve in and contributed to this atmosphere. Electioneering in New York City in 1940, Joseph E. McWilliams of the Christian Mobilizers, an offshoot of the Coughlinite Christian Front, informed an enthusiastic crowd that "I am the anti-Jewish candidate for Congress!" McWilliams was defeated, but others with much the same viewpoint held seats in the national legislature. Republican Congressman Jacob Thorkelson of Montana detailed the conspiratorial operations of the "invisible government," an imaginary power structure which he linked to the "communistic Jew" and to "Jewish international financiers." Mississippi Democrat John Rankin favored the House with a fantastic eulogy of the religious-minded Stalin, a gentile, whom he contrasted with the murderous Trotsky, a Jew.[22]

Observation of organized anti-Semitic movements of the period reveals one side of the picture of prejudice against Jews. The German-American Bund, composed mainly of lower-middle-class German-born residents of the United States, in effect formed the American Nazi movement. Uniforms, swastika armbands, Nazi flags, Storm Troop units, the Nazi salute, goose-step marching, a score of camps for drill and for youth indoctrination served notice of the plans that these Hitlerites had for America. About 40 percent of Bundist strength was concentrated in the New York City area, especially Brooklyn, with sizeable contingents also in Detroit, Chicago, Philadelphia, and other cities. Estimates of the Bund's size varied. Fritz Kuhn, the American *Führer* until his sentencing to Sing Sing Prison in late 1939 for embezzlement of Bund funds, reported a membership of 8,300 to the Department of Justice in late 1937. To his followers, Kuhn is said to have claimed 180,000 to 230,000. More reliable estimates placed the number at about 25,000, including perhaps 8,000 uniformed Storm Troopers.[23]

The Bund blared propaganda through a youth magazine, a newspaper, and numerous public meetings. Praise of Nazi Germany, condemnation of Communism, concern to keep the United States neutral in the face of Nazi expansion in Europe, and denunciation of alleged Jewish control of the American government and economy accounted for the bulk of Bundist discourse. At a 1939 Americanism rally in honor of Washington's birthday, 20,000 Nazi sympathizers met in New York's Madison Square Garden to heil Hitler, boo President Roosevelt, and thunder applause at the mention of Father Coughlin. In a sideshow to the main event, Storm Troopers tried to eject newspaper columnist Dorothy Thompson for laughing loudly when a speaker declared that white Christians adhered to the Golden Rule because of their superior racial heritage. The boisterousness of Bund members was reflected in a series of disputes with American Legionnaires in 1938, culminating in a brawl between some of the war veterans and some uniformed Storm Troopers following derogatory remarks about President Roosevelt at a Bund meeting in New York.[24]

By late 1939 the Bund's influence began to fade following the imprisonment of Fritz Kuhn and reports of Bund ties to German government agencies by the House Committee on Un-American Activities. Because of its non-American orientation and program, the Bund could never have become a major force in the United States. But as a transmitter of German anti-Semitic propaganda it achieved a degree of effectiveness.[25]

A more indigenous anti-Jewish movement comprised the Silver Shirt legions of William Dudley Pelley. Born in 1885, Pelley grew up in an austere and religious New England family. Following a few years as an official in his father's business, the Pelley Tissue Corporation, he turned to Hollywood and a more literary application of his talents. As a writer of short stories for magazines and a creator of motion picture scenarios, Pelley achieved solid success in the 1920's. In an article printed in 1929 in *American Magazine,* Pelley maintained that he had recently died for seven minutes, had talked with departed friends, and had returned to earth convinced that the world of spiritualism was the real world. Following this interlude in the supernatural realms, Pelley initiated a movement based on spiritualism, to be accompanied in 1933 by anti-Semitism and a grandiose plan for Silver Shirt rule, including a corporate political and economic system. Early growth was rapid, but its extent is unknown because "Chief" Pelley kept the enrollment totals secret. Estimates for 1934, the peak year of Silver Shirt strength, range from 15,000 to 50,000. Members were mostly Protestants of old American stock, including many former Klansmen. Largely middle class in background, the group embraced numerous ministers and lawyers and tended to attract older people. Major strength was on the West Coast. By 1938 the movement had dwindled to about 5,000.[26]

Pelley's influence lay less in the importance of the Silver Shirts than in the circulation of his prolific literary output. In 1940 a staff member of the Institute for Propaganda Analysis estimated annual sales of all Pelley publications at about one million. The mixture of occultism, anti-Semitism, and easy answers to the unemployment problem attracted this sizeable demand which the "Chief," equipped with his own publishing plant, did not hesitate to meet. Pamphlets like *What Every Congressman Should Know,* with a cover sketch of the Capitol in Washington showing a giant Star of David atop its dome, trumpeted the "facts" about Jewish control of the Federal government, the press and radio, and the economic system. Included in a 35-page section "Jews in Our Government" were "Unofficial President" Bernard Baruch, Cordell Hull, Frances Perkins, and Ambassador William C. Bullitt. Most successful of a long series of periodicals was *Liberation,* a "Weekly Journal of Aggressive Patriotism." Concentrating on such themes as the Jewish-Communist conspiracy and the complete Jewishness of the "Kosher New Deal," *Liberation* spotlighted President Roosevelt's supposed Jewish ancestry, ran a feature called "News Behind the Jews and Jews Behind the News," and, commenting on a series of air crashes in 1938, promised "that as soon as the communistic Jewish Reds are cooped in this country that the accidents of the airways will drop dramatically!" [27]

With an insight best termed unique, Pelley presented his interpretation of the refugee situation. Announcing that seven million refugees had flooded the United States, the "Chief" saw them all as Jewish Communists, part of a conspiracy to take over the country. But, exulted Pelley, the alien Jews soon ran afoul of their American counterparts: "All at once our American sheenies awakened to the fact that these Germanic refugees coming from abroad were not at all satisfied . . . to do as American Jewish leaders instructed." Instead, the "Yiddisher Refugees" demanded important government posts and were telling "top Jews how to run America. . . . Up in Manhattan, Jews . . . suddenly realized that they had pulled Another Great Boner in allowing entrance to these Refugee Kikes. They were demanding Jewish jobs!" And, explained the Silver Shirt leader, American Jews thereafter ceased to call for open doors for refugees.[28]

Always more writer and pipe-dreamer than activist, the "Chief" in early 1940 disbanded the diminishing Silver Shirts but continued to publish. *Liberation* gave way to the *Galilean*, which Pelley in turn suspended in early 1942 after it was banned from the mails for attacking the war as an effort for advancement of British and Russian interests. In August 1942 William Dudley Pelley was sentenced to a 15-year prison term for criminal sedition.[29]

Unquestionably the most influential anti-Semitic leader was the Canadian-born priest, Father Charles E. Coughlin of Royal Oak, Michigan. His weekly tabloid, *Social Justice,* had a circulation variously estimated at from 185,000 to 350,000. Coughlin's Sunday radio broadcasts reached the public through more than 40 stations and necessitated employment of a staff of over 100 to handle the mail response. A Gallup poll reported that during December 1938 3.5 million people tuned in regularly and 15 million had heard one or more broadcasts. Sixty-seven percent of the regular audience and 51 percent of occasional listeners approved of the radio priest's opinions.[30]

Turning to outspoken anti-Semitism only in 1938, Coughlin rapidly generated a large Catholic anti-Semitic movement and changed the complexion of organized anti-Jewish agitation, previously mainly Protestant. The Michigan priest's power quite likely grew out of his ability to relate anti-Semitism to economic fears and resentments born of the depression. He alleged that international Jewish-Communist control of the financial system explained the economic insecurity of the working classes. Employment of Jewish refugees worsened the situation.

In the summer of 1938 *Social Justice* printed large parts of the long-discredited *Protocols of the Elders of Zion. The Protocols,* a document forged by officials of the Russian secret police and first published in 1905, purported to be plans for world domination drawn up at a secret Jewish conclave in Switzerland in 1897. Anti-Semites circulated the spurious document widely as proof of a Jewish world conspiracy.[31]

In late 1938 the radio priest moved to newer sources of material. In the wake of a wave of violent Nazi persecution of Jews, a Coughlin broadcast minimized the attacks and explained them as a defensive reaction by Germans against Jewish-inspired Communism. Newspapers, analyzing the priest's charges, found them based on Nazi propaganda. Further inquiry showed that an anti-Semitic article in *Social Justice* was almost a verbatim copy of a speech made by German Propaganda Minister Joseph Goebbels in 1935. At this juncture WMCA in New York and some other radio stations demanded pre-examination of Coughlin's addresses. When the priest refused, several stations stopped carrying his broadcasts.[32]

In the meantime, Christian Front organizations had been developing with Father Coughlin's encouragement. Composed mainly of Irish Catholics, mostly from lower- and lower-middle-income groups, and including many laborers, the associations grew strongest in New York City. Large Coughlinite followings also arose in other eastern cities. The New York City Christian Front group, which had been holding street meetings and urging a "Buy Christian" campaign, seized upon the WMCA dispute as a rallying point. In December 1938 it initiated mass picketing of the radio station on Sundays. Efforts to sell *Social Justice* on the streets increased. Christian Fronters participating in both projects made a practice of shouting anti-Jewish slogans such as "Down with the Jews" and "Send Jews back where they came from in leaky boats." One object of the verbal abuse was to provoke responses from Jewish passers-by, thus providing excuses for beatings. Forty to fifty of these turbulent street meetings each week continued to occur well into 1940. Though the 12,000 Fronters in New York formed the most active contingent, the Philadelphia group took part in street fights and spread anti-Semitic propaganda. In Baltimore, the Christian Front pressed the issue of hiring Jewish refugees. Cooperation between the Christian Front and the German-American Bund occurred in New York where Bundists joined street meetings and took part in the picketing of WMCA.[33]

In January 1940 a group of Christian Fronters in Brooklyn was arrested and charged with conspiracy to overthrow the government. Carried away by talk of Communists rising in arms, some young Fronters had heeded calls to form rifle-drilling "sports clubs" in order to be prepared, as Coughlin had warned might be necessary, to meet force with force. Seventeen were arrested after the Federal Bureau of Investigation discovered plans for a series of bombings and a reign of anti-Jewish terror calculated to foment sufficient confusion for the schemers to take over the government. Father Coughlin at first denied any relationship with the suspects, but a week later announced that he stood by them. One defendant committed suicide, charges were dropped against two others, nine more were acquitted, and the government discontinued the cases of the remaining five some six months after the juries failed to reach verdicts in their trials.[34]

The *Tablet,* weekly organ of the Brooklyn Roman Catholic diocese, wholeheartedly supported Father Coughlin and regularly printed his broadcasts. Not dependent on Coughlin for its opinions, this paper of 100,000 circulation was anti-Semitic in its own right, although it tried to disguise this penchant by repeated reference to its "Jewish friends" as well as by publication of letters from Jews similar to the communication which named Father Coughlin as "the best friend of the Jews in the country." [35]

Few Catholic editors or members of the hierarchy felt impelled to denounce Father Coughlin's anti-Semitism. Some exceptions among the Catholic press were the *Commonweal,* the *Catholic Labor Leader,* and the *Catholic Worker.* The Right Reverend Msgr. John A. Ryan, director of the National Catholic Welfare Conference, publicly criticized Coughlin's views. An effective statement by George Cardinal Mundelein of Chicago in late 1938 asserted that Father Coughlin was not authorized to speak for the Catholic Church and did not represent more than his own private opinions. Coughlin's broadcasts, nevertheless, continued until September 1940, when, reportedly, pressure from his superiors in the Church forced him off the air. *Social Justice* persisted into the spring of 1942 when it was suspended from the mails. After the issue of April 20, Father Coughlin fell into public silence.[36]

The Reverend Gerald B. Winrod of Wichita, Kansas, held the largest consistent following of Protestant anti-Semites. Although Winrod's Defenders of the Christian Faith had no organization as such, readers of his monthly periodical constituted his legions. With a circulation of 100,000, *Defender Magazine* featured fundamentalist Bible study, prophecy, missionary news, and Editor Winrod's views on world events.[37]

The Jewish-Communist conspiracy to rule the world was a major theme in Winrod's writing. *Defender Magazine* reprinted Father

Coughlin's statement on the *Protocols of the Elders of Zion* and the editor advised that the radio priest was "undoubtedly informed regarding international Jewish control." Just as world Jewry had forced American entry into the First World War through its control of the press, said Winrod, so the same people, in league with the Communists, were provoking war against Germany, simply because the Germans had broken Jewish control and set up a gentile economic system. The "Hidden Hand" of international Jewry operated everywhere; Jews even controlled the modernist Protestant Federal Council of Churches. Some insight into the conspiracy mindedness of the Defenders as well as an indication of the mental level of either the readers or their editor is afforded by an article entitled "Strange Isn't It?" "Is there a silent, subtle, unconscious Satanic intelligence at work under the surface? . . . How can the *sameness* outlined below otherwise be explained? Is it a mere coincidence?" Then followed a table with a column for each of four men: Mussolini, Stalin, Hitler, and Roosevelt. Under each name was listed the man's birth year, the year he came to power, the number of years he had been in power, and his age. Amazingly, these four items in each case totaled 3,880. By dividing 3,880 in half the reader would obtain the current year, 1940! One can imagine the typical Defender in his armchair, agog at this astounding discovery, and wonder whether Winrod was simply showing contempt for his followers or whether he could really have been dull enough not to have seen that a person's birth year added to his age will produce the current year and that the same result is obtained by combining the year in which a given event occurred and the number of years which have passed since that event.[38]

In addition to the four movements sketched above, more than 100 smaller anti-Semitic organizations operated in the United States in this period. George Deatherage of Albans, West Virginia, leader of the Knights of the White Camellia, distributed, among other literature, the German propaganda newssheet *World Service*. George W. Christians adopted Hitler's distinctive moustache and coiffure. James B. True, Jr., coiner of the term "refu-Jew" and representative of that nether world of protofascists who expected the Jewish conspiracy to burst into violence momentarily, turned out his *Industrial Control Reports* amidst a collection of reportedly patented "kike killer" clubs.[39]

Organized anti-Semitic groups were unable to unite their efforts. Why? The answer involves two principal factors. First, there was too much disparity in the make-up of the different organizations. Anti-Semites in the South, West, and Midwest were generally fundamentalist Protestants and anti-Catholic as well as anti-Jewish. While appreciative of the endeavors of the Coughlinites, they could not be expected to work in close harmony with Catholics. The nativism of the fundamentalists was another important element in their failure to join hands with the alien-flavored Bund and the Irish groups of the east coast. The second main barrier to a unified anti-Semitic or fascistic movement was lack of a leader acceptable to all. Most of the *Führers* were unwilling to take a back seat, and all of them, financially dependent on their own followings, hesitated to risk loss of that security.[40]

Yet, gropings toward an anti-Semitic, fascistic coalition developed. An American Christian conference, held in Kansas City in August 1937, mustered only a small attendance. A similar gathering in Chicago in November 1940 disbanded after holding only two of its nine scheduled days of sessions. At one time in 1939 signs pointed to the possible emergence of a man on horseback in the person of Major General George Van Horn Moseley (USA, retired) who called for Federal armed force to smash the Jewish-Communist conspiracy. But Moseley's stock declined when a dramatic appearance before the House Committee on Un-American Activities brought public attention to his ludicrous belief that conspirators were plotting to poison him. Had Gerald B. Winrod not lost his race for the Republican nomination for United States Senator in the Kansas primaries of 1938, he might have been in a position to have taken charge of a unified fascistic movement. William Dudley Pelley, however, had further reservations about the leader of the Defenders. Attending a Winrod religious address to evaluate the Kansas preacher's fitness for the chieftainship, Pelley was appalled to hear Winrod say that as a fundamentalist he must accept Bible prophecy which indicated that there would be 144,000 Jews among those saved at the end. On hearing this, the Silver Shirt leader decided that the Kansan would not do. " 'Winrod can't put that over,' said Pelley; 'that's too damn many Jews.' " [41]

Although organized anti-Semitism was more obvious and more often dramatic, the memberships of the hate groups by no means represented the total of anti-Jewish feeling in the United States. Prejudice against Jews permeated large sectors of the general population. While it is impossible to gauge this diffuse sentiment, some results of opinion polling provide useful indications.

The American Jewish Committee, with cooperation from major public opinion surveying organizations, has since 1937 kept close track of American attitudes toward Jews. A great many of the findings of these national opinion polls have been summarized in a study by Charles Herbert Stember and others entitled *Jews in the Mind of America*. One great advantage of the information presented in the Stember report is that the same or similar questions on a given issue were asked over a period of years, thus providing a valuable sequence of public opinion. In the matter of popular concepts regarding Jews, five polls from March 1938 through April 1940 consistently found that about three fifths of the respondents believed that Jews had objectionable qualities. When those holding this viewpoint were asked what traits they disliked in Jews, the most frequent answers given were greed, dishonesty, and aggressiveness.[42]

Nine surveys, extending from early 1938 through early 1942, showed that between one third and one half of the people questioned agreed that Jews had "too much power" in the United States. These and other polls indicated that this supposed Jewish power was thought to lie mainly in the areas of finance and business. Indeed, at least in part because of propaganda efforts by organized anti-Semitic movements, polls in 1940 and 1941 reported that from 17 to 20 percent of the populace looked upon the Jews as "a menace to America." In comparison with other "nationality, religious, or racial groups in this country," Jews were believed to be slightly more of a threat than Germans and far more dangerous than Catholics or Negroes.[43]

Indication that hostility toward Jews was reaching an ominous level came from a series of ten surveys conducted between 1938 and 1941. These polls found that a consistent 12 to 15 percent of the people questioned were ready to support a general anti-Semitic campaign. From 1939 through 1941, an additional segment of about 20 percent expressed itself as sympathetic toward such a venture. Surveys made in 1940 and 1941 showed that approximately 30 percent of the respondents would actively have opposed such an undertaking. These results point to the alarming conclusion that as much as one third of the American population was prepared to approve an anti-Jewish movement, nearly the same proportion would have stood against such action, and the remainder would have been little concerned. Parenthetically, although anti-Semitism reached a high level in the 1938 to 1941 period, anti-Jewish feeling continued to increase during the war years and arrived at its summit only in 1944. *Jews in the Mind of*

*America* shows that in the later 1940's prejudice against Jews declined sharply and throughout the 1950's it continued to undergo a slower, but consistent, decrease.[44]

Further evidence of the strength of anti-Semitism in the United States in the late thirties and early forties is revealed by activities of those organizations most heedful of the plight of refugees.

## THE RESPONSE OF THE GROUPS WHICH SUPPORTED REFUGEES

That anti-Semitism was a major element in public resistance to immigration of refugees can be deduced from the fact that people most concerned about refugees worked hard to de-emphasize the Jewish aspect of the problem. The previously mentioned pamphlet *Refugee Facts* took pains to distinguish between "Jews by religion" and other refugees of part Jewish ancestry who were "Jewish" only by the definition of Hitler's racial laws. The brochure, consequently, could state that almost one third of the refugees from Germany in 1938 were Christians. The YWCA pamphlet *Meet the Refugees* stressed that Department of Labor statistics showed 25 percent of the refugees were "of the Christian faith." In the matter of the proportion of refugees which was Jewish, the view of the general public that most refugees were Jews was more correct. A study made soon after the war indicated that some 80 percent of refugees in the United States were Jewish, while Protestants accounted for nine percent and Catholics for six percent.[45]

At times, the endeavor to de-emphasize the Jewishness of the refugee influx turned into an attempt to soft-pedal the existence of any refugee immigration into the United States. An effort was made to discourage newspapers from reporting the docking of ships bringing the fugitives. Behind this strategy lay anxiety that the public, exposed to story after story of ships unloading refugees, would believe the flow of immigrants really was a flood, particularly a Jewish flood. Friends of the refugees feared a negative public reaction might develop, setting the stage for tighter immigration legislation.[46]

Looking back from the present, aware of the fate which awaited Europe's Jews, it is not difficult to be critical of the strategy of muting the refugee issue. Because that approach accepted the idea that widening the quotas for adults was not a possibility, it appears to have been defeatist. Yet, to many supporters of the refugees, the real struggle was to keep the quotas intact in the face of a hostile Congress and to see that these quotas were filled despite various administrative difficulties. The unemployment situation joined strong currents of nativism and anti-Semitism to exert powerful pressures on Congress to stop immigration—or so it seemed to many informed people concerned about refugees. In their thinking, circumstances demanded primary attention to avoidance of the buildup of popular support for anti-immigration legislation which might well result if the general public felt that refugees were flooding the United States.

The policy of avoiding pressure for widening the quotas for adults and of minimizing the numbers and Jewishness of the refugee influx was by no means a Jewish phenomenon only. Rather, this strategy of de-emphasis seemed wise to most groups which supported refugees, including the American Friends Service Committee, the Young Women's Christian Association, the American Committee for Christian Refugees, and the Foreign Language Information Service.[47]

On the other hand, in view of the very great solicitude for the persecuted Jews of Europe shown by American Jews and by their press, the general absence in Jewish publications of this period of appeals for a more generous American refugee policy is particularly striking. For example, the *National Jewish Monthly,* organ of the B'nai B'rith lodges with memberships comprising 90,000, gave major coverage to the desperate plight of refugees. Yet the magazine sounded no call for liberalizing the United States refugee program, and the few muted complaints made about it were typically in the form of quotations from such sources as the *New Republic* and the newspaper *PM*. The only quota that the *National Jewish Monthly* spoke about raising was that of the United Jewish Appeal for funds for refugee relief. At the same time, this magazine was outspokenly critical of the British policy of tightly restricting Jewish immigration into Palestine.[48]

A similar pattern of compassion for the persecuted, little criticism of American refugee policy, no pressure for a more generous United States program, and extremely sharp castigation of British Palestine policy appears in other Jewish periodicals. *Opinion,* "a Journal of Jewish Life and Letters" with a strong Zionist bent, was enthusiastic about a conference which "demonstrated that the American Jewish Community can 'rise to the occasion' when the call goes out for aid to needy brethren overseas." The delegates "passed resolutions which assailed immigration restrictions in Palestine, urged establishment of a Jewish State in Eretz Yisroel, and endorsed America's policy of all-out aid to Britain." But of American immigration restrictions there was no mention.[49]

*Congress Bulletin,* weekly publication of the American Jewish Congress, also exercised caution regarding the question of refugees entering the United States. Most overtly active of the major Jewish organizations, the American Jewish Congress provided leadership for such undertakings as the boycott of German imports and mass meetings in protest against Britain's Palestine policy. Not reluctant to criticize the less outspoken methods of some other Jewish groups, the Congress itself agreed that

> there was a great deal of necessary caution exercised on the part of responsible Jewish organizations while a Commission of the United States Congress was studying the Wagner-Rogers Bill for the admission of 20,000 nonquota German children into this country. . . . Now the Committee has recommended the adoption of the Bill and it seems that the cautious restraint on the part of liberal and Jewish groups may be eased in order to help the passing of the Bill in the House.[50]

The American Jewish Committee, a leading organization for defense of Jewish rights, preferred to function more quietly, often through direct contact with leading people of public influence. The Committee's "refugee misconceptions campaign" was a carefully planned effort to correct impressions that refugees were entering the United States in large numbers, were displacing American workers, and constituted an exclusively Jewish problem. Many of the projects involved preparation of materials to be used by or issued through other media then the publicity outlets of the Committee itself. For instance, *Refugee Immigration—Facts and Figures,* an attractive pictorial pamphlet emphasizing the smallness of the refugee influx, appeared under the combined imprint of a Catholic, a Protestant, and a Jewish refugee aid agency. An article in *Current History* magazine in 1939, stressing the limited numbers of the refugees and their positive effect on the economy, was prepared, in close cooperation with the Committee, by Henry Smith Leiper, associate secretary of the Federal Council of Churches. Radio broadcasts by Walter Winchell and Albert Einstein relied on material offered by the American Jewish Committee.[51]

The effort to counter popular animosity toward entrance of refugees into the United States had still other features. The National Refugee Service worked hard at resettling newcomers in communities away from the east coast. Among several reasons for this program was the wish to avoid concentration of refugees in such areas as New York City. There the inclination to form enclaves fed stories of an alien flood, and their employment in noticeable numbers led to agitation against the immigrants as an economic threat. These factors not only brought hostility to the refugees and strengthened tendencies toward cutting off immigration, but also contributed to an increase in anti-Semitism in general.[52]

The various refugee agencies often coordinated their activities in carrying out these plans. Cooperation was not infrequent between several Jewish groups and the American Friends Service Committee (AFSC), an organization established in 1917 to put Quaker social concerns into practice. In a joint venture with the National Refugee Service, the Friends set up hostels in the Midwest as way stations for immigrants being resettled from the east coast. When, in early 1939, the Quakers received permission to administer relief to Jews in Germany, the American Jewish Joint Distribution Committee provided the bulk of the funds for the project. In the publication of the pamphlet *Refugee Facts,* the AFSC agreed to a request from the American Jewish Committee that the brochure be printed under the name of the Quaker group. The American Jewish Committee had drawn up the booklet as part of its campaign to correct misconceptions about refugees. The American Friends Service Committee made minor changes, had the statistics verified, and composed a short introduction to *Refugee Facts* which then appeared under the imprint of the Quaker organization. The American Jewish Committee assumed expenses for printing, distribution from AFSC offices, and secretarial help to care for the response to the pamphlet.[53]

Before concluding that playing down the refugee issue and its Jewish aspect comprised an excessively defensive policy, one must try to visualize the milieu of the late 1930's and early 1940's as perceived by supporters of the refugees. As has been seen, the setting was hardly favorable to either the refugees or their friends. But while the American scene afforded little room for optimism, the situation in Europe presented far bleaker prospects for the political and religious outcasts.

Chapter 2

# The World Scene

After coming to power in early 1933, the German National Socialist Party initiated 12 years of domestic oppression by moving to realize two of its long-standing objectives. In pursuit of the first, complete control by the party, the Nazis sought to suppress all dissent by subjecting present and past anti-Nazi politicians, authors, clergymen, and labor leaders to arbitrary seizure, imprisonment, torture, and death. In pursuit of the second, the racial purity of the German people, the Nazis sought to eliminate the Jews from their midst by an intricate variety of measures which by 1938 entailed the same terrorism accorded political enemies of the Reich. Both programs of persecution combined in the early years to produce a steady rivulet of emigrants, more Jewish than not because there were many more Jews than active anti-Nazis. When the campaign against the Jews turned to large-scale terror in 1938, the refugee flow out of Germany failed to become a flood only because the dikes and dams of the world's immigration barriers held firm.

Jews, including "non-Aryans," constituted less than two percent of the Reich's population in 1933.[1] Despite relatively small numbers and a high degree of assimilation, German Jewry was easily singled out because of its geographic and occupational concentration. Over 70 percent of this minority group lived in the 12 largest German cities and more than 60 percent of gainfully employed Jews were in commerce and trade. Many others followed professional vocations, especially law and medicine.[2]

German anti-Jewish measures, initiated in the spring of 1933, set into motion the first wave of refugee flight, an exodus which totaled perhaps 50,000 by the year's end. On April 1 the Nazi Party sponsored a National Boycott Day aimed at Jewish stores, products, lawyers, and doctors. Less than a week later, the Law for the Restoration of the Professional Civil Service was promulgated, excluding from public service nearly all people who were not Aryans. At one stroke, Jews were removed from administrative, judicial, public educational, and government clerical and laboring positions, as well as from railroad and postal service, public banks, and all other state and municipal functions. A series of decrees then followed cutting Jews off from medical practice involved with the public health service, from the press, theater, radio, and cultural pursuits generally. Colleges and universities received orders to limit Jews to one and one-half percent of new student enrollments. It was in this initial burst of persecution that the public burnings of Jewish books took place. Although these early decrees did not include expropriation of Jewish businesses, popular pressure, often encouraged by competitors of the Jews, and backed by boycott efforts, had begun to bring about the process of "Aryanization" or transfer of Jewish enterprises to non-Jews.[3]

Emigration in response to the earliest stages of persecution was facilitated by the situation then in effect regarding removal of property from Germany. After paying a 25 percent flight tax, refugees could generally take the rest of their capital out with them. But the picture soon changed as government manipulation of currency and exchange regulations served to confiscate larger and larger proportions of the emigrants' wealth. A refugee's capital, after deduction of the flight tax, could be converted into foreign currency only at rates set by the German government. By 1938 the rate had fallen to about ten percent, in effect a confiscation of the remainder of the capital. And in June of that year Germany prohibited further removal of capital from the country by emigrants.[4]

The second phase of the "cold pogrom" opened with the adoption of the Nuremberg Laws in September 1935. Under these measures the distinction between Aryans and Jews was clarified, since part-Jews ("non-Aryans") were relegated to the same legal status as Jews, both groups losing their citizenship and falling into the position of a subject caste. Intermarriage and sexual relations between Aryans and Jews were forbidden and German women under the age of 45 could no longer work in Jewish homes. "Aryanization" of Jewish businesses continued apace, usually at the behest of the Nazi Party, though expropriation was still not part of official policy. One result of the early years of persecution was that by 1937 one third of Germany's Jews required financial assistance, supplied by the German and overseas Jewish communities. Another outcome was that about 135,000 Jews emigrated from Germany between Hitler's rise to power and the end of 1937.[5]

In 1938 the government's policy of economic strangulation came into full sway. A decree in April ordered that all Jewish property valued at over 5,000 reichsmarks ($2,000) be registered with the government within two months. In November this information proved useful in facilitating the levying of a fine of one billion reichsmarks on Jewish holdings. The fine, an indemnity for the murder on November 7 of a German Embassy official in Paris by a Jewish youth, followed a night and day (November 9–10) of nationwide violence against the property and persons of Jews. On the same day the fine was ordered, a Decree for the Elimination of Jews from German Economic Life was handed down. By January 1, 1939, Jews were no longer to own retail stores or export, mail order, or other distribution businesses. These enterprises, then, had to be sold to Aryans, obviously at a loss. In addition, Jews were not to serve as managers or to hold other leading positions in any businesses. Prior to the events of November, decrees barring Jews from law and medical practice had been issued. By the end of 1938 the economic position of Germany's Jews was untenable: for the most part employment was available only in performing services within and for the Jewish community, a community whose resources were rapidly dwindling.[6]

Before focusing on the responses of other countries to the refugee problem prior to 1939, attention should center briefly on events in Austria earlier in 1938. On the twelfth of March Nazi troops occupied Austria without resistance. The following day union with Germany was proclaimed. And on the fourteenth Adolf Hitler arrived in Vienna to take formal control. For Austria's 180,000 Jews the *Anschluss* meant immediate persecution. Anti-Jewish measures which had evolved in Germany over a five-year period went into effect in Austria in two or three months. Severe dislocation of Jewish business resulted. Plundering and violence against Jews, not directed by the new government but also not inhibited by the police, were widespread. Mass arrests of Jews and anti-Nazis occurred. As a consequence, thousands crowded foreign consulates seeking immigration permits. Other hundreds chose suicide; in March the *New York Times* reported that up to 170 Jews were taking their own lives each day. April in Austria saw inception of a new Nazi technique, that of expelling refugees from the Reich without the papers required for entry into another country. Storm Troopers left 51 destitute Austrian Jews on a breakwater in the Danube at the frontier of Austria, Hungary, and Czechoslovakia. Forced out of Czechoslovakia, the fugitives entered Hungary, whence they were driven back to Austria and imprisonment by the Nazis. More fortunate were the few thousands who escaped illegally across borders into Switzerland and France before increased police guards sealed those frontiers. In the year following the *Anschluss,* nearly 100,000 Austrian refugees did succeed in emigrating. In the autumn of 1938 scenes of persecution not unlike those in Austria followed Nazi occupation of the Sudeten areas of Czechoslovakia after their cession to Germany at the Munich Conference. Meanwhile, based on experience gained in the 1920's, steps had been taken on the international level to assist the victims of Nazi persecution.[7]

## WORLD EFFORTS TO MEET THE REFUGEE PROBLEM 1933–1938

In the aftermath of World War I a succession of refugee problems arose. The Russian Revolution displaced White Russians; Turks persecuted Armenians; many Bulgarians, Greeks, and Turks found themselves under hostile rule because of boundary changes resulting from Balkan wars. The League of Nations accepted these early challenges. While the arrangements made were not always very favorable, by 1930 most of these hundreds of thousands of refugees had at least found new homes. Credit for this accomplishment, one of the League of Nations' few successes, belonged principally to Dr. Fridtjof Nansen, noted Norwegian polar explorer, who was League High Commissioner for Refugees from the inception of the office in 1921 until his death in 1930. Nansen located jobs and loans for refugees as well as places for their resettlement. He also devised the "Nansen passport," an identifying document for stateless persons, which won the acceptance of over 50 nations in 1922 and helped solve a major problem for refugees whose homelands had disowned them. By 1931 the League foresaw virtual solution of the refugee problem within seven years and accordingly arranged to disband the Nansen Office for Refugees at the end of 1938.[8]

While refugees of the 1920's found a world comparatively willing to accept them after the manpower losses of the World War, those who fled Nazi persecution confronted a world deep in depression. Nor was the economic situation the only disability which faced the new High Commission for Refugees (Jewish and Other) Coming from Germany which the League of Nations established in October 1933 to parallel the Nansen Office's responsibility for earlier fugitives. In order to avoid obstruction by Germany, the new agency was created as an autonomous entity and not located in Geneva. It thereby lost much of the moral authority attached to the Nansen Office. The High Commission even had to obtain its operating funds through private contributions. The functions of the agency, initially directed by an American, James G. McDonald of the American Foreign Policy Association, were basically twofold. First, the High Commission, though not itself directly involved in refugee relief or settlement projects, endeavored to stimulate fund-raising activities of private refugee aid organizations and to coordinate their efforts in the areas of migration, retraining, and resettlement. As a second task, McDonald undertook to negotiate with governments regarding passports, work permits, and admission of groups of refugees. As a rule efforts to gain acceptance of substitute documents for Germans who could not acquire or renew passports were successful. But almost nothing could be accomplished toward obtaining permission for gainful employment of refugees in the transit countries; that is, in Germany's neighboring nations which accepted refugees with the understanding that they would resettle overseas as soon as feasible. Attempts to find lands of final settlement met with a fair degree of success, partly because the flow of German refugees was not unmanageably large before 1938. Even so, resettlement by 1936 was becoming more difficult as receiving countries, such as those of Latin America, were increasingly insisting that they had room only for agricultural workers. German Jews did not have such a background, though retraining centers for refugees were in operation in Germany and in some transit countries.[9]

With the promulgation of the Nuremberg Laws, McDonald perceived that the Nazi objective was nothing less than to force the Jews out of Germany. In the face of what would clearly become a much more critical refugee problem, the High Commission was hampered by lack of authority because of its autonomous status. McDonald resigned at the end of 1935 in protest against the weak position of the agency. In his communication to the League of Nations, he pointed out that while private refugee aid organizations could probably keep abreast of the present emigration problem, the increasing need which would in all likelihood soon be forthcoming would overwhelm them. Aiming at the source of the difficulty, McDonald called for "friendly but firm intercession with the German Government, by all pacific means, on the part of the League of Nations" and its members and other states in order to convince the Germans to modify their refugee-producing policy. This exercise of "moral authority" he saw as within the province of the League since the refugee exodus constituted "a danger to international peace." Although the League of Nations did not undertake to influence German policy, it did provide the new High Commissioner, Sir Neill Malcolm, with funds for administration of the agency which was thenceforth closely connected with the world organization.[10]

By 1936 it was obvious that the refugee problem would not be solved by the end of 1938 when the Nansen Office and the High Commission were scheduled to disband. In addition, concern was beginning to develop for unification of the League's refugee efforts. The outcome of two years of deliberation on the matter was a proposal in May 1938 that the two League refugee agencies be discontinued as scheduled and replaced by one new office. In September the League Assembly approved the plan, and the office of High Commissioner for Refugees, with Sir Herbert Emerson at the head, came into being on January 1, 1939. The duties of the new agency were to provide legal protection to refugees, to help coordinate the humanitarian work of private refugee aid organizations, and to assist both private groups and governments in their efforts to facilitate emigration and settlement.[11]

While the League was spending 1938 trying to decide what to do about continuance of its refugee endeavors, the German-Austrian *Anschluss* had precipitated a major crisis in the refugee problem. In many quarters it was felt that the League of Nations' machinery and the private organizations would be unable to meet the challenge. Particularly, the League's efforts were weakened by its inability to negotiate with Germany regarding the refugee issue and by the absence of the United States from the world organization. Consequently, when President Roosevelt called a 32-nation conference for July 1938 with the purpose of forming another international refugee organization, the response was favorable. Although the Intergovernmental Committee on Refugees, the fruit of the July conference, was an admission that the League was inadequate to the refugee task, the delegates who brought the new committee into being repeatedly specified that its efforts would complement, not supplant, those of the League. Qualms about overlapping responsibility ended when, in February 1939, Sir Herbert Emerson, head of the League's newly formed High Commission for Refugees, was also named director of the Intergovernmental Committee on Refugees. Although the two offices remained distinct, full coordination of activity was assured.

What were the results of the League's endeavors to help refugees from Nazism? The responses of various countries, as shown by the numbers of fugitives taken in, provide an indication of the extent to which these efforts were successful. Estimates placed the total number of refugees, Jewish and non-Jewish, who had left Germany from Hitler's accession to power until the beginning of 1938 at 150,000. At this point, Palestine had absorbed the greatest number, 42,000. The United States, having accepted 30,000 to 35,000, was the second largest receiving country. The other major overseas area of settlement, South America, had taken about 20,000, the majority going to Brazil and Argentina. Inclusion of those who moved to South Africa and other non-European destinations brings the number of refugees who had been transplanted overseas to nearly 100,000. Of the roughly 50,000 remaining in Europe, it is impossible to know how many were satisfactorily settled and how many were considered temporary guests. In the case of the western European nations, the prevalent view was that most German refugees were expected to emigrate overseas as rapidly as possible, thereby making room for more refugees to utilize these countries of transit. France, which due to a falling birth rate and a tradition of asylum had been very generous toward Russian, Armenian, German, and Spanish refugees in turn, harbored probably 10,000 Germans. Half that many were in Great Britain, and 7,000 more had taken advantage of the Netherlands' very liberal attitude. Perhaps 20,000, almost entirely Jews of non-German nationality, had fled from Germany to their native lands, most returning to Poland.

Two or three thousand, in Austria and Czechoslovakia, were soon caught up in the second wave of flight from the Nazis. These statistics do not tell the full story, for they indicate the situation at only one point in time, the close of 1937. Most of the nearly 100,000 who had settled overseas by then had spent longer or shorter terms in western European countries of transit. France provides an example of this phenomenon. In late 1933 over 30,000 German refugees were in France. Two thirds of them moved on promptly. The remaining 10,000 became a fairly constant total through 1937, with new refugees entering to replace older ones as they proceeded overseas.[12]

By the end of 1937 the refugee situation had been relatively stabilized and until the crises of 1938 (the Austrian *Anschluss* in March and the pogroms throughout Germany in November) the problem of finding places for people who had the means and the desire to emigrate was met rather effectively. The original hospitable feeling on the part of countries neighboring Germany, the fact that the early refugees were able to bring out some capital and consequently were more attractive guests, the nearly open door of Palestine until 1937,[13] and especially the relative smallness of the migration were important factors. As the depression deepened and refugees began to accumulate in the nations near Germany, resistance developed to letting more fugitives enter. As the thirties passed, less and less capital could be removed from Germany. And in May of 1939, soon after the refugee situation had entered an extremely acute stage, the British, who had reduced immigration into Palestine in 1937, set permanent limits on all further Jewish entry into the Mandate. Most important of all was the haunting truth of James G. McDonald's warning of 1935, that the object of Nazi persecution was to rid Germany of Jews, and that, if Germany were not somehow brought to modify that policy, the refugee problem would become Herculean. When the situation did reach these proportions in 1938, the world was unprepared to make the sacrifices that alone could have solved the problem.

The quandary of the German Jews in the 1930's and the world's response to their plight raise two interrelated questions which have roots in the aforementioned events, but which go beyond 1938 in their implications.

WHY DID THE NAZIS PERSECUTE THE JEWS AND WHY
DID NOT MORE GERMAN JEWS EMIGRATE?

A problem of some importance is the German government's intentions toward the Jews. Until 1941 the main purpose of Nazi persecution of the Jews was to force them to leave Germany, not to exterminate them, a fact which warrants repetition because all postwar reflection upon Germany and the Jews is filtered through knowledge of the extermination policy. Awareness of that horrendous plan has a tendency to blur the picture of the events which led up to its inception and certainly it seems plausible in looking back to presume that from the beginning the Nazis were bent on wiping out Europe's Jews. Yet, while isolated statements can be found which hint that certain Nazis, including Hitler, had all along planned mass execution, the whole trend of events and evidence shows that the German government did not fashion the policy of systematic killing until well after the start of the war. True, the Nazis wished to be rid of the Jews, but until 1941 this end was to be accomplished by emigration, not extermination. Without question the Nazi policy of forcing Jews to leave was sometimes ambivalent and self-contradictory. World-wide dissemination of anti-Semitic propaganda and sending refugees penniless to other countries did not facilitate their resettlement. And undoubtedly the oppression had other objects besides forced emigration: it was lucrative, and the Jews provided a useful scapegoat. Nevertheless, the overall picture clearly shows that the original policy was to force the Jews to leave. The shift to extermination came only after the emigration method had failed, a failure in large part due to lack of countries open to refugees.

In 1939 Sir John Hope Simpson, a foremost authority on the refugee problem, wrote that "the deliberate and expressed object of Nazi policy in regard to Jews and 'non-Aryans' is . . . to compel them to emigrate." Soon after the *Anschluss,* the Nazi press warned Viennese Jews that "there is only one possibility for you: emigrate," and the Gestapo followed this up with constant pressure for speedier departures. In 1938, in both Germany and Austria, it became common practice to make release from concentration camp contingent upon agreement to quit the country promptly. Failure to comply brought return to confinement. A circular sent by the German Foreign Ministry to its diplomatic and consular officials in early 1939 stated plainly that "the ultimate aim of Germany's Jewish policy is the emigration of all Jews living on German territory." Even after the war began, the pressure continued. An American Friends Service Committee report in November 1939 stated that Jews "are not only being permitted to leave but are being forced from Germany." The Hitler government continued to encourage emigration of German Jews until well into the summer of 1941. Sealed railroad trains were provided on regular schedule to carry refugees from Berlin to Lisbon via Paris. In October, however, all legal exit from Nazi territories was ended. By this time other trains were being readied, but they would roll to the east and death.[14]

A pattern is evident in the unfolding of Nazi policy toward the Jews from 1933 through 1940. Until 1938 the technique for pushing Jews out of Germany was mainly that of economic and social pressure. When, by 1938, only a quarter of the country's Jews had emigrated, the Nazis shifted to terror to force out the rest. In Austria the new policy took effect with the *Anschluss*. In Germany widespread violence was delayed until the November pogroms. The terroristic approach was effective, but with most Jews finally ready to leave, there were not enough places to which they could go. The fact that the Nazis were again unsuccessful in their plan to force the Jews to emigrate played its part in the emergence of the policy of extermination.[15]

In view of the intention of the Nazis to make life impossible for them in the Reich, why did not more Jews leave Germany while emigration was still possible? One explanation is that the fairly strong financial position of German Jewry helped to cushion the economic persecution. The alternative of moving to a new land with greatly shrunken financial resources looked formidable. Another answer is that many Jews could not really believe that Nazi oppression would continue, much less worsen. Germany, after all, was a land of high cultural attainment. Bruno Bettelheim assigned the term "ghetto thinking" to this inability to comprehend that Hitler intended to be rid of the Jews by one means or another. Condemning it as voluntary ignorance of the rest of the world and of history, he charged German Jews with being "afraid that to know would mean to have to take action." Bettelheim, assuming that some sort of refuge was available for all, asserted that those aware of the realities of the world fled in time.[16] This interpretation is plausible for the years before 1938. But it does not explain why over 200,000 Jews were still in Germany when the war began, a year after violent persecution started.[17]

In truth, the pogroms of 1938 precipitated a rush for safety. In that year 140,000 departed. But too few of these fugitives were able to move overseas. South America doubled its refugee population during the year, but in so doing absorbed only 20,000. Palestine accepted 12,000 legally, along with a significant, but undetermined, number who evaded the immigration authorities. Perhaps 30,000 found their way to the United States. The rest jammed up in the transit countries of western Europe. France's 10,000 jumped to 25,000 and continued to rise. England's 5,000 at the start of 1938 was 25,000 in April 1939. Holland, Belgium, and Switzerland experienced similar surges. As it became clear that there were far too few places overseas for the refugees, these transit countries moved to close the frontiers. And the pressure kept building. Scores of thousands continued to seek immigration permits at foreign consulates, only to be turned down or put on waiting lists filled for years ahead. By the spring of 1939 enough people had applied for visas to the United States from Germany and Czechoslovakia to fill the quotas of those countries for from four to six years. Other quotas were booked further in advance, reaching 25 years in the extreme case of Hungary. Throughout Latin America doors swung shut. Already limited, Jewish immigration into Palestine was stabilized at a low rate by a British government White Paper of May 1939. Ten thousand immigrants would be allowed to enter each year from 1939 through 1944. In addition, 25,000 Jewish refugees could go in as arrangements for their support were made. This total of 75,000 was expected to bring to one third the Jewish proportion of the population of Palestine. Once this point was reached, no more Jews were to enter without Arab consent, which was but another way of stating that Jewish immigration would end. Then, in response to a large influx of illegal immigrants, Great Britian in July 1939 temporarily suspended the entire legal quota for several months.[18]

Unable to locate places of refuge, yet hard-pressed by the Nazis to leave, thousands grasped at desperate solutions. For a time, refugees with sufficient cash were able to buy their way out. Expertly forged passports and other documents could be purchased. Many Latin American consuls sold visas for hundreds of dollars. Cuban transit permits, for example, cost $300 in the spring of 1939.[19]

Others took ship to Shanghai where no visa was needed to land.

The flood tide of this Far Eastern movement occurred in the fall of 1938 when German and Italian vessels, unable to discharge their cargoes elsewhere, unloaded thousands of refugees at the Chinese port. By August 1939, 15,000 Jews who were leading a pitiful existence in Shanghai, many without work, were straining the resources of the Jewish relief agencies. Access even to Shanghai was barred by the occupying Japanese in the summer of 1939, though 3,000 additional refugees entered before the policy was effectively enforced a year later.[20]

Thousands more fled in ships that found no ports at which to land. When the refugee flow became bottled up in early 1939, German steamship companies, seizing the opportunity for profit, and acting with the connivance of the Gestapo, sent boatloads of refugees to Latin America without the documents required for entry. Barges and ramshackle vessels, their owners charging exorbitant prices, carried fleeing Jews down the Danube, across the Black Sea, and into the Mediterranean. Plans called for illegal entrance into Palestine. A few craft sank, drowning several hundred people. Some refugee ships sailed the waters for weeks in search of places to land. Among dozens of examples, two of the best known were the *St. Louis* and the *Struma*.[21]

Despite receiving notice that the Cuban government had nullified all landing permits already issued, officials of Germany's Hamburg-American line permitted the *St. Louis* to set out for Havana in mid-May 1939. On reaching Cuba, 907 of the refugees on board found that they could not land. Negotiations between American refugee aid agencies and the Cuban president came to nothing while the ship, forced out of Havana's harbor, wandered the waters off Cuba and Florida for nearly a week. Finally, as the liner steamed back toward Germany, refugee agencies persuaded the governments of England, France, Belgium, and Holland to accept the fugitives. Because more than 700 of the passengers had already registered for American visas and had their affidavits of support in order, the *New Republic* was outraged that the United States had not taken them in on temporary visas until their quota numbers could have become current. Deplorable as the episode of the *St. Louis* was, fate treated its passengers kindly in comparison with the 769 refugees who rode the *Struma* out of Istanbul late in February 1942. En route from a Rumanian port since December, the *Struma* was sailing for Palestine. Reaching Istanbul, the passengers were forbidden to land unless British Palestine officials would agree to their subsequent entry into Palestine. Although the Jewish Agency for Palestine warned that the only alternatives were drowning or return to the Nazis, the British authorities were adamant. Despite the protestation of the captain that the vessel was unseaworthy, Turkish officials insisted it be towed out of the port. Shortly after reaching open water, the *Struma* exploded and sank, leaving two survivors.[22]

An objective consideration of the emigration situation as it developed soon after Nazi violence became widespread in 1938 would deny Bettelheim's assumption that refuge somewhere, though perhaps far from ideal, was available for all German Jews. True, from 1933 until 1938, when emigration from Germany was not large, refugees generally were able to find new homes. But, even before the rush began in 1938, most countries had made clear their reluctance to take in large numbers of these persecuted people. What would have happened if the Jews to whom Bettelheim ascribes "ghetto thinking" had joined the migration before 1938? Almost surely the result would have been the same as it was when so many of them did try to leave after the pogroms of 1938: they would have found the doors to other lands rapidly closed and themselves stranded in Germany. The long, pathetic list of refugee ships, unable to find harbors open to them, testifies to the fact that the world of the late 1930's and early 1940's was a world without room for the Jews of Germany, not to mention the millions of their coreligionists in Europe.

# Part II
# The Diplomatic Effort

## Chapter 3

# The Intergovernmental Committee

The extreme persecution of Jews and anti-Nazis which followed on the heels of Germany's annexation of Austria in March 1938 rapidly erased all semblance of order from the refugee exodus. Reacting swiftly, the Roosevelt Administration within eleven days of the *Anschluss* invited 29 European and Latin American countries, Canada, Australia, and New Zealand to a proposed conference to facilitate emigration of refugees from Germany and Austria and to establish a new international organization to work toward an overall solution of the refugee problem. To assure both Americans and foreigners that no country would be called upon for major sacrifices, the invitations and other United States government pronouncements regarding the conference stressed that financing of refugee migration would continue to be borne by private organizations and that "no country would be expected or asked to receive a greater number of immigrants than is permitted by its existing legislation." The United States on its part contemplated no increase in the quotas, although President Roosevelt in his press conference following issuance of the invitations did indicate that the German and Austrian quotas would soon become fully available. In practice this move constituted an important gain for refugees since it ended the policy begun in 1930 of keeping immigration well below the quota limits by means of the "likely to become a public charge" clause. In late April another administrative step facilitated immigration from Austria, then the center of heaviest Nazi pressure for departure. A Presidential Proclamation merged the small

Austrian quota with that of Germany, opening the combined allotment to both German and Austrian refugees.[1]

Some observers saw other factors than sympathy for refugees involved in Roosevelt's summoning of the international conference. The editors of *Time* magazine believed that basically the proposal had been an attempt "to think up a practical way to express the U.S. Government's disapproval" of the *Anschluss*. *Newsweek* asserted that the move was part of an Administration plan to swing public opinion away from isolationism and toward "active opposition to 'international gangsters.'" Views expressed since by a member of the American delegation to the conference indicate that these comments contained an element of truth. An interpretation widely circulated in 1938 held that articles by Dorothy Thompson, emphasizing the need for a vital international organization to coordinate all refugee migration efforts, had stimulated the President's action in initiating the conference. But, as shown in a State Department memorandum of late 1938 summarizing the year's refugee program, the Administration's concern was less positive than appeared on the surface. The memorandum stated that from early 1938 the Administration had been under increasing pressure, especially from Dorothy Thompson and "certain Congressmen with metropolitan constituencies," to assume the leadership of world efforts to deal with the refugee question. After the Austrian *Anschluss*, demands mounted and gave every indication of becoming "both exceedingly strong and prolonged." As a result, the report continued, leading State Department officials, including Secretary Cordell Hull, Undersecretary Sumner Welles, and Assistant Secretary George S. Messersmith, concluded that a strategy far preferable to trying to hold off this pressure would be "to get out in front and attempt to guide" it, mainly in order to forestall moves for more liberal immigration legislation. Welles, according to this account, suggested an intergovernmental conference and Roosevelt approved the proposal.[2]

Actually, the evidence available provides no insight into the President's reasons for approving the proposal, for the records do not indicate the basis upon which the State Department persuaded him to accept the idea. A humanitarian motivation on Roosevelt's part may by no means be ruled out. Despite the State Department's analysis of pressures, consideration of the political realities of 1938 points to the conclusion that Roosevelt stood to lose more by taking the lead in calling the conference than he could gain. The pressure groups which the State Department wished to neutralize, obviously composed mainly of liberals and Jews, were certainly not impotent. But it is difficult to conceive of their having turned against the Roosevelt Administration under virtually any circumstances. On the other hand, there was crucial support to be lost, especially among isolationists and restrictionists, by taking a prominent part in efforts which would appear to assist refugees. In fact, both the summoning of the conference and the opening of the quotas to full use, a move coupled with the conference in the public mind, exposed the President to strong criticism.

The invited nations reacted favorably to the conference call. Within a month most had agreed to attend. Italy alone refused. Rumania, which had not been included in the plans in any way, asked that it be ranked with Germany and Austria as a refugee producer so that it could "dispose" of a number of its Jews. Although politely rejected by the State Department, the Rumanian request exemplified one of the dilemmas which constantly haunted thoughtful advocates of aid to refugees: If efforts to care for Germany's unwanted peoples should succeed, would not other countries be encouraged to make life impossible for minorities within their boundaries? [3]

In the United States the President's actions to facilitate migration of persecuted people seemingly drew a very positive response. General press coverage was heavy and almost wholly favorable. Important national organizations swiftly registered approval. For example, the executive committee of the Federal Council of Churches, representative of 20 Protestant denominations, was emphatic in its endorsement. The Young Women's Christian Association, assembled in its national convention, praised the plan for an intergovernmental conference. *Commonweal,* a Catholic weekly review, announced support for the project. The National Association for the Advancement of Colored People expressed satisfaction with the President's refugee plans. Organized labor, long restrictionist, also commended the steps taken by the Administration. Although convinced that unemployment ruled out any widening of the quotas, William Green of the AFL approved Roosevelt's proposals to facilitate movement of persecuted people from Germany and Austria and asserted that the United States should take the lead in offering them refuge. John L. Lewis, head of the CIO, also supported the new efforts to aid refugees.[4]

Applause was by no means unanimous in the United States. The

New York state convention of the Veterans of Foreign Wars disapproved of the President's extending a welcome to refugees and passed a resolution calling for an end to all immigration for ten years. In the circular "America—The World's Almshouse," the American Coalition of Patriotic Societies, "an organization to coordinate the efforts of civic and fraternal societies to keep America American," assailed the President's plan and urged the public to prevail upon Congress "to stop the leak" in the walls keeping foreigners out "before it becomes a flood." Criticism of the liberalized refugee policy also appeared in the Jesuit weekly, *America.* Late in July it warned of a "notable increase in the number of foreigners . . . during the past four or five months," mentioned reports that refugees from Germany and Austria were "pouring into the country on every boat from Europe," and stated that "quota restrictions from certain countries have been arbitrarily set aside with Government connivance." The Brooklyn *Tablet* asserted that taking in the homeless was a "work of mercy" and thus "commendable," but went on to ask if "true mercy . . . wrecks its own house to provide a doubtful shelter for another." [5]

Some voices in Congress also questioned the Roosevelt Administration's refugee policy. When the matter of appropriations for American participation in the international refugee conference reached a House subcommittee, Democrat Edward T. Taylor of Colorado wanted assurance that no changes in the quota laws were contemplated and that the proposed international meeting did not constitute "an invitation to use the United States as a dumping ground for all of these people." A public letter to Secretary of State Cordell Hull from Congressman Martin Dies (D.) of Texas sharply criticized the Administration's plan. Claiming that the outcome of the conference would be that the United States alone would provide for a more generous policy, Dies declared that instead the government's duty to the unemployed required an end to the influx of foreigners. Sympathizing with refugees, Dies suggested that Americans help them settle in Paraguay, a country which needed people to colonize its open lands. [6]

In an address to the House, Thomas A. Jenkins (R.) of Ohio delivered a more outspoken assault on the President's refugee program. Expressing clearly the anger of restrictionists at Roosevelt for ending the policy of keeping immigration well below the quota limits, Jenkins maintained that the President's proposals would "violate the immigration policies under which the Nation is supposed to have been operating for the last 7 or 8 years. . . . For years the policy has been to stay within 10 percent of quotas." Because of unemployment and relief conditions in the United States, the Ohio Republican felt the new immigration policy should be reversed. Jenkins also announced his fear that Roosevelt would next give Secretary of Labor Frances Perkins free rein to admit refugees as temporary visitors, a category without numerical limitations. In common with many other restrictionists, Jenkins believed incorrectly that the Department of Labor issued visitors' visas. As with all visas, the State Department assigned these temporary entrance permits through its consular officers. The Labor Department supervised only renewal of visitors' visas.[7]

Indication of general public feeling about refugee immigration appeared in a *Fortune* poll reported in July 1938, the month the intergovernmental conference occurred. Two thirds of the respondents (67.4 percent) agreed that "with conditions as they are we should try to keep them out." Only 18.2 percent took a position comparable to that of President Roosevelt, that "we should allow them to come but not raise our immigration quotas." Far less, 4.9 percent, wanted to "encourage them to come even if we have to raise our immigration quotas." The other 9.5 percent did not know where they stood on the issue.[8]

In April, closer to the initial announcement summoning the conference, the editor of the Brooklyn *Jewish Examiner* conducted a private survey of opinion regarding the possibility of raising immigration quotas 50 or 60 percent to allow entry of more refugees. Perhaps surprisingly, only two of six Jewish congressmen who replied to the inquiry favored the proposition and one gave qualified approval, while two opposed the idea and one was noncommittal. One of these congressmen thought it especially inadvisable for Jews to propose increased quotas at that time because of growing opposition to the Administration's recent steps to help refugees. Another felt that an effort to widen the quotas would ruin what possibilities already existed for aiding victims of Nazi persecution. Three rabbis declared that pressure for allowing entry of increased numbers of fugitives from Hitler would set off widespread public antagonism and could end in hurting the cause of the refugees.[9]

Through the spring of 1938 the Roosevelt Administration prepared for the conference at Evian. In April the President asked nine distinguished Americans to talk with him about formation of a national committee to coordinate the work of private refugee agencies in the United States and to advise the Administration in its efforts to assist refugees. In a memorandum written to brief the President before the gathering, Undersecretary of State Sumner Welles revealed the State Department's anxiety about possible public impressions that the Administration was contemplating any further widening of the portals. Welles's memorandum emphatically counseled Roosevelt to turn a deaf ear to any suggested changes in United States immigration laws or practices. At the meeting, the President spoke of his hope that the projected national committee would serve as a liaison between American private refugee agencies and the intergovernmental commission expected to arise out of deliberations at the forthcoming conference at Evian. He implied that the main task would be to secure financial support from the private organizations for programs developed by the intergovernmental commission. In reply to the question of possible government funds or loans to help finance the overwhelming task, the President answered

> that he felt that at least for the present it would be unwise to put forward any proposal which would occasion public dispute and controversy such as a change in the immigration quotas or appropriations or loans from public funds.

From this meeting emerged the President's Advisory Committee on Political Refugees, an organization vitally concerned with the Administration's refugee program through the rest of the Roosevelt years. In mid-May, at its first official meeting, the group elected James G. Mc-Donald, former League of Nations High Commissioner for Refugees, as chairman and Samuel M. Cavert of the Federal Council of Churches as secretary. Included among nine others on the committee were Hamilton Fish Armstrong, editor of *Foreign Affairs;* Paul Baerwald, chairman of the American Jewish Joint Distribution Committee, a leading refugee relief agency; Joseph P. Chamberlain, professor of public law at Columbia University; and the Most Reverend Joseph F. Rummel, Archbishop of New Orleans and chairman of the Committee for Catholic Refugees from Germany.[10]

Myron C. Taylor, who had recently retired as chairman of the board of United States Steel, agreed to serve as chief American representative at the intergovernmental conference, held in July at the

French resort town of Evian-les-Bains. Delegates from 32 nations participated. In addition, Poland and Rumania, anxious to arrange emigration of Jews from their countries, sent observers. Even Germany, approving of the assembly at least to the extent of being happy to supply the refugees which were its *raison d'être,* allowed representatives of German and Austrian Jewry to attend. Members of about 40 private refugee aid agencies appeared as guests and submitted memoranda of suggested action to a conference subcommittee set up to receive their reports. Unfortunately, a tendency toward disunity flared up among Jewish rescue organizations present at the conference. As a result, the 21 Jewish private groups in attendance could not unite on any set of plans to submit to the assembly. *Congress Bulletin,* weekly publication of the American Jewish Congress, later decried this "disintegration and rivalry" at Evian, calling it a "spectacle of Jewish discord and disruption." The *Day,* a New York Jewish newspaper, referred to the situation as a "disgrace." Reports from the conference stated that prolonged disputes over minor items among representatives of the Jewish agencies there were taxing the patience of governmental delegates.[11] Distressing though this performance was, perhaps one could at least draw from it the consolation that it disproved with certainty the notion of a united Jewish international power relentlessly pursuing its alleged goal of world domination.

In the opening public speech of the conference, Myron C. Taylor stated that the United States contribution lay in making the German-Austrian quota of 27,370 fully available. As the sessions proceeded, delegate after delegate excused his country from any increased acceptance of refugees. The British representative declared that for the most part the overseas territories were either already overcrowded, not suited to European settlement, or unable to accept many refugees because of political conditions. Some areas, such as parts of East Africa, might offer possibilities, but only for limited numbers. He excluded Palestine from the Evian discussion entirely. England itself, being fully populated and in the throes of the unemployment problem, was not available for immigration. The delegate from France stated that his country would do what it could, but had already reached "the extreme point of saturation as regards admission of refugees." The Belgian emissary reported that the same condition prevailed in his nation. The Netherlands could receive more immigrants only as refugees presently in Holland moved on to lands of final settlement.

Australia could encourage no large amount of immigration because, "as we have no real racial problem, we are not desirous of importing one." New Zealand's representative maintained that on account of economic problems only a limited number could be accepted into his land. He went on to characterize the Evian Conference as a "modern 'wailing wall.' " Because of the depression Canada had almost no room for immigrants. For the Latin American countries, unemployment was the main factor in the need to keep immigration at a low rate. The Dominican Republic, one of the last states to report, alone offered any substantial encouragement, volunteering to contribute large but unspecified areas for agricultural colonization. After most of the statements had been made, Sir Neill Malcolm, League of Nations High Commissioner for Refugees, told the delegates that the series of speeches had shown, as his investigations since 1936 had indicated, that large-scale settlement overseas was quite unlikely, at least for the present. The reporter for *Newsweek* expressed it more bluntly:

> Chairman Myron C. Taylor, former United States Steel head, opened proceedings: "The time has come when governments . . . must act and act promptly." Most governments represented acted promptly by slamming their doors against Jewish refugees.[12]

Before adjourning, the Evian Conference established a new permanent Intergovernmental Committee on Refugees and commissioned it to negotiate on two fronts. One task was to "approach the governments of the countries of refuge with a view to developing opportunities for permanent settlement." The other step aimed at persuading the German government to cooperate in establishing "conditions of orderly emigration," which particularly meant an effort to induce the Nazis to permit removal from the Reich of a reasonable amount of refugee property. The two objectives were interrelated: observers reasoned that if refugees were able to bring capital with them, potential receiving countries would be more interested in opening their doors. Terminating the conference on an optimistic note, Myron C. Taylor declared that the meeting had been only a beginning and that with permanent machinery being set up the outlook was promising for bringing about "a real improvement in the lives and prospects of many millions of our fellowmen." [13]

People concerned about the plight of the refugees recognized the importance of having had the problem accepted as an international responsibility. They also pointed to the new Intergovernmental Committee as a step forward, especially since, unlike the League of Nations' refugee organs, it could depend on American participation and could negotiate with the German government on the refugee issue. Nevertheless, the bulk of informed opinion agreed that the Evian Conference had failed almost completely in its major task, that of finding places to which refugees could go. Reporting on a thorough survey of editorial opinion, the *Contemporary Jewish Record* pointed out that a large proportion of the American secular press was dissatisfied with the outcome of the conference. Catholic, Protestant, and Jewish publications expressed the same disappointment. Commenting on the Evian Conference a few years later, President Roosevelt blamed the meager results of the meeting on the "overly cautious" attitudes of most other nations regarding acceptance of refugees.[14]

THE INTERGOVERNMENTAL COMMITTEE ON REFUGEES

True to the inauspicious circumstances of its birth at the Evian Conference, the Intergovernmental Committee on Refugees (ICR) did not accomplish much in its nine-year career. Recipient of little real authority, and for years no funds except a minimum for administration, the performance of the ICR failed to extend far beyond talk and paperwork. After the war former Undersecretary of State Sumner Welles wrote:

> The committee could have been responsible for an outstanding humanitarian achievement prior to and during the war years, but . . . the final results amounted to little more than zero. The Government of the United States itself permitted the committee to become a nullity.[15]

Most active during the 13 months of its existence which preceded the German invasion of Poland, the Committee saw the onset of hostilities cut short nearly all the work it had been able to initiate. George Rublee, an American international lawyer and the ICR's first director, can hardly be blamed for the small success which came of his efforts to negotiate with Germany and to persuade member nations to accept larger numbers of immigrants. Appointed in August 1938, Rublee set up offices in London and, despite his 70 years, attacked the refugee problem with energy and apparently with the belief that real progress was possible.

Rublee's first project, instituting negotiations with Germany for a plan of orderly emigration of refugees with part of their capital, encountered four months of delay. The initial obstacle was inability to assemble the five officers of the ICR for the first planning meeting with Rublee. Great Britain, the United States, and the Netherlands were willing to commit themselves to the program of the Committee at least to the extent of naming permanent representatives. France and Brazil, the other nations expected to send officials, were not. After a week's hesitation France relented. On August 31 the officers met with Rublee, despite the absence of a Brazilian delegate.[16]

Plans to begin overtures to the German government regarding talks with Rublee then had to wait over a month as the Czech crisis, eventuating in the Munich agreement, pushed all other European diplomatic action into the background. Two weeks later, in mid-October, the State Department and Rublee agreed that the British and American Ambassadors in Germany should immediately sound out the German government on the question of discussions with Rublee in Berlin. Once again, critical time had been lost, in this case because of stalling by the Chamberlain government which was anxious not to jeopardize its policy of amicability with Germany. At last, partly in response to a special communication from Roosevelt asking Chamberlain to approach Hitler personally on the matter, contacts with the German government commenced on October 18 with assistance from the British Ambassador in Berlin.[17]

Once the British were disposed to be helpful, the Germans chose to delay. Then, after two more weeks of waiting, Rublee began to receive intelligence that the Nazis were making plans for possible interviews with him. By the end of another week, these rumors became more concrete. Unfortunately, at that point, in early November 1938, the death of a German diplomat at the hands of a half-crazed Jewish youth set off large-scale violence against Jews throughout Germany. These pogroms threw the whole refugee situation into confusion and further retarded Rublee's mission.[18]

Finally, in mid-December, Dr. Hjalmar Schacht, president of the Reichsbank, ostensibly visiting London in regard to business with the Bank of England, arranged to present a plan to Rublee as a basis for negotiation. Schacht informed Rublee that he would be welcome in the German capital if discussion of the proposal seemed in order. The Schacht Plan provided for emigration over a three-year period of the 150,000 German-Jewish men and single women of working age. Another 250,000 people, made up of dependent women and children, would remain until the workers were settled and able to bring them out. The last 200,000 Jews and non-Aryans were old people and would have to stay in Germany, but persecution would end.[19]

In outlining the financing of his plan, Schacht estimated the value of Jewish property in Germany at about six billion marks. Under his proposal, one and one-half billion of this would be placed in a trust fund in Germany. Jews outside Germany would then raise an equivalent amount in foreign currency. This capital, in the form of a loan secured upon the Jewish property held in trust, would be available to emigrating Jews to use in establishing themselves outside Germany. Interest and amortization of the loan would be charged against the Jewish property in the trust fund. These payments would, of course, have to be made in foreign currencies, but, because of Germany's critical shortage of foreign exchange, the Nazis were unwilling to allocate any of the proceeds of their normal exports to facilitate operation of the Schacht Plan. Consequently, Schacht's proposal stipulated that the non-German currencies needed to service the projected debt would have to come from an increase of German exports over their usual level.[20]

Plainly Germany would be contributing little by this plan. Repayment of the large loan of foreign currency would be contingent upon increased sales of German goods in foreign markets, sales which could lead to opening new permanent outlets for German exports. An obvious consequence would be major harm to movements which were boycotting German goods in the United States and elsewhere.[21]

Resistance to the Schacht proposal appeared swiftly. Jewish leaders in Britain and France rejected an Intergovernmental Committee suggestion that a group of prominent American, British, French, and Dutch Jews meet to consider the plan. They feared a body of that sort "would lend an air of credulity to the idea that there is such a thing as world Jewry." The American State Department concluded that the loan would be impossible to raise under the conditions in the plan which was commonly looked upon as a ransom scheme by which Jewish refugees would be released in return for foreign cooperation in building German exports. Spokesmen for the American Jewish Congress and other groups supporting the boycott of German products joined liberal voices like the *New Republic* and the *Nation* in denouncing the proposal as refugee barter, extortion, and blackmail.[22]

Nevertheless, George Rublee spent much of January 1939 in Berlin negotiating with Dr. Schacht and, after Schacht's dismissal from the Reichsbank, with Helmuth Wohlthat, a German official representing Hermann Goering. To the surprise of many people, Rublee obtained modification of the earlier German offer. The new proposal, which came to be called the Rublee Plan, provided for establishment of a trust fund of at least 25 percent of Jewish property in Germany. This fund would pay for German-produced equipment and capital goods to facilitate settlement overseas of the 150,000 German Jews of working age. In effect, refugees would be able to take a portion of Jewish capital out of Germany in the form of usable equipment. Credits in the trust fund could also pay for the emigrants' transportation and freight expenses in Germany and on German ocean vessels. Once the workers were established abroad, their dependents, numbering about 250,000, would join them. The plan contemplated formation of a private international corporation to carry out purchase of capital goods and to manage related financial arrangements outside Germany. The 200,000 older Jews who were to remain in Germany would be allowed to live peaceably and, if unable to work, would be supported from Jewish property in Germany other than that in the fund for emigration.[23]

The Rublee Plan specified that the German-made goods involved must be used only for equipping emigrants or developing refugee colonization projects. In this way the most controversial aspect of the Schacht Plan, the question of increased foreign sales of German goods, was avoided. But Schacht's original proposal had aroused so much suspicion in regard to refugee negotiations with Germany that the Rublee Plan also met distrust in many quarters. The editor of the *Nation* saw it as an improvement over the earlier proposal, but even so as "an undisguised ransom scheme" and "still detestable" because acceptance of it would mean recognition of the Nazi policy of confiscation of Jewish property. The Voluntary Christian Committee to

Boycott Nazi Germany called for rejection of the Rublee Plan as did the Joint Boycott Council of the American Jewish Congress and the Jewish Labor Committee.[24]

*Congress Bulletin*, the publication of the American Jewish Congress, in February 1939 maintained that "the new scheme loses none of the objectionable features included in its predecessor, the Schacht Plan." But, the following week, Rabbi Stephen S. Wise, president of the Congress, admonished that the plan should be deliberated with an open mind, and an editorial recommended "careful and thorough consideration" of any proposal that might hold the least hope of saving hundreds of thousands of lives. Yet, two weeks later, this publication pointed to "the universal condemnation of the new Nazi ransom scheme," only to follow a fortnight afterward with complaint that the plan, now described as a "dubious consolation," had "disappeared into thin air." Finally, in May, *Congress Bulletin* approvingly printed an editorial from the Zionist *New Palestine* which asserted that no such agreement should be made with Hitler. Jewish opinion in general reached the same conclusion.[25]

*Congress Bulletin*'s ambivalence typified that of many people concerned about the plight of refugees, including those who decided to support the Rublee Plan. For example, columnist Dorothy Thompson, who had repudiated the Schacht Plan, thought the concessions gained by Rublee were important enough to warrant acceptance of the offer despite its shortcomings. She argued that, although the plan might increase German exports, it would prevent "wholesale suicides," and that a quarter of Jewish capital in goods was better than the little or nothing which was the clear alternative. Miss Thompson concluded that, "at any rate, it is easy to tell people inside a fortress to die for a principle rather than accept compromise." [26]

The State Department and the Intergovernmental Committee on Refugees approved the Rublee Plan. George Rublee, feeling that he had completed the limited mission to which he had agreed the previous summer, resigned as director. Sir Herbert Emerson then added the directorship of the ICR to his duties as League High Commissioner for Refugees. The President's Advisory Committee on Political Refugees and the ICR immediately initiated steps toward establishment of the private international corporation which under the Rublee Plan would administer purchase of supplies and capital goods for resettlement of refugees.[27]

Unfortunately, more than five months elapsed before the new organization took form. In late April 1939, nearly three months after the Germans had agreed to the Rublee Plan, Wohlthat expressed bitter disappointment to ICR negotiator Robert Pell that nothing concrete had yet developed regarding the private corporation. Wohlthat and Goering, concerned about adverse effects of Nazi violence on German foreign relations and foreign trade, were caught between the Intergovernmental Committee's inaction and the growing strength of forces in Germany which wanted to seize or destroy all Jewish property. Pell told Wohlthat that "a great deal of resistance had had to be overcome in the beginning," but the delay would soon end. In large part lack of progress was certainly due to the resistance that Pell mentioned. On that same date in late April the State Department was informing President Roosevelt of Myron C. Taylor's efforts to set up the corporation. Taylor had met "great reluctance in Jewish circles" because of fears that formation of such a corporation would bring accusations that "international Jewry" really existed, that it would imply approval of Nazi confiscation of Jewish property, and that implementation of the plan "might in some way assist the German Government." But by mid-April Taylor had succeeded in persuading some 70 American Jewish leaders that these fears lacked basis, and plans for the international interdenominational refugee foundation began to take shape. More than another month passed while people in England working toward the same end inched toward agreement on disputed details with the American group. Finally, on July 20, 1939, the new corporation, called the Coordinating Foundation, came into existence.[28]

Six weeks later war broke out in Europe, Britain and France withdrew from all commitments to aid emigration from the Reich, Germany in effect repudiated the Rublee Plan while reaffirming its desire to evacuate Jews, and the Coordinating Foundation and the Intergovernmental Committee went into virtual dormancy.[29] Assurance that the Nazis would have upheld their end of the agreement if arrangements for refugee resettlement had been made more swiftly is, of course, impossible. Yet, in view of the obviously critical nature of the problem, it is tragic that so little was accomplished in the year before the war began.

Throughout the months that the Intergovernmental Committee was dealing with Germany and devising plans to finance emigration, negotiations were also underway to try to find places to which refugees could go. But these endeavors were fighting the tide, for soon after the Evian Conference many ICR members, particularly Latin American countries, increased their immigration restrictions. One factor in the unwillingness of Latin American nations to take more refugees was the feeling widely held by their governments that the United States and Britain wished to push most of the problem onto them. Nor were the British Dominions, seen as another hopeful possibility, more cooperative. For instance, negotiations produced openings for 25 settlers to go to Kenya with the possibility that later their families might be allowed to follow. In a message to the State Department soon after the pogroms of November 1938, George Rublee emphasized the "indifference of the participating governments" and stated that except for the United States and the British Isles "doors have been systematically closed everywhere . . . since the meeting at Evian." [30]

Met in all directions by rising barriers to immigration, yet facing a problem vastly aggravated in November of 1938 by widespread Nazi terror against Jews, the Intergovernmental Committee increased its interest in colonization projects for refugees. Undoubtedly a desperate lack of any other solution induced the often unrealistic discussion of refugee havens which ensued. Isaiah Bowman, president of Johns Hopkins University and probably the foremost expert of the period on land settlement problems, had edited a thorough survey of world land settlement possibilities in 1937. Bowman concluded that "new land will accommodate too slow and small a stream of population to be of real social importance to the countries of origin." Chapter after chapter held out little hope except for a few small-scale opportunities. *Science News Letter* reported in December 1938 that three population experts whom it had interviewed had all stated that empty lands offered no solution to the refugee problem. The high costs of such settlement, lack of background of most refugees for such a life, absence of transportation facilities in proposed areas, the unsettled argument about adaptability of white people to tropical climates, questions of diseases and insects, unwillingness of nations to allow entry of groups large enough to resist absorption, and the extremely slow development of such colonies were among realistic factors cited by several writers. Myron C. Taylor of the Intergovernmental Committee, in early October 1938, saw "little promise" in mass migration projects, though he felt conditions required that no possible contribution be overlooked. But by mid-1939 the situation had become so hopeless that a message written by the State Department and signed by the President for Taylor's guidance on a forthcoming trip to Europe on refugee matters declared that "the problem in its larger aspects appears almost insoluble except through a basic solution such as the development of a suitable area to which refugees could be admitted in almost unlimited numbers." [31]

Only the circumstances of blank walls on all sides could have made such utopian solutions seem feasible. Plans appeared from all directions. Newspapers and magazines carried maps pinpointing the locations of brave new refugee worlds which were to arise in such tropical paradises as the Orinoco lowlands and the plateaus of southwest Africa. For months the State Department pursued with full seriousness and conscientious concern the phantom of a Jewish homeland in Angola. Prime Minister Antonio Salazar of Portugal was not at all interested, although Bernard Baruch and other Jewish leaders were. President Roosevelt dispatched a personal note to Mussolini to inquire about the possibilities of refugee settlement in Ethiopia. Although the President was "particularly struck with the appropriateness" of a plateau in the southwestern part of that colony and extending into Kenya, Mussolini rejected the idea and proposed instead the open areas of Russia and North America. Ambassador William Phillips, receiving the reply, asserted that "we Americans seemed already to be doing our part in that we had already a large Jewish population." The strenuous efforts in behalf of refugees led a writer for the *Jewish Workers' Voice* to comment on the benefits of being stateless:

> Powerful nations, enjoying sovereignty and freedom, have only their own countries to fall back upon. But Jewish refugees have a choice of many lands to pick from. If one prefers the humid heat of the jungles of Guiana, he is welcome to it. If someone else's taste runs to tsetse flies and similar blessings of East Africa, they are at his disposal. Verily, it is good to be a refugee. [32]

Despite the unrealistic aspect of the colonizing proposals, they did, in addition to providing a ray of hope in an otherwise almost totally dark picture, have the advantage of drawing support from groups with divergent viewpoints. The British government, especially after the November 1938 pogroms, hastened to inquire into refugee settlement possibilities in British Guiana, Northern Rhodesia, Tanganyika, and other places. The American State Department worked diligently on several colonization plans. Herbert Hoover in 1940 foresaw a state in the Central African highlands for ten million war victims. The United States Congress, hostile to any widening of American quotas for refugees, strongly supported Jewish settlement elsewhere. In October 1938 nearly half the members of Congress signed a petition calling on President Roosevelt to urge Great Britain not to carry out a rumored forthcoming stoppage of immigration to Palestine. Restrictionists like Congressmen Dies and Jenkins wholeheartedly favored colonization of refugees in uninhabited areas outside the United States. Even outspoken anti-Semites like the Christian Mobilizers advocated a haven for Jewish refugees in British or French Guiana or Kenya.[33]

Franklin Roosevelt, perhaps because of his interest in things nautical, geographical, and tropical, was intrigued by land resettlement schemes until his death. Soon after the start of the war, at a conference of the Intergovernmental Committee held in Washington at the President's invitation, Roosevelt, with accurate insight, declared that in the aftermath of the conflict the world would face a problem of 10 to 20 million refugees. The President called upon the ICR to begin scientific surveys of uninhabited areas in preparation for postwar resettlement of these millions. In December 1939, undeterred by the complete failure of his Ethiopia proposal of a year before, Roosevelt talked of one or two large settlements, covering a million square miles and supporting millions of people, where refugees might develop a "self-sustaining civilization" of their own. In 1940 Roosevelt brought Henry Field, an archaeologist and anthropologist of the Chicago Museum of Natural History, to Washington and put him to work on the secret "M" Project. Field and his staff were to compile a file of studies on settlement possibilities throughout the world. In action until late 1945, "M" Project produced 666 studies which were nearly totally useless because, among other reasons, they were kept classified until 1960. Field reported in 1962 that one of Roosevelt's plans for the postwar period had been a project to use desalinated water to make the North African deserts into fertile agricultural areas served by air-conditioned cities.[34]

President Roosevelt's most persistent hopes for refugee colonization centered on Venezuela, particularly the Orinoco River valley. During the autumn of 1938 the President asked geographer Isaiah Bowman for information on the Orinoco country. Bowman sent a long and discouraging letter summarizing the negative settlement potentialities in the region. Roosevelt, noticing that Bowman's report discussed only the lowlands north of the Orinoco, immediately responded with a request for data on the higher terrain across the river. Apparently prospects south of the Orinoco were no better, for a few weeks afterward Bowman forwarded a 26-page survey of "Settlement Possibilities in Africa." Slow to surrender his Venezuela vision, four years later an undaunted Roosevelt was corresponding with Aleš Hrdlička of the Smithsonian Institution on the question of postwar land settlement in South America with emphasis on the Orinoco basin.[35]

With support and cooperation from the Roosevelt Administration, the Intergovernmental Committee considered a procession of possible refugee colonization havens. Foremost among them were Northern Rhodesia, Tanganyika, Kenya, Nyasaland, the Philippine Islands, British Guiana, and the Dominican Republic. The greatest attention and hope focused on the British Guiana and Dominican Republic plans.[36]

An Anglo-American committee of experts, with an Army engineer and two airplanes on loan from the United States War Department, travelled to British Guiana in early 1939 to assess the suitability for settlement of 40,000 square miles there which the British had offered. Most of the land was within five degrees of the equator and 250 miles from the sea. Means of transportation to the coast, obviously crucial to any proposed settlement, were limited to airplane, a canoe and motor launch combination in the wet season, and a crude cattle trail suitable for horses and pack animals. After considerable searching, the commission located some mountain valleys with good soil in this region. The survey team's report concluded that conditions warranted further study and experimental small-scale settlement in order to determine what the actual possibilities were. Accordingly, planning began for settlement of 5,000 selected young colonists at an estimated cost of three million dollars. Despite the guarded optimism of the survey commission, some observers were very skeptical in view of the equatorial climate and the danger of tropical diseases. Yet, although the outbreak of war multiplied problems, plans went forward to send the first 500 settlers by June 1940. A report the following November that a small refugee settlement had been planted 50 miles from the coast marked the end of the dream of a major refugee haven in this tropical region.[37]

Soon after the Evian Conference, the Dominican Republic made a confidential offer to the Intergovernmental Committee to receive 50,000 to 100,000 refugees as agricultural colonists. An important motivation behind the overture was General Rafael Trujillo's wish to increase the white population of his country. Early State Department doubts regarding the proposition melted as other doors shut and the November 1938 pogroms increased the need for places of refuge. In March 1939 the President's Advisory Committee, in close cooperation with the State Department, sent a commission, including experts from the United States Department of Agriculture, to survey the potentialities for refugee settlement. The commission reported that 29,000 families could eventually be accommodated and recommended a trial settlement of 200 families.[38]

The President's Advisory Committee then approached James N. Rosenberg, a lawyer and chairman of Agro-Joint, a Joint Distribution Committee subsidiary which had successfully settled 50,000 Jewish families on the land in Russia between 1924 and 1938. With encouragement and help from President Roosevelt and the State Department, Rosenberg obtained assurances of cooperation from the Dominican government in the fall of 1939 and went on to establish the Dominican Republic Settlement Association, Inc. (DORSA), financed largely by Agro-Joint funds. In January 1940 a contract between DORSA and the Dominican Republic assured full citizenship and all civil, religious, and economic rights to the settlers. Trujillo provided a personal estate of 26,000 acres at Sosua, on the north shore of the island, accepting stock in the corporation as payment. The Sosua site included 5,000 acres of cultivable fields, good timberland, sufficient water, buildings enough for 200 people, and a harbor ten miles from a deep sea port. A prevailing sea breeze brought dependable relief from the semitropical heat. Large adjoining tracts of land, mostly government owned, would be available for later expansion. The colony enjoyed a tax-exempt status, valid as long as it adhered to its agreement to avoid undertakings which would compete with Dominican business.[39]

In view of the cooperation of the Dominican government, the

continuing support of the United States Departments of State and Agriculture, the careful investigation and planning, and the favorable features of Sosua itself, one might expect that if any refugee haven were to succeed this one would. In fact, supporters of the project and many others looked upon Sosua as a test tube, important because it would prove to other Latin American nations that refugee colonization was workable and could be beneficial to the country involved. Settlement of a first group of 500 selected refugees began in March 1940. Unfortunately, wartime transportation difficulties delayed the arrival of colonists. By June of 1942, only 472 refugees were at Sosua, and the total probably never reached much above 500. Despite hard work and a degree of progress, Sosua scarcely proved to be the example that would open other doors. Aside from its small size, problems of discipline and administration, as well as of refugees using the Sosua opportunity as a steppingstone for immigrating to the United States, hurt the colony. With time also came the realization that good soil at the site was limited. In 1941 the Brookings Institution conducted a comprehensive survey of refugee prospects in the Dominican Republic and concluded that the country as a whole could absorb only about 5,000 refugees and that the Sosua tract had received virtually all the settlers it could support.[40]

From the vantage ground of the present, the unrealistic nature of the various plans of colonization is made crystal clear by the fact that, despite the tremendous need for refugee havens, none materialized except for the small settlement at Sosua. Again, although studies to make way for such projects continued through the war, colonization of new territories played almost no part in the migrations connected with the huge displaced persons problem after the end of hostilities.

As for the Intergovernmental Committee on Refugees, the opening of war halted its efforts to facilitate emigration from Germany. The Committee then worked to resettle refugees from countries of transit to receiving nations overseas, but even on this problem accomplished little. In 1943, after the German policy of extermination of Jews had become clear, the ICR tried to augment its program, but remained rather ineffectual. Awakening after the war, the Committee was more successful in helping resettle displaced persons. At the end of June 1947, the Intergovernmental Committee was disbanded, its functions taken over by the International Refugee Organization.[41]

Meanwhile, between 1938 and 1940, these nearly fruitless diplomatic efforts to move victims of Nazism into other countries were paralleled by a series of vain attempts by some Americans to prod Congress into liberalizing United States policy toward entry of refugees.

Part III

# The Effort in Congress

Chapter 4

# Charity Begins at Home

Soon after the pogroms of November 1938, the *Nation* predicted accurately that "liberalization of the immigration laws is an idea which most politicians regard as too hot to handle, and it would take an unmistakable demonstration of public opinion to change this attitude." Except for the Wagner-Rogers Children's Bill, the few efforts made to modify the immigration laws generated little support. The children's bill did attract major backing, but not the "unmistakable demonstration" that Congress apparently required.[1]

In the wake of Germany's annexation of Austria in early 1938, two Democratic congressmen from New York submitted refugee bills to the House of Representatives. Samuel Dickstein proposed that, when the fiscal year 1938 ended on June 30, the United States combine all countries' unused quota allotments for that year and make them available to refugees. Emanuel Celler's measure provided exemption for refugees from the clauses of the immigration law which excluded any person likely to become a public charge, any alien whose passage was paid by an organized group, and any minor unaccompanied by a parent. The Celler bill would also have empowered the President to widen quota limits for refugees.[2]

Hearings on these bills, scheduled for April 20, 1938, never occurred. Early in the month a conference representing several important Protestant, Catholic, Jewish, and nonsectarian refugee aid agencies met in New York and unanimously agreed that hearings on the Dickstein and Celler bills would be harmful. The conferees felt that restrictionists would use the occasion to broadcast their views and that the resulting publicity could hurt President Roosevelt's plans for the forthcoming Evian Conference. They pointed out that the President's proposal had already aroused criticism, that the Administration had side-stepped much more objection by emphasizing that the immigration laws would remain unchanged, and that efforts to modify the laws in favor of refugees would stir up further opposition to what the United States was even then doing. Consequently, the people at the meeting decided to make two moves. First, any organizations having personal contacts with Celler or Dickstein would try to convince them to call off the hearings. Second, a letter would be sent to Dickstein, chairman of the House Immigration Committee, asking him to drop the hearings and mentioning that if they did take place groups represented at the meeting might send witnesses to testify against the proposed bills. The letter, representing 14 organizations, went to Dickstein, with copies to Celler and Secretaries Hull and Perkins. In addition, a State Department official approached the other Jewish congressmen, advised them of the risks involved in the proposed hearings, and obtained their agreement to work against permitting such bills to come up. These actions succeeded, for the House Immigration Committee soon called off the hearings, stating that measures to aid refugees should properly wait until the intergovernmental refugee conference had acted.[3]

After the Evian Conference the Celler and Dickstein bills remained buried. Apparently the only group to give further support to either proposal was the Jewish People's Committee, a Communist front, which sent petitions in favor of Dickstein's bill to the President in June 1938 and again in early 1939. Then in January 1939 Celler introduced a bill to allow entry of all refugees except those with physical, mental, or moral defects. Fugitives coming to the United States under Celler's new proposal would have been assigned to a probationary status for five years before receiving regular, permanent immigrant standing. But in late February Celler announced he would not press his refugee bills because of popular antipathy to such proposals in the South and West. Some of his House colleagues had advised Celler that if his bills came up other measures to halve the quotas or stop immigration entirely would reach the floor and very likely pass.[4]

Because supporters of refugee entry looked upon reduction or closure of immigration as a real and constant threat, they felt impelled to arrange their activities with an eye to this danger. Restrictionists, riding an undercurrent of antirefugee feeling, emphasized their propositions that aliens caused unemployment and that the most effective solution would be to stop further immigration and deport as many noncitizens as possible. Support for these proposals could be mustered easily in Congress because, as Senator Lewis B. Schwellenbach (D.) of Washington declared in 1940, condemnation of aliens

> is perhaps the best vote-getting argument in present-day politics. The politician can beat his breast and proclaim his loyalty to America. He can tell the unemployed man that he is out of work because some alien has a job.

Accordingly, each legislative year witnessed the introduction of numerous measures to stop immigration and to deport noncitizens. The year 1939 was representative in this respect. Among the multitude of antialien bills proposed in the first session of the Seventy-sixth Congress were one by Congressman B. Frank Whelchel, a Democrat from Georgia, to end all immigration for five years and another with the same goal by Republican Senator Rufus C. Holman of Oregon. Representative John J. Dempsey, New Mexico Democrat, saw his measure to deport and exclude aliens who advocated "any changes in the American form of government" pass the House but die in the Senate. Congressman Stephen Pace, Democrat of Georgia, offered a bill which at the close of 1939 would simply have ended all immigration and deported all aliens.[5]

Most seriously regarded of the antialien proposals of 1939 was a cluster of five measures presented to the Senate by Democrat Robert Reynolds of North Carolina and co-sponsored in the House by Joe Starnes, Democrat of Alabama. The Reynolds bills would have reduced the quotas 90 percent, halted permanent immigration for ten years or until unemployment fell to three million, and provided for fingerprinting and annual registration of all aliens. The packet also included deportation of aliens who received public relief or whose presence was "inimical to the public interest."[6]

A Senate Subcommittee on Immigration held three days of hearings on Reynolds' bills in March 1939. Labor Department representatives spoke against all five of them. The CIO opposed the deportation measures and the AFL stood against compulsory fingerprinting of aliens. Other testimony against the proposals was scant, largely because several of the groups concerned about refugees avoided the hearings in order not to give Senator Reynolds an opportunity to use cross-examination of witnesses as a vehicle for antirefugee publicity. On the opposite side, restrictionist forces appeared in strength. The American Coalition of Patriotic Societies, the American Legion, the Junior Order United American Mechanics, the Immigration Restriction League, Inc., the Ladies of the Grand Army of the Republic, and others urged enactment of all five bills. Actually, as supporters of a liberal immigration policy had feared, these hearings turned into something of a sounding board for antirefugee feeling. Senator Reynolds, who was not a member of the subcommittee, stepped in, took the helm, and steered the proceedings into a series of his favorite channels. He declared that ships loaded with refugees were docking in Cuba where the passengers planned to await their chance to slip into the United States. Reynolds implied that they would join other thousands who were supposedly infiltrating the country by eluding the immigration patrol. Restrictionists complained that refugees were pouring in with visitors' visas, that the Labor Department refused to deport aliens, and that foreigners were depriving American citizens of jobs.[7]

The platform provided restrictionist views when immigration legislation came up for discussion was only one worry of people concerned about refugees. The very existence of bills such as those proposed by Senator Reynolds deterred application of pressure to liberalize the immigration laws. If a measure to facilitate refugee entry had reached the floor of Congress, counter efforts to cut drastically or completely to end immigration would very likely have developed. Fear centered on the possibility that exclusionist support might snowball and a very restrictive law be passed. Many backers of a liberal refugee policy agreed with Dorothy Thompson that raising the issue of enlarging the quotas would be "political dynamite." Shortly after the pogroms of November 1938, a representative of the American Friends Service Committee stated in a memorandum that "to our knowledge, no one is trying to change the quota. It is considered highly dangerous to attempt such a step, and might jeopardize even the present quota." James L. Houghteling, Commissioner of Immigration and Naturalization, reported to President Roosevelt in January 1940 that he had attended all the 1939 sessions of the Immigration Committees of both houses of Congress. Houghteling concluded that "the tendency of a considerable part of Congress was toward the reduction of existing immigration quotas. The chance of any liberalizing legislation seemed negligible." [8]

The strength of congressional opposition to increased immigration explains why no major effort occurred to widen the quotas for adult refugees. But, despite the handicaps, friends of the victims of Nazism did decide to press for legislation to permit entry of 20,000 children outside the quota limits. The main impetus for this action arose from a series of tragic events in Germany in late 1938.


## THE NIGHT OF BROKEN GLASS

Without any warning, on the night of October 28, 1938, the Nazis rounded up 12,000 Polish Jews living in Germany, many of them German residents for over 20 years, transported them to the Polish border, and left them there virtually unsheltered and unsupplied. Among the deported Jews were the parents of 17-year-old Herschel Grynszpan, then living in Paris. The youth, upon receiving news of the fate of his parents, determined to kill the German Ambassador to France. On November 7 Grynszpan went to the German Embassy. When the third secretary, Ernst vom Rath, approached to ask his business, Grynszpan shot him. Two days later vom Rath died. The same night, November 9–10, and on into the late afternoon of the tenth, assaults on Jews and Jewish property swept through Germany. [9]

During the time of Broken Glass, called *Kristallnacht* in Germany, Storm Troopers and others, armed with crowbars and axes, smashed Jewish shops and encouraged looting by the gathering crowds. Police failed to appear. Most of Germany's synagogues burned while firemen acted only to protect nearby non-Jewish property. Nazis invaded and wrecked Jewish homes. Terrorists even damaged Jewish hospitals, old people's institutions, and children's boarding schools and beat their occupants or forced them out into the night. At least 20,000, and perhaps as many as 60,000, Jews were arrested without charges and placed in concentration camps, their whereabouts unknown to their relatives. Reliable British sources told of the beating and killing of many of these prisoners. For example, guards beat to death 12 of a group of 62 Jews delivered to the Sachsenhausen camp. By mid-December news reports mentioned that the ashes of some Jews who had disappeared at the time of Broken Glass were being sent to their families upon payment of a three mark fee.[10]

Propaganda Minister Paul Joseph Goebbels termed the violence a spontaneous outburst of popular anger resulting from the vom Rath murder. At the time, most observers pointed out that the actions were obviously well organized and could not have been impromptu. William L. Shirer has shown how German documents, released since the war, prove that the Nazi government sponsored and carefully planned the pogrom.[11]

Further retaliation against Jews followed rapidly. As retribution for the killing of vom Rath, the Reich levied a fine of one billion marks (about 400 million dollars) on German Jewry. The government ordered Jews to repair damage inflicted on their residences and businesses. Insurance due them went instead to the state. Other decrees virtually eliminated Jews from German economic life, and measures of social and cultural discrimination were promulgated. German schools had to dismiss their few remaining Jewish students. In most cases Jews were thrown off government poor relief. They were excluded from theatres, concerts, cultural exhibits, and public libraries. Jewish occupants had to vacate certain areas of Berlin within seven months. The Nazis even declared that, because of the vom Rath murder, Jews were "unreliable and unfit to own and drive automobiles," and withdrew these privileges also.[12]

The November violence shocked the world. The British Ambassador to Germany later compared its effect with that of the sinking of the *Lusitania* and the killing of nurse Edith Cavell in World War I. In sympathy, Holland, Belgium, Switzerland, and France allowed thousands of Jews to enter without funds or passports, and, after closing the borders, continued to permit illegal immigrants to remain if they would stay in government camps. For a time England was accepting immigrants at the same rate as the United States.[13]

In the United States, reaction against Nazi terror was strong and outspoken. The press, religious and civic groups, labor organizations, the American Legion, and public officials protested. Herbert Hoover, Alfred M. Landon, Alfred E. Smith, William Green, John L. Lewis, and many other leading figures joined in expressions of outrage. Throughout the country protest meetings took place. President Roosevelt declared: "I myself could scarcely believe that such things could occur in a twentieth-century civilization." [14]

In a sharp slap at the Nazis, the President summoned home Hugh R. Wilson, American Ambassador to Germany. Technically, Wilson returned for consultation. In fact, the move amounted to a recall and was generally interpreted in that way. While this maneuver must have distressed isolationists, most of the press vigorously supported the President. A Gallup poll found that, of respondents who expressed an opinion, 72 percent approved "temporary withdrawal" of the ambassador "as a protest." Yet, although the *Kristallnacht* had thrown the refugee problem into a much more critical phase, Roosevelt reiterated the position he had taken when summoning the Evian Conference. Asked whether he would recommend relaxation of the immigration laws for the benefit of refugees, the President replied: "That is not in contemplation; we have the quota system." To a telegram from Democratic Senator James F. Byrnes of South Carolina, pledging cooperation in obtaining legislation to increase the German quota, Roosevelt responded with a noncommittal note of appreciation. But on November 18 Roosevelt did announce that in view of conditions in Germany the government would allow the 12 to 15 thousand refugees already in the United States on visitors' visas to remain by means of extensions of their permits.[15]

Although a Gallup survey taken soon after the Night of Broken Glass showed that 94 percent of those questioned who held an opinion disapproved of the German treatment of Jews, and 97 percent condemned Nazi persecution of Catholics, a dissonant reaction was quite vocal in some circles. Rev. Gerald Winrod, leader of the Christian Defenders, was upset that the press should go into "hysterics" because "shop windows are smashed in Germany," while almost no voice had spoken out against massacres of Christians by Communists in Russia and Loyalists in Spain. Since early 1938 the Brooklyn *Tablet* had sporadically complained that oppression of Christians in Mexico, Spain, and Russia hardly occasioned a raised eyebrow, while the American press and United States government officials regularly denounced persecution of Jews by the Nazis. After the November pogroms, this charge became a major theme in the *Tablet* for weeks. Why, inquired the *Tablet*, was news of persecution of Christians generally suppressed, while each day brought forth "a morning, noon and night denunciation of the lesser persecution of our friends, the Jews"? Why didn't the Administration call its ambassadors home from Mexico, Spain, and Russia in the face of widespread murder of Catholics? Father Coughlin pressed the same points in *Social Justice*. Indication that this indignation was having an effect on the public appeared in a letter to presidential secretary Marvin McIntyre. From Detroit the writer cautioned that at several midwestern mass meetings of protest against Nazi actions he had noticed Catholics asking why Roosevelt was silent when priests were killed and churches burned in Spain and Russia. A judge in St. Joseph wrote McIntyre that at the Michigan American Legion convention he had observed severe criticism of the President's refugee policy by a large proportion of both Catholics and Protestants.[16]

In other quarters a wave of sympathy for the persecuted people of Germany aroused calls for a more liberal American refugee program. The *Commonweal*, a Catholic weekly, advocated suspension of quota limits for the benefit of refugees. The *Catholic Worker* urged that America's doors swing open to all refugees. A *Collier's* editorial spoke for widening the gates. Peace organizations suggested a special session of Congress to increase the quotas. The *New Republic* recommended transfer to persecuted Germans of the unused immigration allotments of other countries. Taking uneasy notice of such tendencies, the Protestant *Christian Century* declared that America's pressing economic and social problems required "that instead of inviting further complications by relaxing our immigration laws, these laws be maintained or even further tightened." [17]

One of the most tragic consequences of the time of Broken Glass was the fate of thousands of German children. Beset by hunger, excluded from schools and playgrounds, constantly subject to bullying, not knowing, in many cases, when or if their fathers would return from concentration camps, great numbers of boys and girls led a wretched existence. Understandably, despite the heartbreak involved in separation, many parents were soon pleading with refugee agencies to take their children away to safety. A woman wrote to a children's relief organization in Amsterdam:

I just heard that the husband of my cousin has been arrested. My cousin herself, as a result of the dreadful happenings, lost her mind and had to be taken to an asylum. The children are left without any help. .

Newswriter Quentin Reynolds reported that, among a group of 500 of these boys and girls taken into England, less than ten percent knew the whereabouts of their parents. In Germany to arrange for emigration of children, English social workers found it impossible in many cases to trace the parents of their charges. From the Netherlands came information that numbers of young refugees were "simply put on a train and sent to Holland in the hope that they would be looked after." A Quaker engaged in relief work in Germany stated that "it is a very common thing for parents to come to us and say: 'Can't you take our children and send them where they will be safe?' " Meanwhile, in the United States, concern for these German boys and girls began to crystallize.[18]

ORIGINS AND RECEPTION OF THE WAGNER-ROGERS BILL

In the aftermath of the November pogroms, many Americans hoped the wave of public sympathy for the victims of Nazi terror could be turned into practical help. Most advocates of a more liberal refugee policy agreed that the mood of Congress precluded any change in the quota system in favor of adult refugees. But the pitiful circumstances of thousands of German children led to the thought that Congress might be willing to open the door to a limited number of these boys and girls without charging them to the quota. Responding sympathetically to the idea, Senator Robert F. Wagner, a Democrat of New York, and Representative Edith Nourse Rogers, a Republican from Massachusetts, in February 1939 introduced identical bills to permit, over a single two-year period, entrance outside the quotas of a total of 20,000 German refugee children aged 14 or younger. These resolutions provided that the young refugees must "be supported and properly cared for" by responsible private agencies or individuals, thereby assuring that they would not become public charges. Nor would the United States government incur any other expenses involved in the proposal. This bill, then, constituted the first serious attempt to liberalize the Immigration Act of 1924.

By late November 1938, Secretary of Labor Frances Perkins had been considering introduction of legislation for nonquota entry of German children. And on December 10 the *Nation* had pointed to England's acceptance of thousands of child refugees and had advocated that the United States take at least 15,000. But the Wagner-Rogers Bill actually had its source in a meeting held in mid-December at the New York City apartment of Dr. Marion Kenworthy, director of the Department of Mental Hygiene of the New York School of Social Work. Out of this interdenominational gathering, attended by several leading social workers as well as by some jurists and people of other callings, grew the Non-Sectarian Committee for German Refugee Children. Although the committee did not formally organize until ten weeks later, an interim group began immediately to develop plans for reception and care of refugee children and for enactment of enabling legislation. Unofficial offices were set up in New York and Washington.[19]

Working in cooperation with religious leaders, the interim committee circulated to a select list of Protestant and Catholic clergymen a statement calling on Americans and their Congress to open the United States to some of the refugee children. Signed by more than 50 prominent churchmen, the document was delivered to the White House as a petition and released to the press on January 9, 1939. Before long, welfare and religious organizations began to receive offers from American families to take young refugees into their homes. By mid-April, 1,400 of these unsolicited invitations had come from 46 states. Within three weeks the number approached 5,000. On February 8 the Executive Council of the AFL and John L. Lewis for the CIO made public their acceptance of possible legislation on behalf of refugee children. The following day Senator Wagner introduced his bill, soon to be supported by Mrs. Rogers' companion measure in the House.[20]

In the meantime, the interim committee had obtained sponsorship for its program from outstanding American citizens representing all major religious faiths, both major political parties, and numerous vocations. Early in March the Non-Sectarian Committee for German Refugee Children formally came into existence, headed by a distinguished group of co-chairmen: His Eminence George Cardinal Mundelein, represented by Bishop Bernard James Sheil of Chicago, Canon Anson Phelps Stokes of the Washington Cathedral, Governor Herbert

H. Lehman of New York, William Allen White of Emporia, Kansas, Dean Helen Taft Manning of Bryn Mawr College, and President Frank Porter Graham of the University of North Carolina. Acting executive director was Clarence E. Pickett of the American Friends Service Committee. The national committee, numbering more than 70 members, included such prominent Americans as Marshall Field, Rev. Harry Emerson Fosdick, actress Helen Hayes, President Robert M. Hutchins of the University of Chicago, the recent Republican candidates Alfred M. Landon and Frank Knox, President William A. Neilson of Smith College, George Rublee, Rev. Dr. Maurice S. Sheehy of the Catholic University of America, Rexford G. Tugwell, and Mrs. Stephen S. Wise. In its initial press release the new committee announced its support of the Wagner-Rogers Bill and its intention to develop a practical program for placement of child refugees in American homes.[21]

In late March, 20 leading child welfare specialists, who for over two months had been maturing plans for care of the young victims of persecution, presented their completed proposals to the Non-Sectarian Committee. Drawn up in consultation with the Federal government's Children's Bureau, the suggested procedures aimed at placing the child refugees in homes of their own faiths throughout the United States. Entrusting selection of the children in Europe to the American Friends Service Committee, the Non-Sectarian Committee expected to assume temporary care upon arrival and financial responsibility throughout the project. Existing qualified local child welfare agencies, many of which had already volunteered to help, would investigate the offered homes and handle placement and continuing supervision of the young refugees. Centrally indexed full case records to be kept on each child would facilitate contact between parents and children whenever possible.[22]

For a measure not considered major legislation, the Wagner-Rogers Bill drew endorsement from an extraordinarily broad cross section of individuals and organizations. In labor circles, Alexander F. Whitney, president of the Brotherhood of Railroad Trainmen, and David Dubinsky of the International Ladies' Garment Workers' Union joined the AFL and CIO leadership in support of the resolution. Political figures besides those already mentioned included Herbert Hoover, Governor Luren Dickenson of Michigan, former Governor Philip La Follette of Wisconsin, and Mayor Fiorello La Guardia of

New York City. The New York State Senate passed a resolution in favor of the Wagner-Rogers Bill. Among a large number of religious organizations backing the proposal were the Federal Council of Churches and many individual denominational groups. Numerous women's associations expressed approval. Conspicuous among social service bodies taking a stand for the measure were the YWCA and the National Child Labor Committee. Uniting with Helen Hayes in her support of the bill were several other actors, including Don Ameche, Jean Arthur, Joe E. Brown, Irene Dunne, and Henry Fonda. From Massachusetts came an announcement that Mrs. Calvin Coolidge and other Northampton women had made plans to care for 25 of the young refugees.[23]

Editorial reaction to the proposal was widespread and virtually unanimous in approval. At least 85 newspapers from 30 states and the District of Columbia supported the resolution. Despite the strength of restrictionist views in the South, 26 Dixie newspapers, representing every southern state except Arkansas and Mississippi, favored the children's bill.[24]

But opposition formed almost immediately. Patriotic orders, restrictionist associations, and the American Legion struck back to preserve the nation against the threat of inundation by 20,000 alien children. John B. Trevor, head of the American Coalition of Patriotic Societies and father of the national origins principle which formed the keystone of the Immigration Act of 1924, issued a circular rebuking Senator Wagner and Mrs. Rogers for daring to sponsor such a bill while the nation contained "a mountain million of neglected boys and girls, descendants of American pioneers, undernourished, ragged and ill." Trevor called for protests to Congress "to protect the youth of America from this foreign invasion." The Ladies of the Grand Army of the Republic closed ranks with the Junior Order United American Mechanics, the Patriotic Order Sons of America, the Daughters of the American Revolution, the United Daughters of 1812, and numerous other patriotic societies to secure the country against the foreign children. The American Legion, then one million strong, joined the columns of the opponents of the Wagner-Rogers Bill.[25]

The strength and influence of these patriotic organizations in the 1930's should not be underestimated. Obviously, any endeavor backed by the American Legion and the Daughters of the American

Revolution was heir to substantial power. But many other groups, though less well known, also commanded devoted followings. For instance, the Junior Order United American Mechanics, a fraternal and patriotic society, had fought for immigration restriction since its formation in 1853. In the late 1930's membership, heaviest in Pennsylvania, Ohio, and the upper South, stood at nearly 200,000. The Junior Order counted several congressmen among its members. Five state organizations which had seceded from the main council of the Junior Order in the 1890's agreed fully with the parent body on immigration legislation and lent the weight of their 150,000 members to the forces against the Wagner-Rogers Bill. Inclusion of the Daughters of America, its women's auxiliary, would place the total numbers connected with the Junior Order United American Mechanics in 1939 at close to half a million people.[26]

Uniting the political influence of dozens of patriotic associations were two organizations which functioned as what might be termed legislative holding companies. The largest, the American Coalition of Patriotic Societies, operated from Washington. On its board of directors were representatives of 115 patriotic and fraternal organizations with total memberships of about two and a half million. The function of the American Coalition was to carry out policies upon which the member organizations could agree. A main sphere of activity involved legislation and one area of consistent unanimity among the various societies was immigration restriction. In New York City the Allied Patriotic Societies, established in 1922, served in a similar fashion as a policy clearing house for about 30 patriotic associations in the metropolitan area. Coordinated action by the member groups resulted, especially on the battle lines of immigration restriction.[27]

## THE BILL ON THE FIRING LINE

Foremost among weapons used to fight the child refugee proposal was the argument that "charity begins at home." A flood of concern burst forth for sharecropper and city poor children. "Shall we sentence these slum children to crime, poverty, and hopelessness while we import children from a foreign country?" asked the American Immigration Conference Board, Inc., in a handbill entitled "America's Children Are America's Problem! Refugee Children in Europe Are Europe's Problem!" Asserting that "American Children Have First Claim to American Charity," the circular, in logic repeatedly echoed by restrictionists, insisted that "if homes are available for the adoption of alien children, Americanism demands that needy American children be adopted into them." No amount of argument that sharecropper and slum parents would not consent to having their children moved into the homes of others, or that the demand for adoptable children in the United States was far greater than the supply, could dent this line of reasoning in the least. Nor did it seem to make much difference that most leading child welfare workers, unquestionably strongly dedicated to the well-being of American children, agreed with Katharine F. Lenroot, chief of the United States Children's Bureau, that entry of 20,000 refugee boys and girls "would not lessen in the slightest degree the care and protection afforded a single American child." Of all the arguments offered by opponents of the Wagner-Rogers Bill, the one about its depriving American children was most effective with the public.[28]

Part of the support which had been anticipated for the bill failed to materialize because of a belief in some circles that the proposal would lead to the breakup of German families. For example, the director of a charities organization in Pittsburgh criticized the bill on the ground that keeping families together was preferable despite the material privations that might befall them. Clarence Pickett and other American Friends Service Committee personnel, having observed conditions in Germany, reported that thousands of children were already experiencing the insecurities of a shattered home life. Other thousands had lost parents to concentration camps or suicide. Quaker estimates indicated that as many as 100,000 to 130,000 children were living under conditions which made emigration without their parents seem far more desirable than remaining under the Nazis. An English child refugee agency reached the more conservative conclusion that 40,000 to 70,000 should be brought out.[29]

Although Quaker reports on the situation in Germany came directly from their staff involved in emigration and relief work, not everyone found the evidence conclusive. Msgr. Michael J. Ready, general secretary of the National Catholic Welfare Conference, sought accurate information about the Wagner-Rogers Bill for presentation to a meeting of the Administrative Board of Bishops to be held in mid-April 1939. In a letter to Senator Wagner, Msgr. Ready stated he had been unable to confirm that conditions in Germany necessitated bringing thousands of child refugees to the United States. He asked the senator to provide him with more complete authentication. Wagner arranged for Clarence Pickett to meet with Msgr. Ready. After the conference, Senator Wagner wrote to Msgr. Ready expressing his own conclusion that the plight of children in Germany made the legislation urgently necessary. Adding that the measure was permissive and in no way compelled emigration or placed pressure on any family or organization, Wagner conveyed his hope that the Administrative Board of Bishops would grant the bill sympathetic deliberation. In reply, Msgr. Ready informed Wagner that Pickett had been unable to convince him of need for the proposed legislation.[30]

Nearly a year later, in February 1940, the Most Reverend Joseph F. Rummel, Archbishop of New Orleans, expressed doubts about bringing young refugees to the United States. Archbishop Rummel, whose chairmanship of the Committee for Catholic Refugees from Germany and whose membership on the President's Advisory Committee on Political Refugees testified to his concern for fugitives from Nazism, questioned the social and moral validity of a program that would divide families by moving children 3,000 miles away from their parents. Surprisingly enough, Archbishop Rummel had been among the churchmen who in January 1939 had signed the petition to President Roosevelt calling for entry of refugee children. The wife of a former German high court official who had sent her son to the United States before the onset of war had felt quite differently. Offering a bouquet of flowers to the social worker who had been helping to arrange the departure of her child, the mother had said: "It is unspeakably hard to send my boy away, and yet I am so thankful that he has the opportunity to go and build up a new life over there!" [31]

In the meantime, during the spring of 1939, the Non-Sectarian Committee had been broadening its efforts for the children's bill. The leaflet "Suffer Little Children," presenting the case for the proposal, was circulated, as were printed copies of the statements of Senator Wagner and Mrs. Rogers, the clergy petition, and a sheet of excerpts from newspaper editorials endorsing the measure. Sporadically sent to a mailing list, the committee's news bulletin reported on the progress of the bill and urged communication with congressmen. Lists of members of the immigration committees of both houses accompanied typewritten form letters calling for active support of the Wagner-Rogers Bill. Labor leaders, prominent liberals, churchmen, and notable educators received requests that they encourage national legislators to back the proposal. These steps to generate pressure on Congress met with some success, for in April Representative Samuel Dickstein found it "almost impossible to keep up with the mail" on the child refugee measure and Representative Anton Maciejewski (D.) of Illinois reported receiving 260 letters in one morning, all favoring the bill.[32]

State branches of the Non-Sectarian Committee took shape in Ohio, Michigan, Texas, Illinois, Minnesota, Colorado, Utah, and California. Enjoying the support of well-known movie stars and such leading citizens as Los Angeles Times publisher Harry Chandler, Judge Goodwin J. Knight, John Steinbeck, and Stanford University president Ray Lyman Wilbur, the California division was particularly active. In response to efforts of the California group, the state legislature, with only one negative vote in each house, passed a resolution requesting Congress to enact the children's bill. Through the cooperation of many California newspapers, numerous editorials favorable to the Wagner proposal appeared in the state. The California branch supplied special material to the press, circulated a newsletter, and sent out speakers. Perhaps most important was the intensive effort, through a variety of channels, to influence the California delegation in Congress. This pressure, according to the California division's executive secretary, brought solid progress and some clear commitments in the endeavor to win Congressional backing for the Wagner-Rogers Bill.[33]

The main lobbying effort for the child refugee bill centered in Washington. In large part labor and usual overhead costs were supplied free of charge, enabling the Non-Sectarian Committee's Washington office to operate on small funds. In late March a private polling service, engaged to test sentiment regarding the bill in the upper house, reported "a preponderant feeling in the Senate that this subject is 'too hot to handle.' " Only 45 senators were willing to reveal their views; of these, 21 favored the measure and 24 opposed it. In actuality, opposition was much stronger than appeared on the surface. The polling service pointed out that many of the 49 senators who were approached but refused to take a stand did comment that they were against "letting down the immigration bars in any degree." The survey bureau concluded that the bill at that time stood little chance of passage.[34]

Analysis of the poll indicates, as might have been expected, least backing for the Wagner-Rogers Bill in the South. Less than 15 percent of the southern members of the upper house took a stand in favor of the measure. About one fourth of the senators of both the Northeast and the Far West supported the proposal. Unexpectedly, in view of isolationist influence in the Midwest, the main strength of the bill appears to have been among senators from that region. Nearly one third of the midwestern senators approved the measure. A breakdown by party shows that one fourth of the Democrats were behind the children's bill in contrast to less than one tenth of the Republicans. One third of the nonsouthern Democrats favored the proposal.[35]

The poll turned up a few surprises. Senator Arthur Capper, Republican of Kansas, who less than a year before had advocated tighter immigration policies, approved of the Wagner-Rogers Bill. Pressure applied by William Allen White contributed to Capper's shift. On the other hand, Senator James F. Byrnes of South Carolina, who four months earlier had suggested to President Roosevelt that he ask Congress to widen the quota for German refugees, would not take a position on the children's bill. The same unwillingness to express his opinion came from Progressive Senator Robert M. La Follette, Jr., of Wisconsin, although his brother Philip appeared at hearings on the measure in April to testify in its support. Senator Lewis B. Schwellenbach of Washington disappointed sponsors of the bill by his opposition, though he reversed his stand later.[36]

The Non-Sectarian Committee correctly perceived from the survey that the bill was in a very weak position in the Senate. With hearings due to begin in less than a month, attempts to develop support on Capitol Hill, particularly within the Senate Committee on Immigration, were intensified. For instance, in the endeavor to bring Republican Senator Warren Austin of Vermont into the camp, the committee sought the aid of Dorothy Canfield Fisher. Proponents of the bill hoped that through Senator Lister Hill, Democrat of Alabama, some influence could be brought to bear on Democrat Richard B. Russell of Georgia, chairman of the Senate Immigration Committee. The tactics of those working for the bill seem to have been successful. In any event, although only four of the fourteen members of the

Senate Committee on Immigration favored the refugee measure, the three senators appointed to a subcommittee to participate in joint hearings were all supporters of the Wagner-Rogers Bill.[37]

Late in April four days of hearings took place before a joint subcommittee of the immigration committees of both houses. Two factors set the tone of these hearings. One was the make-up of the subcommittee: of the three senators and five representatives only one man was not sympathetic toward the bill. The other factor was the planning of the Non-Sectarian Committee regarding presentation of testimony favorable to the measure. In order to demonstrate a broad spectrum of support, as well as to provide clear evidence of the need for the bill and the practicality of the plans developed for the young refugees, a carefully selected succession of witnesses appeared. Quaker and Unitarian relief workers and former Wisconsin governor Philip La Follette, all recently returned from Europe, described conditions under the Nazis which made removal of the German children imperative. Three child welfare experts, including Katharine Lenroot, chief of the United States Children's Bureau, vouched for the adequacy of the plans formulated for care of the young refugees. In a significant shift from labor's traditional restrictionism, the AFL and the CIO each sent a representative to testify for the measure. College educators; members of women's organizations; and Protestant, Catholic, and Jewish clergymen spoke in favor of the Wagner-Rogers Bill. The appearance of Helen Hayes added color to the hearings. The actress introduced herself as the mother of two children and pleaded for entry of the young refugees.

Opposition to the bill consisted almost entirely of spokesmen for patriotic and restrictionist organizations and the American Legion. Some of their arguments simply repeated the usual restrictionist litany. Others reflected new reasoning particularly fitted to the Wagner proposal. A few were absurd, such as the assertion that, since the bill did not specify that the children must be refugees, 20,000 young Nazis might come over. And, as in all restrictionist discourse on the Wagner-Rogers Bill, witnesses repeatedly invoked their contention that the coming of 20,000 boys and girls would somehow deprive poor American children.

Displaying a nimble versatility, opponents of the bill objected that it would tear German families apart by separating children from their parents, yet suggested an amended version which would reserve places for the same children, but not for their parents, within the regular quota. Some witnesses chided supporters of the measure for limiting its scope to German boys and girls. With Spanish, Chinese, Ethiopian, Russian, and numerous other hundreds of thousands of children suffering, they maintained that one should not single out the Germans for help. Such discriminatory legislation was unthinkable and, since all were not welcome, none should come. At the same time, they asserted that the move to bring in 20,000 German children was really an entering wedge calculated to produce the initial break which would be expanded ultimately into total destruction of the immigration walls. In other words, restrictionists claimed, backers of the Wagner-Rogers Bill actually were aiming to bring in all the world's suffering children, and millions of adults as well. Although "charity begins at home" formed the main theme in the fight against the children's bill, a careful reading of the joint hearings leaves the strong impression that restrictionists were concerned most of all that passage of the bill might start to undermine the Immigration Act of 1924.[38]

While almost no overtly anti-Semitic statements came out in the testimony against the Wagner-Rogers Bill, the *Nation* stood on safe ground when it charged that a "subtle and effective argument is the *sotto voce* contention that this is a Jewish bill. The implication is that all the children are Jewish." In many quarters this was reason enough for keeping them out. At the joint hearings, Francis H. Kinnicutt, president of the Allied Patriotic Societies, put heavy stress on the predominantly Jewish composition of refugee immigration into the United States and presented a table to substantiate the point. Referring to job competition, John B. Trevor of the American Coalition of Patriotic Societies stated that "the American-born child in many places must yield to the foreign-born refugee because of race affinity." Miss Margaret Hopkins Worrell, spokeswoman for the Ladies of the Grand Army of the Republic, stopped in midsentence by a congressman when she protested that Congress might "decide to admit 20,000 German-Jewish children," proceeded to argue with the legislator when he pointed out that "they are not all Jewish." In a statement not made at the hearings, but given in an address before the convention of the United Daughters of 1812 held in Washington the same week, Mrs. Arthur J. O'Neill, president of that organization, advocated a resolution opposing the Wagner-Rogers Bill. Pointing out that most of the child refugees would be Jewish, and noting that the United States is predominantly Christian, the speaker concluded that America's needy ought to be cared for before taking in new foreigners.[39]

By repeatedly emphasizing that large numbers of the German boys and girls involved were Christian, sponsors of the children's bill revealed their awareness and their anxiety that anti-Jewish feeling was a real obstacle to the measure's passing. Most of these Christian boys and girls were "non-Aryans"; that is, children who were not Jewish by religion, but who had Jewish forebears. Estimates of the proportion of the children who were Jewish by religion ranged from 50 to 60 percent. Senator Wagner, Clarence Pickett, and others emphasized that selection of the boys and girls should be based on their need to emigrate and not on their "race or religion." Still, privately, some members of the Non-Sectarian Committee were by late June concerned because relief workers abroad had noted a smaller proportion of non-Aryans than had been expected among children needing to emigrate. They felt that a more equal division between Jews and non-Aryan Christians would have a better effect on Congress and on the American public.[40]

Once completed, the joint hearings became the subject of evaluation in both camps. John Cecil, president of the American Immigration Conference Board, described witnesses who supported the bill as "sob sisters" who had been "appealing to the emotions" of Congress. The *Junior American,* monthly periodical of the Junior Order United American Mechanics, observed that "the early part of these hearings was given over to somewhat of a stage show," but when, in the final two days, "the working class of people, including the Junior Order, American Legion, Veterans of Foreign Wars and patriotic societies generally began to fire and fight the measure, the tables seemed to turn." Hinting at questionable motives, the same article mentioned that prominent people who were supporting the Wagner-Rogers Bill were without doubt "in the employ of large interests in this country." But only J. H. Patten of the Immigration Restriction League, Inc., author of the theory that Secretary Frances Perkins was born of Russian immigrant parents, had the perspicacity to discover that the conduct of the hearings, other activities of the Non-Sectarian Committee, and the history of former anti-immigration battles added up to a pattern of foreign conspiracy. Patten maintained that European countries, especially England, France, and Holland were trying, if not plotting and planning, to dump refugees on us and are really back of all this high-pressure propaganda with such expensive headquarters in New York City and here in Washington, . . . where had been conducted the same "Wine, Women and Alien Lobby" that was finally revealed back of the White, Williams and Sterling refugee bills in 1922 and 1923. . . . All this lobbying and propaganda which is shown up in the Congressional Record in the form of editorials that disclose a common origin and source, ought to be investigated. . . . Such an investigation ought to particularly deal with . . . where they get all this money to try to influence Congress to pass this Wagner Resolution.

Further "evidence that foreign governments must be back of this Wagner Resolution" included presence at the Non-Sectarian Committee's office of a Mr. Rothschild who "could scarcely speak good english [sic]"; the revelation that Erich Warburg, who was also at the office, "is foreign born and if a citizen, has just been naturalized"; and the disclosure that others reportedly on the premises were connected with "Communistic and Internationalistic front organizations." Patten placed within this category the American Civil Liberties Union, the Women's International League for Peace and Freedom, and the Foreign Language Information Service.[41]

Clarence Pickett, spokesman for the Non-Sectarian Committee, concluded that the opposition at the hearings "did not seem to be very effective," predicted that the subcommittees would report the bill favorably, cautioned that the full House Immigration Committee was a "much more dubious" proposition, and warned that Senator Reynolds had threatened a filibuster if the bill should reach the Senate floor. Characterizing the hearings as "impressive," the Washington correspondent for the social work journal *Survey Midmonthly* commented in late April on the progress of the measure. Because of the effective work of its sponsors in organizing support and in presenting to the public the carefully formed plans for the child refugees, this observer reported, the bill, which had looked hopeless one month before, had advanced to the point where it stood "possibly an even chance" of being enacted.[42]

In early May each subcommittee unanimously reported the bill favorably to its respective full committee. The few amendments suggested by the joint subcommittee served simply to clarify technical problems and did not weaken the measure. But the apparent success of the Wagner-Rogers Bill in the hearings jolted its opponents into intensified activity. Attacks on the measure became more outspoken, often coming to the surface in the form of letters to the editor. Part of the newly invigorated opposition was anonymous and fell into the category of biased emotionalism. A *New York Herald Tribune* editorial noted that "it is rather surprising how much bad but bitter argument has been evoked by the Wagner bill" and went on to comment that the entrance of 20,000 boys and girls "is being opposed with as fiercely narrow a sincerity as if they were an invading host." The leader of the Washington office of the Non-Sectarian Committee thought the expanded drive against the measure had been launched because restrictionists "who felt that the bill would not even get this far are becoming pretty concerned." In mid-May, the American Legion's legislative representative in Washington reacted to what he saw as rapid progress of the Wagner-Rogers Bill by calling on the 58 departments and 11,580 posts to act swiftly to block the measure. He suggested that members contact congressmen by telephone, telegraph, and letter.[43]

Further trouble for the children's bill was brewing in the House Committee on Immigration and Naturalization. Not convinced that four days of joint hearings had been sufficiently conclusive, the full House committee conducted five more days of testimony. In many ways the new hearings, held in late May and early June, were a repeat production. As before, the Non-Sectarian Committee planned carefully; its only major shift in strategy involved a special effort to have several Southerners testify. In general, both sides again aired the same arguments.[44]

For the restrictionists, most of the same people, representing the same organizations, reappeared for the second round. Very likely the testimony of James L. Wilmeth of the Junior Order United American Mechanics provided the clearest insight into the reason behind the tenacious efforts to keep 20,000 children out: "We are afraid to lift the quota. We are afraid to see it lifted. We don't know where it will end." [45]

The Non-Sectarian Committee had changed its cast a great deal, but its performance also largely repeated the April effort. A fresh slate of outstanding child welfare workers vouched for the practicability of the care plan for refugee children. A new group of clergymen, three Protestants and a Catholic, testified in favor of the bill. Once more, representatives of the AFL and the CIO spoke in support of the measure. Coming before the committee "as an American and as a father" of four children, two of them adopted, actor Joe E. Brown asked that Congress open the door to 20,000 young refugees. Of 30 witnesses who advocated admission of the children, 10 were Southerners, including Frank Porter Graham, president of the University of North Carolina, and Homer P. Rainey, president-elect of the University of Texas.[46]

Despite similarities between the two sets of hearings, the atmosphere of the second hearings differed greatly from that of the first. The joint subcommittee had been sympathetic toward the measure and had even occasionally rebuked restrictionist witnesses. But the full House committee included several congressmen who, openly antagonistic to the Wagner proposal, did not hesitate to express their hostility in sharp and at times rude questioning of witnesses who favored the bill.[47]

Several members of the House committee dwelt on the "charity begins at home" theme. Republican John Z. Anderson of California was concerned about American refugees, the "million and a half people . . . wandering around our own country at the present time without shelter, without necessary food, without proper clothing." Congressman Anderson asked if it was not "a rather sad commentary on our country" that people had offered homes to foreign children when American boys and girls were so much in need. Manifesting the same solicitude for the poverty-stricken children of the United States, Iowa Republican Henry O. Talle wanted to know "how many of those homes that might admit those [refugee] children will not admit the needy children in our own country." Cliff Clevenger, Republican from Ohio, emphasized that his thinking in reference to the Wagner-Rogers Bill was closely related to his concern for the working man. Two months before, Anderson, Talle, and Clevenger had demonstrated their regard for the poor by voting against a bill to provide supplementary funds to keep WPA workers on the job through the fiscal year of 1939.[48]

Edward H. Rees, Kansas Republican, was disturbed about how "hundreds of thousands of these children and parents of these children that don't have just even a meager supply of food, shelter, and clothing" would feel about it if the country admitted 20,000 refugee children. On the deficiency appropriation bill for WPA funds, Congressman Rees had two months earlier managed to appear on both sides of the issue. Rees first voted for a motion to send the WPA bill back to committee and probable death. Immediately after this motion had failed by a margin of more than two to one, the bill itself went through with Rees's help. In 1937, Representative Rees had followed the same procedure of voting for recommittal, seeing that motion fail overwhelmingly, and then shifting his support to the measure in the matter of the Bankhead-Jones Farm Tenant Bill, another proposal to aid American poor.[49]

Despite their concern that entrance of unaccompanied refugee children would deprive needy American boys and girls, several committee members suggested granting the German children first preference within the regular annual quota. Spokesmen for the Wagner bill declared they could not support the measure with such an amendment because it would displace endangered German adult refugees from the visa waiting lists. In an attempt to satisfy supporters of the bill and still keep the quota system intact, Congressman William R. Poage, a Democrat from Texas, presented an arrangement for partial mortgaging of the German quota. Under the Poage plan each of the 20,000 refugee children would be issued a temporary visitor's visa, valid until six months after the child's twenty-first birthday. Upon reaching the age of 21, the young refugee could apply for citizenship and would then receive preference within the current German quota and with it the right to permanent residence. The Non-Sectarian Committee would have agreed to this proposed amendment since it postponed assignment of regular quota places to the children for at least seven years, by which time the refugee emergency, they hoped, would have ended.[50]

Although proponents of the Wagner-Rogers Bill felt their willingness to accept the Poage compromise might enhance the measure's chances of enactment, they were not overly optimistic. Commenting at the end of May on opposition shown at the hearings by members of the House Committee on Immigration, Clarence Pickett reported that some of these congressmen were definitely hostile to the bill and committed to vote against it. In Pickett's opinion the American Legion had by then become the main force against the resolution. He felt uncertain about the bill's reaching the House floor.[51]

Clarence Pickett was not alone in his analysis. A statement made at the House committee hearings by Colonel John Thomas Taylor, spokesman for the American Legion, conveying his "full confidence that this committee will not report out a bill at all," had elicited from Chairman Samuel Dickstein of New York some sharp cross-questioning and a remark which indicated the weak position of the bill in the 21-man committee. Dickstein had said:

There has been a rumor around the Capitol here, and there was before we started the hearings, that this committee was pretty well controlled to kill this legislation. In fact, they talked about having 11 votes in their pockets.

A private poll known to the State Department reflected the accuracy of the rumor. The poll found eleven committee members against the bill, eight for it, and two absent. By mid-June the Senate looked even more doubtful than the House. And a week later Quaker workers in Germany, who would have selected the children if the bill had succeeded, were told: "Don't count on its passing. It's going to be a close matter." [52]

In fact, when the full Senate Immigration Committee did vote on the resolution, it was "a close matter." But, despite important progress made since March in drawing support to the Wagner-Rogers Bill, the gains were insufficient. On June 30 the Senate committee reported the bill favorably, but only after amending it to death. The revised measure granted first preference to the children, but they would be counted as part of the regular annual German quota. No mortgaging provision softened the blow. Expressing his own feelings and those of the Non-Sectarian Committee, Senator Wagner announced that the changed bill was "wholly unacceptable." Because the amended version would remove endangered German adults from their positions on the far overfilled quota list, Wagner preferred "to have no bill at all." He voiced his understanding that the Senate committee's action had occurred when some of its members were absent and asserted that he would urge reconsideration by the complete committee. [53]

The paralyzing amendment had passed by only a narrow margin, and, as Senator Wagner indicated, a number of committee members were absent from the session. [54] Poor attendance reflected the quandary of several senators who usually backed Wagner on social legislation and did not like to vote against him in this case. Yet they felt they would be criticized at home if they supported the measure. Consequently, some of the senators avoided the issue by failing to attend the committee session.[55]

Soon after the Senate committee had acted, sponsors of the Wagner-Rogers Bill initiated efforts to salvage the measure. At first they hoped the bill could be brought to the Senate floor, repaired there with a mortgaging plan like Poage's replacing the immigration committee's vitiating amendment, and then passed. On the House side a substitute resolution including Congressman Poage's compromise was introduced in mid-July. Within days the futility of these moves became apparent and, as Congress neared adjournment, backers of the child refugee plan decided to let the matter drop for the time being.[56]

Senator Robert Reynolds proclaimed in his *American Vindicator* magazine that, "although not successful in killing the resolution entirely," he and others had forced the crippling change. To the general press he announced his satisfaction because he knew supporters of the measure would not accept the committee's amendment. The *Nation* concluded that ruin of the Wagner-Rogers Bill had been the Senate committee's intention as evidenced by its simultaneous approval of another measure combining the children's bill with two of the five antialien bills earlier authored by Senator Reynolds. The resulting proposal provided for registration of aliens and a five-year ban on all quota immigration, but would have granted special entrance permission to the 20,000 children. In its report the Senate committee explained its generosity: "This is a humanitarian gesture of sympathy to enable these 20,000 children . . . living in Germany under tragic conditions to find a home." Although the first session of the Seventy-sixth Congress left in its wake these two devastated versions of the Wagner-Rogers Bill, sponsors of the children's resolution had not yet lost hope.[57]

## AFTERMATH AND CONCLUSIONS

The Non-Sectarian Committee worked through the summer of 1939. With congressmen at home, strategy turned to formation of additional state divisions and diversion of lobbying efforts more to the local level in order to develop pressure on enough lawmakers to set the stage for a stronger push when Congress reconvened. Despite the costs involved in the new approach, the committee proceeded to assign salaried organizers to the South, Midwest, Far West, and other regions. An experienced publicist took charge of the entire operation.[58]

Just as the Non-Sectarian Committee's new projects began to gather momentum, the war opened and the campaign for the children's bill came to a halt pending clarification of the refugee situation. When the committee learned that Congress would reconvene in September, it briefly deliberated, but rejected, the possibility of pressing the Wagner-Rogers Bill at the special session. By November this judgment had been reconfirmed, and, in fact, the group never attempted to revive the proposal. Behind this decision lay the committee's belief that "pressure for this Bill would constitute a hazard to the general immigration situation" because "such a move would rouse to life antialien bills of all kinds." Back in July, in a strong statement in *Newsweek* in favor of the Wagner-Rogers resolution, Raymond Moley had referred to the same apprehension when he maintained that the real obstacle to the measure was "fear that debate in the open will loose the tongues of certain members of Congress who are itching to burn verbal fiery crosses." [59]

An indirect cause for abandoning the bill arose out of growing strictness by the State Department and its consular service in regard to issuing visas to refugees in general. Requirements for affidavits of support from American residents, necessary to assure the consulates that prospective immigrants would not become public charges, increased in stringency after the war started. As a result, a great many refugees, when their turns on the quota list arrived, unexpectedly found their applications rejected on account of unsatisfactory affidavits. Many of these people had been planning to emigrate as families. Since the State Department was willing to cooperate in a plan by which children of these refugee families might come in separately under affidavits supplied by American refugee organizations, the Non-Sectarian Committee decided to redirect its energies and child placement and care plans to such a program. State Department concurrence in the new endeavor derived from the department's reasoning that assurances of support for children need not be as rigorous as those for adults. Quite as important was the department's feeling that entry of children was much less likely to arouse antagonism in Congress than immigration of adults. Of course, the children would come as regular quota immigrants.[60]

Through the fall and winter of 1939 the Non-Sectarian Committee discussed plans to reorganize for the new undertaking. In order to make contributions for the revised program deductible for tax purposes, a different committee, unconnected with legislative efforts, had to be developed. After many delays, the Non-Sectarian Foundation for Refugee Children was incorporated in April 1940, backed by a distinguished group of sponsors which included Eleanor Roosevelt, Albert Einstein, Governor Herbert Lehman, George Rublee, and leading educators as well as prominent clergymen of the three main faiths. The new organization, oriented toward smaller ambitions than the Non-Sectarian Committee, contemplated care of only 500 children the first year.[61]

Before the Non-Sectarian Foundation was a month old, the Nazi blitzkrieg had overwhelmed the Low Countries and was rapidly vanquishing France. Again, as in September 1939, the emigration situation collapsed into temporary confusion and the new organization found itself unable to carry out any of its plans. Consequently, the foundation reduced its staff and budget to a stand-by basis at the end of May. Then, in June, responding to German bombing of Britain, several groups sprang up in the United States with a common interest in evacuating English and possibly other European children to safety in America. In this movement the Non-Sectarian organization played its last role. Spearheaded by many of the same people who had worked for the Wagner-Rogers Bill, and called together by Eleanor Roosevelt, groups interested in bringing over British and other boys and girls met and established the United States Committee for the Care of European Children. The new association absorbed the Non-Sectarian Foundation as its child care division and served until 1953 as America's foremost agency for home placement and supervision of unaccompanied child refugees.[62]

Why did the Wagner-Rogers Bill, despite the important backing it attracted and the really modest numbers for which it asked succor, fail even to reach the floor of Congress? Strong currents of nativism, anti-Semitism, and economic insecurity which were important features of American life in the late 1930's furnish the basic explanation. Nativists looked on the children's bill as an emotional stratagem to force a foot into the door. Once pried open, they reasoned, the door would swing wide and foreigners would flood the country. Because many understood the measure to be a bill for Jewish children, anti-Semitic feelings of all degrees tended to aid the restrictionists' cause. Although the unemployment argument could not have been too effective in itself, the economic situation provided a foundation for the slogan which served as shield against the alien threat. A *Miami Herald* article of April 1939, reporting interviews with eight people regarding the child refugee bill, noted that the five persons who opposed the resolution "were unanimous in citing the need for measures to relieve suffering in the United States before attempting to aid the unfortunate in other countries." [63]

The results of two opinion surveys cast doubt on whether support mustered for the Wagner-Rogers Bill, though widespread and articulate, reflected majority sentiment among the general population. A poll of 1,000 women, mostly housewives, conducted in late May 1939 by the *Cincinnati Post,* showed 77.3 percent opposed to allowing entrance of "a considerable number of European refugee children" outside the quota limits. The survey registered approval of such a move by 21.4 percent, with only 1.3 percent failing to answer.[64] A Gallup poll taken in January 1939 had found much the same sentiment. Asked for their views regarding a proposal "that the government permit 10,000 refugee children from Germany to be brought into this country and taken care of in American homes," 26 percent of the respondents signified approval, 66 percent opposed the plan, and 8 percent held no opinion.[65] In January 1939 the plight of refugees was still much in the press and in the public eye because the Night of Broken Glass and the economic and other oppressive measures which followed it were not far in the past.

In addition to suffering from opposition, the Wagner-Rogers Bill was hurt by lack of support from the Administration. The Department of Labor maintained strict neutrality in regard to the measure, although Secretary Frances Perkins favored it. When Katharine F. Lenroot, chief of the Children's Bureau, appeared before the congressional committees to testify for the resolution, she pointed out that she spoke for herself, not the Administration. In the hearings on Robert Reynolds' five antialien bills, senators carefully cross-questioned officers of the Immigration and Naturalization Service about the Labor Department's position on the Wagner-Rogers Bill. Repeatedly these officials answered that the Labor Department had submitted its report on the Wagner proposal without supporting or opposing it.[66]

The Department of State, the other executive agency closely affected by the children's bill, opposed the plan from its inception. The formal letter communicating the department's recommendations to the Senate Committee on Immigration adhered to impartiality, although it did point out that processing an additional 10,000 visas per year would entail a serious problem in terms of administration and would require increased staff and office space. But actually the State Department quietly discouraged the bill. Late in December 1938 the President's Advisory Committee on Political Refugees, interested in possible legislation to allow entry of 27,000 child refugees outside the quota, considered recommending that the President sponsor such a bill. The State Department strongly disapproved the idea, warning that any move to change the immigration laws at all would be likely to arouse discussion which could lead to enactment of tighter restrictions. The President's Advisory Committee yielded to the State Department's feeling that neither the Advisory Committee nor the President should sponsor a children's bill.[67]

When, in January 1939, an early draft of Wagner's bill came before Assistant Secretary of State George S. Messersmith, he advised against introducing the measure in Congress. Messersmith claimed that any step to liberalize immigration limitations would result in even more restriction. In addition, he feared that passage of the Wagner bill would not only increase administrative problems, but would also encourage more European governments to persecute Jews.[68] Late in the spring, officers of the State Department conveyed to Senator Wagner unofficially their great concern that, if the Wagner-Rogers Bill should reach the floor of Congress, it could become the legislative vehicle for restrictionists who were urging elimination of all immigration quotas. The department therefore advised against pressing for consideration of the bill.[69] Wagner of course continued to work for the measure. In the fall, before deciding definitely to abandon the bill, the Non-Sectarian Committee learned that another drive to pass it would meet active State Department opposition, apparently again due to fear that such an effort would stir up an antialien storm.[70]

From the White House came only an impartial silence. A member of the House Immigration Committee complained that he was unable to obtain the views of the Administration on this issue. While the President was on a Caribbean cruise in February 1939, Mrs. Roosevelt cabled to ask him if she could tell Undersecretary of State Sumner Welles that they approved passage of the children's bill. Roosevelt cabled back that "it is all right for you to support child refugee bill but it is best for me to say nothing till I get back." Evidently it remained best to say nothing, for, in June, Roosevelt received a memorandum from his secretary reporting that Representative Caroline O'Day (D.) of New York had asked if the President would give her his views on the bill. The Chief Executive penciled on the message: "File No action FDR." Fresh from the bitter battles of the 1938 elections, Congress in 1939 had a more conservative complexion than before and was intent on asserting its independence from strong executive leadership. Political crosscurrents unquestionably made it difficult for Roosevelt to back this comparatively minor legislation which was very unpopular in some quarters and which Congress generally saw as too hot to handle.[71]

The official silence of Eleanor Roosevelt is harder to unravel, especially in view of her strong personal approval of the Wagner-Rogers Bill. In January 1939 the First Lady enthusiastically became a sponsor of the child refugee plan, but said she was not free to make her position public until Congress enacted the bill. Still, in reply to a question about the children's bill at a mid-February press conference, she stated that "it seems to me the humanitarian thing to do." About a week later occurred the exchange of cables with the vacationing President which seemingly cleared the way for the First Lady to back the measure openly. Yet, some misgivings on the part of Mrs. Roosevelt or the Chief Executive must have cropped up, for her public sponsorship of the resolution never materialized. Upon establishment in 1940 of the Non-Sectarian Foundation, which was completely divorced from legislative activity, Mrs. Roosevelt immediately and openly became one of its honorary vice presidents.[72]

Several countries opened their doors in varying degrees to children who fled Germany without their parents after the Night of Broken Glass and the ensuing repression had shattered their family life. Until September 1939, when the war ended immigration to Britain, England had taken in more than 9,000 of the young refugees. Figures for other nations extend only into May 1939. By then Holland had received 2,000, Belgium 1,500, France 600, Sweden 250, and the

United States 240. In addition, many other children came to the United States with their families during this period. The 240 who arrived without their parents entered by special arrangement with the Department of Labor and were charged to the quota.[73]

Recognizing that Congress would not permit increased immigration into the 48 states, various people turned their attention toward the sparsely-settled territory of Alaska as a possible haven for some of the refugees.

# Chapter 5

# The Outer Ramparts Hold

In the weeks and months following the time of Broken Glass, discussion of potential havens for the victims of Nazi persecution occasionally centered on Alaska. Only eight days after the November 1938 pogroms swept Germany, Democratic Congressman Charles A. Buckley of New York wrote to President Roosevelt suggesting settlement of refugees in Alaska. Contrasting the northern territory's small population with its wealth in resources, Buckley concluded that immigration would be good for Alaska, as well as for the refugees, and offered to introduce a bill to exempt the territory from regular quota limitations. In his reply, prepared by the State Department, the President rejected Buckley's proposal because such a step "would in effect make Alaska a foreign territory for immigration purposes, which would obviously be out of the question." [1]

At his press conference two weeks after the *Kristallnacht*, Secretary of the Interior Harold L. Ickes, responding to a question regarding possible use of American possessions for refugee settlement, said he thought that Alaska had room for immigration and that a plan for refugees to go there might deserve study. As a matter of fact, the Department of the Interior very soon undertook an inquiry into the potentialities of Alaskan development, including the role of immigration in such a venture. Nine months later, in August 1939, the department released the results of its investigation in a publication entitled *The Problem of Alaskan Development*. Commonly known as the Slattery Report, because Undersecretary Harry Slattery had signed the introductory note, this booklet outlined the riches in newsprint and other forest products, tin, seafood, fur, and several additional resources which awaited fuller development in Alaska. Pointing out that the vast territory contained only 60,000 inhabitants, the report went on to discuss Alaska's slow population growth. Hinting broadly at the value of an influx of refugees, the document referred to the "disastrous effect" wrought on Alaskan development by the Immigration Act of 1924 and declared that application of the quota restrictions "to an underpopulated territory whose future well-being depends on new immigration and new capital is extremely questionable from the standpoint of national policy." The Slattery Report noted the unbalanced nature of Alaska's economy, in which fishing and mining, mainly limited to summer work, accounted for 95 percent of employment, and urged establishment of year-round industries based on processing raw materials.[2]

Having sketched the potential for Alaskan development and some of the obstacles impeding it, the Interior Department's paper offered recommendations for an orderly flow of manpower and capital to the territory. New settlements, it advised, should be based on such industries as wood, minerals, fish, fur, and tourists, with agriculture limited to the needs of the Alaskan market. To sponsor these enterprises the report suggested "public purpose corporations," privately financed, but chartered by the Federal government. These proposed businesses would operate under limitations established by Congress regarding permissible types of industries and the kinds of settlers to be employed. Concerning sources of investment capital, in what was at least a partial reference to philanthropic groups interested in assisting refugees, the booklet mentioned that "men of vision who have allowed humanitarian considerations to influence their use of economic power" were interested in the "human values as well as purely economic values" involved in Alaska settlement plans.[3]

As to prospective colonists, the report anticipated that the majority of the "hundreds of thousands of pioneers" would come from unemployment rolls in the United States. But, in cases where not enough Americans were qualified and willing to accept positions in the new industries, it suggested modification of such "artificial limitations" as restrictive immigration laws in order to allow "skilled labor from the four corners of the earth" to fill employment requirements. Continuing this obvious reference to refugees as a source of manpower, the Slattery Report discussed Alaskan attitudes toward "organized immigration of new settlers of various races, creeds, and stations," and made a dubious case for its conclusion that, partly because of Alaskan tolerance, "the people of Alaska, then, want to see their land populated and it makes little difference whether this population comes from the United States or from abroad." [4]

Within the Department of the Interior, *The Problem of Alaskan Development* did not go unquestioned. Ernest Gruening, director of the Division of Territories and Island Possessions and soon to become governor of Alaska, sharply criticized the Slattery Report in a memorandum to Secretary Ickes. Asserting that the study smoothed over problems and placed Alaskan development possibilities in an overly favorable light, Gruening charged that the letter of transmission accompanying the document hid its purpose which was actually to assist refugees. Gruening objected to possible legislation based on the Slattery Report because it would make Alaska an exception to the immigration quota laws. He maintained that such a measure would violate the Interior Department's policy that territories should receive treatment equal to that of states, and that it would be basically undesirable as well as generally resented throughout Alaska if a class of immigrants was set up which had to remain in the territory, turning it into a virtual concentration camp. Several weeks later the department's Supervisor of Alaskan Affairs, Paul W. Gordon, expressed similar opinions. [5]

In a rebuttal sent to Ernest Gruening, Harold Ickes wondered why Gruening thought the objective of helping refugees had been hidden, since the report itself, the press release referring to it, and newspaper comment on it had all pointed out that some arrangement for refugee entry to Alaska was part of the plan. Ickes cited pages in the report where warnings appeared regarding several problems involved in Alaskan development. As to the concentration camp argument, the secretary felt it was "pretty remote from reality." [6]

Harold Ickes thought highly enough of the report to want to place it before the Intergovernmental Committee on Refugees, meeting in Washington in October 1939. He passed the idea on to President Roosevelt who forwarded the suggestion to Undersecretary of State Sumner Welles for advice. As in the case of Congressman Buckley's letter of nearly a year before, the Department of State was negative about plans for moving refugees to Alaska. Replying rapidly to the President's inquiry, Welles stated that both he and Secretary Hull counseled rejection of Ickes' idea. They felt that submission of the report to the Intergovernmental Committee might stir up "a great deal of unnecessary excitement" in the United States by giving a false impression that thousands of refugees would be entering Alaska. The State Department was apprehensive about "the inevitable implication that great quantities of refugees would soon be pouring from Alaska into the United States proper." Welles recommended that the Interior Department submit the report to the ICR at some other time "when there would be less likelihood of misunderstanding on the part of public opinion in this country." [7]

Despite his acceptance of State Department advice regarding the response to Congressman Buckley and the handling of Secretary Ickes' suggestion concerning the Slattery Report, President Roosevelt may personally have favored refugee settlement in Alaska. In any event, Harold Ickes, after discussing the issue with Roosevelt in early November 1939, declared himself "astonished at the thought that the President had given to a comparatively minor problem . . . and his cleverness in working it out." Roosevelt's plan, according to Ickes, involved moving 10,000 settlers into Alaska during each of the next five years. Half would come from the United States and the other half from abroad, the aliens entering Alaska outside the quotas, but according to the same nationality ratios by which the quota system admitted immigrants to the United States. With such an arrangement the President thought only about ten percent would be Jewish, a result which would "avoid the undoubted criticism" that would arise "if there were an undue proportion of Jews." This system would also prevent formation of any national enclaves which might resist Americanization. From Ickes' version of this conversation, Roosevelt seems to have had in mind eventual admission to Alaska of several thousand fugitives from Nazism. But the Chief Executive never took an open position on the question of refugee immigration into Alaska.[8]

Public reception of the Slattery Report was generally positive because of the popularity of the idea of Alaskan development. Even the Junior Order United American Mechanics, aware that the bait included refugee settlement, weakened its restrictionism fleetingly and declared that "surely, it would seem that in our great possession of Alaska there is ample opportunity for men and women who have . . . the frontier spirit." Widespread newspaper publicity greeted release of the document. Before the Slattery Report was six months old the Interior Department had received over 4,000 letters in response to it, less than one percent critical. Editorials, which had by then appeared in 388 newspapers, were overwhelmingly favorable.[9]

Meanwhile, in August 1939, only two days after release of the study, the Secretary of the Interior had announced that his department was drafting a measure to permit refugee entry into Alaska outside the regular quota limits. The proposed legislation, as Ickes informed Republican Senator Robert A. Taft of Ohio, "rather closely" followed recommendations put forward in the Slattery Report. Most likely the whole Alaska development scheme was devised with the plight of European refugees foremost in the minds of the planners. A reading of the Slattery Report, especially the parts dealing with immigration and refugees, leaves little doubt that one of its important purposes was to prepare the way for a refugee bill. Whatever uncertainty might persist after studying the document is dispelled by Ickes' statement in his *Secret Diary* that the report "grew out of the idea of taking care of a certain number of refugees despite our quota laws." [10]

News in August 1939 that a refugee bill for Alaska was under preparation aroused immediate opposition. Within a few days the pressure of this reaction forced the Interior Department to deny that it was planning wholesale immigration of refugees into Alaska. Still, Senator Robert Reynolds' *American Vindicator* insisted that the proposal was another "opening wedge" to bring in hundreds of thousands of aliens and warned: "Alaskans, you had better be on your guard." They already were, according to an article in the *New York Times*. The writer reported numerous protests from Alaskans against possible entry of large numbers of refugees and pointed out that some of this resistance was "based on racial grounds." [11]

Months later, in February 1940, the Department of the Interior finally completed preparations for placing the Alaska Development Bill before Congress. A press release issued on February 11 claimed broad editorial support for and wide popular interest in the proposed plans for Alaskan colonization. Secretary Ickes asserted that most opposition came from a few Alaskans who feared that a population increase would endanger their control of the territory's resources. On March 13, acting on behalf of Senator William H. King (D.) of Utah, Senator Robert F. Wagner (D.) of New York introduced the bill. The next day Representative Franck Havenner, California Democrat, submitted the same measure to the House.[12]

The King-Havenner Bill would have based Alaskan growth on privately financed "Alaska development corporations" to be chartered by the Department of the Interior. To make sure these new operations would not interfere with existing United States or Alaskan business, the measure limited the chartered corporations to such enterprises as agriculture, processing of forest products, mining, fisheries except salmon, fur farming, and services for other settlers. Under the proposed legislation, refugees between the ages of 16 and 45 who qualified for the new jobs could come to Alaska outside the immigration quota limits. But for five years these refugees would have to restrict their employment to the same lines of work as those permitted the development corporations. Each approved immigrant could bring his wife and children with him.

Other features of the King-Havenner Bill indicate that its sponsors tried to learn from the failure of the Wagner-Rogers Bill. To head off the "charity begins at home" and "refugees take jobs" arguments, drafters of the Alaska Bill framed their plan to include poverty-stricken and unemployed Americans. First preference for at least 50 percent of the new jobs had to go to American citizens, if they were qualified for the work. Supporters of the legislation felt they held a trump card to play against standard restrictionist arguments, for this plan would create jobs for Americans. Anticipating nativist denunciation of the bill as a wedge to break down immigration walls, the writers of the measure included a requirement that refugees who entered Alaska under its provisions stay there for at least five years. After that, only when the quota of a refugee's native country was unfilled could he obtain a permanent visa, gain citizenship, and then move freely in the United States. In effect, entry of these refugees would be mortgaged against future quotas.[13]

The King-Havenner Bill failed to attract widespread support. The Non-Sectarian Committee, which had championed the Wagner-Rogers Bill, discussed the Alaska Bill at some length, was unable to develop much enthusiasm, and did not take a stand for it. The American Committee for Christian Refugees decided against any action as an organization. The *Nation* did not mention the proposal. The *New Republic* carried only an article by a conservationist against the Interior Department's entire Alaska settlement scheme and a letter in rebuttal to the article.[14]

But the Alaska Bill was not without friends and the Interior Department did not stand alone in its plan for territorial development.

As early as February 1939 new groups interested in Alaskan colonization began to form. Several, but not all, of these associations were primarily concerned with rescue of refugees. In general, the functions of these organizations were twofold: to work for passage of legislation similar to that envisioned in the Slattery Report, and to develop financing for the proposed settlement projects. In carrying out their plans, the groups received full cooperation from the Department of the Interior.[15]

By August 1939, when the Slattery Report appeared, a coordinating committee of colonization associations had emerged in New York City. Within two months the organization took the name National Committee for Alaskan Development and issued a statement which faithfully reflected the Slattery Report. By January 1940 another New York group involved in refugee aid, the Roland German American Democratic Society, threw its support to the National Committee. Out of this merger of interests came the Alaskan Development Committee. Sponsors of the new organization included Harry Slattery, President Frank Kingdon of the University of Newark, theologian Paul Tillich, lawyers, businessmen, motion picture stars Paul Muni and Luise Rainer, as well as officers of the National Refugee Service, the American Committee for Christian Refugees, the American Friends Service Committee, the United Czechoslovak American Societies, and the Federal Council of Churches. With offices in Washington and New York, the Alaskan Development Committee became the main private group pressing for passage of the King-Havenner Bill.[16]

The Alaskan Development Committee also worked on the problem of financial backing for the proposed Alaskan corporations. By early 1940 signs pointed to people concerned about refugees as the main source of this capital. In a memorandum regarding the Alaska Bill, the committee pointed out that American capital was generally little interested in investment in Alaska, but many Americans who were sending large sums abroad for refugee relief would prefer to put the money into projects which would enable the victims of persecution to become self-supporting.[17]

A vigorous opposition arose to counter the meager support which the Alaska Development Bill succeeded in attracting. By far, strongest disapproval came from Alaskans themselves and for the most part centered on the refugee aspect of the measure. Resistance to the proposed legislation developed months before the bill appeared and continued for more than a year. In October 1939 the editor of the *Ketchikan Alaska Chronicle,* in a letter to arctic explorer Vilhjalmur Stefansson, expressed his belief that, despite the Slattery Report's assurances of Alaskan tolerance, residents of the territory were negative toward a settlement plan which included immigration of Jewish refugees. The editor felt that Alaskans had "a tendency to see a difference between 'colonization' and 'immigration,' and a further tendency to see a difference between immigration of Europeans and European Jews." Several months later, a biting editorial in the *Alaska Weekly* asserted that the purpose of the Slattery Report had been simply to set the stage for the King-Havenner Bill, and that the bill was mostly a "verbal smoke screen" to cover the real purpose of the proposal which was "colonizing Alaska with refugees, financed by private capital. That it is Jewish capital and that the refugees to be poured into Alaska if this bill is passed will be Jewish is obvious." The *Alaska Weekly* went on to condemn "opposition to Jewish refugees based on racial antipathy," but stated that the "consensus of opinion" in the territory held "that Jews would be the least desirable of immigrants because of being the least adaptable" to Alaskan conditions.[18]

Several of the territory's chambers of commerce lodged strong protests against the King-Havenner Bill. The Fairbanks group, for instance, passed a resolution opposing the Alaska Bill because, among other reasons, it implied "virtual serfdom" for the refugees, for they would be bound by five-year job contracts. Also, since only charitable groups concerned to aid "refugees of their own race" would be likely to invest in such a plan, the practical result would be to turn Alaska into a "dumping ground for foreign refugees of doubtful capacity for assimilation." The Alaska Miners Association telegraphed Senator King that enactment of the measure would bring disaster to the territory which already had to contend with the problem of thousands of jobless men flocking in. The "old settlers" of Igloo No. 15 of the Pioneers of Alaska objected to populating their land with aliens who "cannot be assimilated in Alaska, and will constitute a menace to our American civilization." Additional resistance to the King-Havenner Bill came to the surface when a subcommittee of the Senate Committee on Territories and Insular Affairs held hearings on the proposal in mid-May 1940.[19]

Only four witnesses appeared against the King-Havenner Bill: Don

Carlos Brownell, mayor of Seward and senator-elect of the Alaska Legislature; Colonel John Thomas Taylor, representing the American Legion; John B. Trevor of the American Coalition of Patriotic Societies; and Anthony J. Dimond, delegate from Alaska to the United States Congress. Both Alaskans stood firmly against further bureaucratic control of the territory by the Secretary of the Interior. Delegate Dimond asserted that the proposal, by establishing separate immigration laws for Alaska, would set it off from the rest of the country, making it into "a sort of a concentration camp or semipenal colony." The American Legion spokesman, sensing danger of fifth column infiltration through Alaska, declared that "instead of opening our doors wider to the Trojan horses of the enemies of our democracy; . . . we should be taking steps to expel them and to close our doors to any more of their kind." Veteran restrictionist John B. Trevor argued against additional entry of foreigners because of the unemployment situation and the fifth column danger. For good measure, Trevor contributed his view that Nazi persecution of Jews had occurred "in very many cases . . . because of their beliefs in the Marxian philosophy." [20]

The Department of the Interior marshalled testimony in favor of the Alaska Bill. Its basic strategy was to bring in numerous government specialists to sketch the advantages of the proposal to the United States. The first witness, Secretary Ickes, introduced the theme by declaring that "if a proposition is good for business, and good for the national defense, and good for the American people, we ought not to turn it down merely because it has some humanitarian by-products." More than a dozen other officials from such agencies as the Departments of Commerce and of Labor, the General Land Office, the Division of Alaskan Fisheries, the Bureau of Mines, the Office of Indian Affairs, and the United States Geological Survey vouched for the practicality and the value to the nation of the projects contemplated in the King-Havenner Bill. Witnesses pointed to excellent opportunities for development of the cod, shrimp, and crab fisheries, the paper and pulpwood industries, mining, fur farming, and other enterprises. They stressed the economic contribution that the new settlements and businesses would make by providing markets and putting the unemployed to work. And they asserted that additional population and improvements such as roads and airports would mean easier defense of a vulnerable frontier. Besides the officials, a few nongovernment people appeared for the bill. Among them were Alvin R. Johnson, director of the New School for Social Research, Clarence E. Pickett of the American Friends Service Committee, and Frank Bohn representing the Alaskan Development Committee.[21]

During the hearings witnesses for the bill repeatedly maintained that its major objective was development of Alaska and that its refugee features were only incidental. For their part, Senators Robert R. Reynolds (D.) of North Carolina and Homer T. Bone (D.) of Washington, subcommittee members who questioned this rationale, pressed these witnesses to agree that the legislation was really aimed mainly at helping refugees. One approach was to demonstrate that the proposed plans for development of Alaska would work just as well without immigrants. This provided grounds for Reynolds to denounce the bill as "just a smoke screen" for refugees "to get in the back door." Senator Reynolds succeeded in bringing the Director of Forests to concede that many unemployed Americans could chop down trees, run pulp mills, and market pulpwood. The chief of the Division of Game Management acknowledged that foreign technicians were not necessary for successful fur farming. To an official of the National Park Service, who was outlining the advantages of having trained European personnel involved in development of Alaskan recreational and tourist facilities, Senator Reynolds pointed out that American ability in that business was proven by the fact that the United States had more tourist houses than all other countries combined. The witness responded that "some of them are not run too efficiently." To this observation Reynolds replied, "No, but very interestingly," a remark which received rapid confirmation when the Park Service official commented, "I will acknowledge I spent a couple of very interesting nights at Valdez." In the end, the witness granted that refugees were not essential to establish recreational enterprises. Senator Bone maintained that agriculture did not require European-trained technicians; that if Bolivians with their level of education could mine and process tin, Americans could also; that thousands "who never saw the inside of a high school" were catching and canning fish.[22]

Arguing in a related vein, Senator Reynolds, joined by Alaska Delegate Dimond, declared the King-Havenner Bill granted nothing new of importance to the proposed development corporations except the right to bring in immigrants. The logical conclusion, Reynolds maintained, was that the bill should be dropped and the potential investors in Alaskan development should go into operation immediately, supplying 100 percent of the new jobs to unemployed Americans. When supporters of the bill pointed out that much of the anticipated capital would be forthcoming only if "specially selected and qualified refugees are admitted," Reynolds had solid ground for charging that the measure was basically a refugee bill. Considering the position in which sponsors of the Alaska Bill had placed themselves by insisting that it was only incidentally a refugee measure, the reasoning that the development plans were quite workable without refugees seemed conclusive.[23]

Yet, in a brilliant rejoinder, Felix S. Cohen, Assistant Solicitor of the Interior Department and co-author of the bill, denied that the primary aim of the measure was to help refugees and stated that the immigration features were simply "an essential means" for carrying out the "fundamental purpose" of the bill, settlement of Alaska. Cohen declared that he and the Interior Department would support the bill even if the immigration clauses were eliminated, provided other means of bringing about Alaskan development, such as tax advantages, were substituted. But he felt the arrangements in the King-Havenner Bill were "superior and preferable from the standpoint of general public policy" to the possible alternatives. One basis for this conclusion lay in the expectation of Cohen and others that some European industries, suited to Alaskan resources, would move to the territory if essential technicians and administrators could also come. Another source of investment capital, "certain individuals who are interested in aiding friends or relatives to escape from certain powers," had obvious ties to the immigration aspects of the bill. In brief, funds available for refugee aid, and some refugee-owned industries, could be diverted to Alaskan development in a way that would also benefit victims of persecution. But this wedding of interests could not occur without modification of the immigration laws. Restrictionists, and a great many Alaskans, were unwilling to pay that price and contented themselves with castigating, in the words of Senator Reynolds, "people in the United States who will put up their money to help foreigners when they won't put up their money to help poor citizens of the United States."[24]

Still, two questions arise regarding the case presented by Felix Cohen. First, if the actual primary concern behind the measure was development of Alaska, was the method written into the King-Havenner Bill really, from a pragmatic standpoint, "superior and preferable" to other possible approaches such as tax advantages? This question has to be considered in the light of Senator Bone's apt observation to Cohen that "the moment this bill emerges on the floor of the Senate the immigration feature will be the point around which the argument will revolve." Undoubtedly sponsors of the measure realized that this sort of debate would occur and that it would handicap the bill's chances of passage. The second question is whether the Alaska Development Bill's provision for refugees actually was simply a device for attracting capital for the "fundamental purpose," building up Alaska. Or did the refugee aspect of the bill—and the bill itself, for that matter—in fact arise out of concern to find a place of safety for victims of persecution? The latter explanation is much more convincing in view of evidence already discussed in reference to the origin and contents of the Slattery Report. Corroboration comes from a statement made by Secretary Ickes in December 1940 that

> even before the refugee pressure for a haven in this free land of ours became as severe as it is, my department had proposed legislation which would provide for a further colonization of Alaska, whose economy would also thereby be greatly improved.[25]

In any event, testimony in favor of the bill did not convince the subcommittee. The Seattle Chamber of Commerce, which stood against the measure, learned from an observer that the subcommittee would pigeonhole the bill because opposition was so strong. Replying in June 1940 to a letter against the bill from the Daughters of the American Revolution, Democratic Senator Millard E. Tydings of Maryland, chairman of the Committee on Territories and Insular Affairs, stated that the measure would probably not get out of the committee. And also in June, Democrat Lex Green of Florida, chairman of the House Committee on Territories, informed correspondents that no hearings on the Alaska Bill would take place in his committee and that enactment was very unlikely. In fact, no further action on the measure ever occurred.[26]

Although the King-Havenner Bill died in the subcommittee, the idea behind it persisted. Harold Ickes spoke approvingly of Alaska as a place of refuge in December 1940. Late in January 1941 Representative Samuel Dickstein (D.) of New York submitted a new measure "to colonize Alaska for purposes of national defense and as a market for surplus production." Dickstein's proposal would have made all unused quota numbers of all countries for the preceding six years available to refugees who wanted to immigrate to Alaska and were willing to stay there for five years. Soon, like a formalized dance, the motions of the previous year began almost to repeat themselves. Delegate Dimond asked to be heard in opposition to the bill; restrictionists made their disapproval known; a subcommittee, this time in the House, was named to consider the proposal; and a joint memorial against the measure passed both houses of the Alaska Legislature unanimously. In phrases reminiscent of the argumentation of 1940, the joint memorial declared that the bill would "wreck the economic system of Alaska," make the territory "virtually a concentration or detention camp," change "the culture and economy in Alaska from American to alien," and "convert the Territory into the world's largest and most expensive penal colony." Congressional hearings did not materialize, but otherwise the pattern remained intact as the new bill, like its predecessor, was laid to rest in a subcommittee.[27]

As with the Wagner-Rogers Bill, the Alaska Development Bill foundered on the rocks of nativism, anti-Semitism, and economic insecurity which in the late thirties and early forties loomed in the way of all refugee legislation. Nativists saw the proposal as a means of slipping thousands of aliens in through the Alaskan frontier. And anti-Semites concluded that it was a bill to expose Alaska to an influx of Jewish immigrants. The claim that another move was afoot to dump penniless refugees in the country fed on economic fears which had matured through ten years of depression. Because the bill most affected Alaska, the major response came from residents of that territory. Alaska was immune neither to unemployment problems nor to anti-Semitism. In addition, many Alaskans of 1940, particularly businessmen and politicians, held extremely hostile feelings toward Secretary Ickes and any of his plans. The Interior Department, which played a large part in the administration of Alaska, received heavy criticism from radio stations, newspapers, and chambers of commerce in the region. Furthermore, some of the territory's financial leaders opposed establishment of new industry. Others, merchants, shippers, and state of Washington producers, who lived from supplying territorial markets, disapproved of any farm colonization plans. As a result of this combination of attitudes against Interior Department projects and against refugee immigration, the Alaskan reaction to the King-Havenner Bill was negative. In the States, nativists and anti-Semites, who foresaw a steady leakage of refugees from Alaska into the Pacific Northwest and the rest of the country, made common cause with Alaskan opponents of the measure.[28]

Through the months that they had been devising and pressing the Alaska plan, Harold Ickes and some of his subordinates had been realistic enough not to pin all their hopes for refugee rescue on Congress. Searching for alternatives within existing immigration legislation, Interior Department lawyers concluded that the law had enough elasticity to permit a small influx of refugees into the Virgin Islands as visitors. There they could safely wait for a chance to move to a permanent haven.

Although the Department of the Interior exercised administrative jurisdiction over the Virgin Islands, any plan to move refugees into the Caribbean possession had to conform to the United States immigration code since it applied to the islands as well as to the mainland. Because the quotas were already under heavy pressure, the Interior Department's Virgin Islands project aimed at providing asylum for temporary visitors, a category not subject to numerical limitations. Ordinarily only State Department consular officials, by issuing visitors' visas, could authorize entry of foreign visitors. Consuls were strict in examining applicants and in requiring proof that visiting aliens could and would return to their homelands after a limited period of time. Of course, very few refugees could qualify for visitors' visas.

The Interior Department, devising a different interpretation of the visitor category, wanted to allow a limited number of refugees to "visit" the Virgin Islands without visas until their turns arrived on the waiting lists for permanent quota entry into the United States. Obviously, admission of visitors who had no intention of returning home, but who planned to enter the United States via the Virgin Islands, constituted a new departure in immigration practice. This the State Department would not approve.[29]

But, in the case of the Virgin Islands, the Interior Department was almost in a position to bypass the State Department. A clause in an Executive Order of April 1938 authorized the governor of the Virgin Islands to allow alien visitors without visas to enter the islands in emergency cases. The Virgin Islands Legislative Assembly passed a resolution opening the islands as a way station for refugees. And the governor agreed to sign a proclamation which would put the plan into operation. But the Interior Department decided to delay the proclamation pending settlement of one remaining legal problem. Administrative regulations, long since drawn up to implement the Immigration Act of 1924, included a proviso that aliens who had already applied for permanent quota immigration would void their applications if they entered the United States or any of its possessions as temporary visitors. Since the main purpose of the Interior Department's plan was to furnish a waiting place for people already on quota lists, this stipulation undercut the whole project.[30]

In October 1939 the Department of the Interior opened negotiations with the Departments of State, Justice, and Labor in an effort to have the Virgin Islands exempted from this ruling. The Labor Department approved the Interior Department's request. But the State Department, supported by the Department of Justice, consistently maintained that the change required action by Congress.[31]

Yet, in November 1940 the Interior Department, mistakenly feeling that agreement with the State Department was within reach, moved to put its project into operation. Plans called for taking about 2,000 refugees into the Virgin Islands until they could move to the United States mainland. While in the islands, they would rely on their own financial resources, on those of friends or relatives in the United States, or on help from American refugee agencies. Except for a limited number with special skills, the visitors would be forbidden gainful employment. One important aspect of the project was the expected boost which the influx of support money would give the islands' economy. Also, expansion of housing and recreational facilities to meet refugee needs would, it was thought, help build the Virgin Islands hotel and tourist industries, potentially very important, but lagging because of lack of facilities.[32]

Ward M. Canaday, chairman of the board of Willys-Overland Motors and owner of large holdings in the Virgin Islands, held a different view of the probable economic effects of using the islands as a refugee haven. Canaday warned the Interior and State Departments and President Roosevelt that turning the West Indian possession into a place to unload refugees could give it a reputation which might ruin its attractiveness as a tourist center.[33]

Early in November 1940, Lawrence W. Cramer, governor of the

Virgin Islands, prepared a proclamation permitting selected refugees to enter without visas. On November 12 Assistant Secretary of State Breckinridge Long learned of it. Long, who was continually exercised about possible immigration of Nazi agents, feared that admission of refugees without careful scrutiny by the State Department's consular service would open the Virgin Islands to infiltration by German subversives. He lost little time in spelling out his fears to President Roosevelt who ordered Cramer's proclamation suspended.[34]

Actually, the Interior Department had been working out a special procedure with the President's Advisory Committee on Political Refugees for careful screening of these refugees. Late in November, after it had completed the new safeguards, the Interior Department again sought State Department agreement to its plans for the Virgin Islands. In mid-December the State Department responded with a 15-page opinion by its Legal Adviser making a strong case for the view that refugees under the Interior Department's Virgin Islands arrangement could not, by the nature of their circumstances, qualify as temporary visitors and so were ineligible for entry except as quota immigrants. The final blow came in the form of a memorandum from the President to Harold Ickes. Roosevelt bluntly told Ickes to drop the matter because it was concerned with foreign policy, an exclusive province of the President and the State Department.[35]

Yet, for months Ickes and his Solicitor, Nathan R. Margold, would not admit defeat. Margold, after summarizing the Interior Department's position in a memorandum which Ickes passed to Roosevelt, turned out a 75-page paper defending the legality of the department's proposal. But the Department of Justice closed its file on the question by February 1941 and in April the State Department emphasized that its December decision would stand. Margold and Ickes finally accepted the inevitable and gave up the project.[36]

Why did the Virgin Islands plan come to nothing? Quite clearly, the project's shaky legal basis was a serious obstacle. Admission of aliens without clearance through the American consular service ran against long-established administrative practice. The Interior Department's redefinition of "temporary visitors" to include refugees unable to return home strained the meaning of the term. And regulations cutting incoming visiting aliens off the quota lists for permanent immigration seemed immutable. Yet, the governor of the Virgin Islands, through Executive Order, did have legal authorization to permit entry of aliens without visas in emergency cases. And, before the Virgin Islands project was buried at the end of 1940, the State Department had stretched the rules enough to admit as "temporary visitors" to the United States a few thousand political refugees who had no intention of returning home to Nazi prisons or death.[37]

Consideration of all aspects of the affair leads to the conclusion that, although the Virgin Islands plan collapsed partly because of its questionable legal foundations, an equally important reason for its failure lay in Breckinridge Long's belief that Nazi agents trying to get to the United States disguised as refugees gravely threatened the nation's safety. He was appalled at the thought of aliens entering American territory without first passing through the consular service's scrupulous screening procedures. Long and the State Department felt the risk unjustified, even in the case of the Virgin Islands, 1,000 miles from the mainland. Since the State Department actually administered the immigration laws, in the last analysis it held the authority to decide the fate of the Virgin Islands project.[38]

While the Interior Department's Alaska and Virgin Islands efforts for refugee rescue had been working their way toward final failure, the course of the European war had shifted drastically. In the spring of 1940 the Nazi blitzkrieg swept through western Europe. After France fell, heavy German bombing of Britain in preparation for invasion precipitated in the United States a new refugee movement which, because of its close relationship to the English ordeal, drew very strong public support and remarkably swift action from the Roosevelt Administration and the Congress.

# Chapter 6

# Charity Extends to the Channel

On the morning of April 9, 1940, Denmark awoke to find that the "phony war," which had lasted for the six months since the conquest of Poland, had come to an abrupt end. Without warning and without resistance, German troops moved into the small coastal nation and controlled it before the day was over. Norway, attacked the same morning, rallied from the surprise assault, but in vain. Although hostilities continued into June, Norwegian opposition broke down by the end of April. The blitzkrieg struck Luxemburg, the Netherlands, and Belgium on May 10, and, despite help from French and British expeditionary forces, the three small nations collapsed before the month was out. Four days after the invasion of the Low Countries, German units entered France and an astonished world saw them drive down the Somme Valley to the English Channel in a week. One week later evacuation of Allied forces from Dunkirk was underway, by mid-June Paris fell, and on June 22 France surrendered.

Thousands of German refugees who had previously escaped to the Low Countries and to what became occupied France found themselves again under Nazi control. Many others joined the millions of people of all walks of life who, fleeing the paths of the German armies, choked highways to the south. Total war held the stage as the *Luftwaffe* rained bullets and bombs on civilians streaming along roads or waiting in crowded railway stations. A survivor of the bombing of the Bordeaux station told of a little girl who had been standing near him, "clutching her mother's skirt so as not to get lost. After the explosion, she was still standing there dazed, holding on to a piece of woolen skirt, but her mother—she had been blown to bits." [1]

Americans, aware of the suffering of European civilian populations, wanted to extend concrete aid. At the President's request, Congress amended an unemployment relief appropriation bill, before passing it in late June, to include 50 million dollars for purchase of American agricultural, medical, and other supplies for refugee relief. Earlier in June support had begun to develop in the United States for removal of boys and girls from the war areas. Solicitor General Francis Biddle of the Department of Justice wrote the President suggesting, without result, that Roosevelt ask Congress for authorization to use one million dollars of the 50 million dollar refugee relief appropriation for transportation of young war victims to the United States. Biddle urged sending an American ship to France immediately to evacuate children in critical need in the Bordeaux area. Eleanor Roosevelt, who also advocated government action to facilitate rescue of the children, acceded to the President's request that she delay her efforts in that direction until he and the State Department could form a clear policy on the issue. But for the children in France only immediate steps could have availed. Before the end of June the Nazi grip on France had tightened, making removal of children from that country extremely difficult. In any event, although suffering there continued, the worst horrors of war had moved elsewhere.[2]

Even before France capitulated, Nazi aircraft started to strike England and the Battle of Britain opened. Anticipating invasion as well as air bombardment, the British government in mid-June initiated plans to send thousands of children to safety overseas. After France fell, American concern for war-endangered children quickly narrowed its scope and threw itself behind a movement to bring English boys and girls to the United States. Sympathy for Great Britain rose rapidly enough throughout the country for President Roosevelt to begin releasing military supplies to the British in June. In this atmosphere of growing concern for England, a child rescue movement which combined its own natural appeal with the cause of aid to Britain could not fail to attract a flood of public support.[3]

A Gallup survey published in late June reported 58 percent in favor of allowing English and French children to come to the United States for the duration of the war. The poll also found 25 percent of all those questioned willing to take "one or more of these children" into their homes. Translated into numbers, these results indicated that five to seven million American families were interested in welcoming the children into their households. Conceding the need to allow for a large amount of shrinkage, Gallup still concluded that the number of boys and girls who could possibly come would fall far short of filling the homes which would be opened to them. Although the poll referred to French children as well as British, *Time* magazine mirrored the public mind accurately when it announced that Gallup's survey revealed extensive "U.S. willingness to harbor British children." [4]

As air attacks on Great Britain increased, support for evacuation of English children to the United States grew in the American press. From mid-June into September the *New York Times* gave almost daily coverage to the issue and in the same 12 weeks carried 18 editorials urging swift action to help remove children from England. *Life* magazine printed captivating photographs of British boys and girls who had already come, announced that America had "unreservedly" opened its doors to the young English refugees, and backed the movement for mass evacuation. The *Christian Century*, certain that English children would not compete for jobs and would "place no strain on this country," called for their admission. [5]

In the meantime, at Eleanor Roosevelt's invitation, representatives of various groups concerned about immigration of refugee children conferred for several days in New York City. Out of these meetings emerged on June 20 the United States Committee for the Care of European Children (USC). With Mrs. Roosevelt as honorary president and Marshall Field as president, the new organization concentrated on two major objectives: finding ways to provide sponsorship for British children who had no relatives or friends in the United States, and assuring high standards of care for all boys and girls who arrived. Within two days of its formation, the USC was inundated with offers of 2,000 homes for children. Less than two weeks later the number reached 10,000, a figure which climbed to 15,000 during the next week. Utilizing a professional staff lent by social work agencies, and voluntary labor equivalent to 75 full-time daily workers, the committee through its first weeks fought frantically to catch up with the growing flood of invitations. Endorsement of the USC soon came from overseas when in early July the British government designated it the official agency for reception of children in the United States. Working closely with the Federal government's Children's Bureau, the United States Committee established standards for the cooperating child care organizations which would handle placement and continuing supervision of the children. In England, the government offered to pay ocean passage for children whose parents could not meet the cost and rushed plans to send 15,000 children to the United States and the same number to Canada by the end of August.[6]

As a result of these efforts, mass evacuation of English boys and girls seemed about to commence in early July. But when, as the days passed, the British government did not start the children on their way, American supporters of the movement began to look for the cause. On Saturday, July 6, an article in the *Washington Daily News* by Raymond Clapper blamed the United States immigration law. Although the large British quota, which exceeded 65,000 per year, was adequate, the law stipulated that no more than one tenth of the quota numbers could be issued in any single month. Because the bombs would not wait, Clapper wondered why the Administration had not requested Congress to modify the law and went on to ask: "Why doesn't President Roosevelt, the great humanitarian, do something?" On Monday, the President had White House secretary Stephen Early explain to Clapper that delay regarding the children was due to lack of ships, not to a shortage of visas. Clapper responded that the President could easily obtain a change in the law and that such a step would place responsibility for moving the children clearly on the British. The journalist also mentioned that supporters of Republican presidential nominee Wendell Willkie had become interested and Willkie might propose amending the law as a means of hastening removal of children from danger.[7]

At his press conference on Tuesday, July 9, the President sidestepped questions about complaints that endless red tape was keeping the children out, but did indicate that the shipping bottleneck was the main problem. On Wednesday, a corroborating view came from Joseph P. Kennedy, American Ambassador to England, who cabled the State Department that the obstacle was transportation, not red tape or quota limitations. Kennedy predicted the evacuation plan would be a huge failure because of the ship shortage. Yet, that same day, the United States Committee for the Care of European Children asserted that mass removal of young refugees necessitated changes in immigration regulations.[8]

On Thursday, July 11, a State Department press release concerning British refugee children averred that "all the red tape has been cut and all of the nonessential requirements have been eliminated." The statement emphasized that "any delay that may be occurring . . . is not attributable in any way to American regulations." According to Harold Ickes' notes, at a Cabinet meeting held the same day, Roosevelt raised the problem of evacuation of English children and insisted that lack of convoyed shipping was the real obstruction. Ickes reported that "the President was a little nervous on the subject, but he finally told Hull and Bob Jackson to simplify procedure at this end as soon as possible and to join in a statement to the public telling just what this country is doing." [9]

In accordance with Roosevelt's instructions, and despite the State Department's very recent assurances that no red tape remained uncut, a joint statement by the Departments of State and Justice, dated Saturday, July 13, announced a "simplified procedure" for entry of refugee children. In fact, the new regulations constituted a major relaxation in immigration restrictions for the benefit of "children under sixteen years of age who [sought] to enter the United States to escape the dangers of war." One of the five changes reduced formalities and paperwork involved in granting visas. Another suspended the rule that no child could enter unless he was with or on the way to join a parent. A third modification exempted child refugees from a regulation excluding aliens whose passage was paid by any organization. The other two innovations, those concerning corporate affidavits and visitors' visas, were the most significant. [10]

Usually an immigrant satisfied the legal requirement that he prove himself unlikely to become a public charge by presenting affidavits from friends or relatives in the United States promising financial support for him in case of need. Besides being rather complicated and quite time consuming, this procedure was a practical impossibility for English families who did not have acquaintances in the United States. In order to allow boys and girls of all circumstances to enter, the new regulations permitted an agency such as the United States Committee to bring in thousands of children under a single blanket affidavit which guaranteed their financial support. This "corporate affidavit" would rest on simplified affidavits which Americans willing to care for the children would give to the agency. [11]

Another remarkable change initiated by the new regulations of July 13 allowed issuance of visitors' visas to refugee children "upon a showing of intention that they shall return home upon the termination of hostilities." Since visitors' visas were not subject to numerical limitations, this change enabled the Administration to spike allegations that monthly quota limits were hindering evacuation of British children. The requirement that the children intend to go home after the war satisfied a long-standing State Department policy which restricted issuance of visitors' visas to people who had a homeland to which they could return. Actually, the only children eligible for these special visitors' visas were British boys and girls, for they alone among the war victims still had a country which would agree to take them back. The means by which the Administration divined in July 1940 that Britain would be free to call the children home at the end of the war are undeterminable. If Germany had been victorious, perhaps the Nazis would not have allowed repatriation of English children. If the Administration assumed the defeat of Hitler, seemingly French, Belgian, Polish, and German-Jewish children as well as those of other backgrounds would also be able to "return home upon the termination of hostilities." In any event, although the other four changes made by the new regulations of July 13 applied to all refugee boys and girls, only British children qualified for the crucial visitors' visas. True, in late September non-British children who had reached England became eligible for visitors' visas, but only after the British government had agreed to allow these boys and girls to return to England after the war.[12]

For British children the Administration had obviously opened the doors to a mass migration. But while these developments were unfolding in Washington, the British government, on July 12, announced postponement "for the present" of its evacuation plans because convoys were not available and without convoys the risk of sinkings was too great. Parents able to make their own arrangements and willing to take the chance could still send their children overseas. One reason the British government had entered the evacuation movement, however, had been to stifle criticism by enabling poorer English families to send their children away also. Consequently, suspension of the government's plan once again brought complaints that only children of the rich could reach safety. The negative effect which this situation had on national morale partly explains Prime Minister Winston Churchill's statement to the House of Commons on July 18 that large-scale removal of children was "most undesirable" and that he did not think the military situation required it. In holding the evacuation movement responsible for "a crop of alarmist and depressing rumours . . . detrimental to the interests of National Defense," the Prime Minister indicated that plans to transfer children overseas were feeding defeatist attitudes. Cryptically, Churchill, in answer to a question, mentioned that an offer of American ships to take the children out "would immediately engage the most earnest attention of His Majesty's Government." [13]

In New York City a group of women had anticipated the Prime Minister's remarks about ships and had formed the American Women's Committee for the Release of Mercy Ships for Children to spearhead a crusade for sending United States vessels to transport English boys and girls. Since, except for Red Cross supply ships, the Neutrality Act of 1939 kept American vessels out of the war zones, the Women's Committee determined to build public pressure to change the law so American passenger liners could bring the children out. The ladies opened their campaign with a full-page illustrated advertisement in the *New York Times* asking readers to write or telegraph the President in favor of allowing mercy ships to sail to England. Then a letter to 2,000 women's organizations urged meetings and petitions for the ships. In less than a week, sister organizations appeared in 14 states and an advisory committee of men stepped forward to help with fund raising for the legislative endeavor.[14]

Almost immediately Thomas C. Hennings, Jr. (D.) of Missouri and Emanuel Celler (D.) of New York introduced mercy ships bills into the House of Representatives. Shortly afterward, Carter Glass (D.) of Virginia sponsored a similar measure in the Senate. Hennings' bill, which was the one Congress acted upon, amended the Neutrality Act to permit unarmed American vessels, not under convoy, to transport refugee children under 16 out of war zones, provided the ships sailed under safe-conduct assurances from all belligerent nations. A friendly House Foreign Affairs Committee received the Mercy Ships Bill on Tuesday, July 23. On Wednesday the committee discussed the measure, on Thursday it conducted hearings, and on Friday, at an executive session, it voted without dissent to report the proposal favorably to the House. Action was so rapid that the State Department, which usually communicated its views to Congressional committees by letter, reported by telephone that it had no objection to the measure.[15]

Fearing that the safe-conduct clause in the Hennings Bill might lead to complications, the Women's Committee for the Release of Mercy Ships for Children began in late July to urge deletion of that requirement. A *New York Times* editorial agreed that Congress should not "tie the President's hands" with a safe-conduct provision, but should instead permit him to decide what assurances were necessary and leave it to the Chief Executive and the State Department to work out some arrangement with Germany.[16]

As a matter of fact the President was not at all anxious to take responsibility for a decision to move ships full of children through dangerous waters. At his press conference on July 26 Roosevelt pointed out that, without "reasonable assurance" of safety, it was "a pretty big responsibility for this Government to take, to send ships in there and fill them up with children and then have them sunk." When a reporter asked what would constitute reasonable assurance, the Chief Executive replied that it would depend on the circumstances of each case and that even if the government obtained assurances "it might be still taking a risk to bring children back through that war zone." Again, in his press conference two weeks later, the President emphasized that "nobody, no government, wants to take the responsibility of loading a ship with refugee children and taking them through that war zone unless, first, the safe-conduct was obtained and, secondly, there was a reasonable assurance it would be lived up to." A few days afterward Roosevelt, quite understandably, wrote Democratic Congresswoman Caroline O'Day of New York that he hoped the House version of the Hennings Bill had not left the decision up to the President. Mrs. O'Day reassured Roosevelt that the measure had passed the House "without leaving a bit of responsibility to you or anyone else, except, perhaps, Hitler and Mussolini." She explained that Hennings and she had convinced the Women's Committee that the bill would lose in the House if the safe-conduct clause were removed. A Gallup poll released on August 17 lent support to Mrs. O'Day's argument and to Roosevelt's caution. Of those expressing an opinion, 63 percent approved sending American ships "to bring English refugee women and children to the United States . . . if Germany and Italy agreed not to attack" the vessels. Significantly, a supplementary survey, which omitted the wording about assurances from Germany and Italy, found that the proportion in favor of the proposal dropped to 45 percent.[17]

In the meantime, the Mercy Ships Bill, with the safe-conduct requirement securely fastened, had been following its course through Congress. On Friday, August 2, a week after the House Foreign Affairs Committee reported the proposal out, the Rules Committee voted for early consideration of the measure. Objection by Michigan Republican Fred L. Crawford blocked a move in the House on the following Monday to obtain unanimous consent to bring the Hennings Bill directly to the floor. The next day a delegation of the Women's Committee, "expressing shock" at Crawford's refusal, flew to Washington. On Wednesday the Rules Committee brought in a special resolution requiring action on the bill. This special resolution, which passed early that afternoon, and consideration of the Hennings Bill which followed immediately, precipitated a half day of debate in the House, purportedly on the mercy ships issue.[18]

Although the actual question was on amendment of the Neutrality Act, members of the House rode a variety of hobbies about the chamber floor during the four-hour discussion. No congressman dared take a stalwart stand against bringing in British children, but several made clear their reluctance to permit increased immigration, and some raised the specter of an invasion of hordes of alien boys and girls. John M. Robsion (R.) of Kentucky warned that the bill "would permit all of the children" of any number of European countries (he named seven) to be brought here in American ships. Robsion calculated that "as a matter of fact it would permit millions to come." Matthew A. Dunn (D.) of Pennsylvania wondered whether "it is possible for us to bring every person from Europe over to this country." Butler B. Hare, South Carolina Democrat, asked if Congress ought not set "some limitation as to what countries these refugees should come from." He anticipated that Germany would take the opportunity to "send all of these refugees over here for us to support." In an attempt to keep the influx within bounds, Joshua L. Johns (R.) of Wisconsin offered an amendment to set a maximum of 75,000 children. But the House rejected Johns's suggestion.[19]

To insure that no adult foreigners would enter under cover of the Hennings measure, Republican Thomas A. Jenkins of Ohio proposed the superfluous precaution that all supervisory personnel who sailed with the children would be subject to the immigration laws. Even House approval of Jenkins' amendment did not allay the misgivings of John C. Schafer (R.) of Wisconsin. Schafer wanted the bill to limit adults accompanying the children to American citizens. Since this requirement would complicate the task of organizing transportation, Sol Bloom (D.) of New York protested. Schafer countered by implying that Bloom really objected "because my amendment lets the cat out of the bag, and that the major purpose of this bill is to bring in adult refugees. . . . Without my amendment one or more adults could be brought here for every child." Bloom forced three separate votes on the amendment, but each time Schafer's change carried easily.[20]

Some opposition to the Hennings Bill grew out of fear that it would bring the nation closer to war. Connecting the mercy ships movement with efforts to pull the United States into the conflict, Robsion of Kentucky asked if the purpose in scattering British children throughout the country was "to create another great source of propaganda to involve us in the European war." Other congressmen argued more realistically that, despite safe-conduct assurances, a submarine or mine might sink a ship loaded with children. Americans would naturally blame the tragedy on German treachery and inflamed public opinion could lead to entry into the war.[21]

Although many of the same anti-immigration arguments used in the debate on mercy ships had been very effective against the Wagner-Rogers Bill, they did not prevail against the Hennings Bill. Actually, several opponents of the measure, swept along by the tide of public feeling, announced they would vote for the bill. One congressman summarized their viewpoint: "This bill is unnecessary, it is fraught with danger, yet I am going to vote for it." In the end the measure passed by a voice vote with, according to the *New York Times,* "only a few heard in dissent." [22]

After its rapid trip through the House, the Mercy Ships Bill went to the Senate Committee on Foreign Relations. Immediately the Women's Committee took aim on the upper house. Petitions again circulated. A delegation settled in the capital to interview senators. Co-chairman Mrs. Harold T. Pulsifer arrived in Washington with a nine-year-old English refugee girl who had prepared a speech for the Foreign Relations Committee. The plea was not needed, for the Senate committee hastened to report the bill favorably. When the Mercy Ships Bill reached the Senate floor, Michigan Republican Arthur H. Vandenberg emphasized that the Foreign Relations Committee, often sharply divided, had been "unanimous, completely and enthusiastically unanimous," for enactment of the measure. No objection arose to a request for unanimous consent to consider the bill and the measure passed without debate. On August 27, only six weeks after the Women's Committee had launched its campaign, the bill to amend the Neutrality Act became law.[23]

With this legislative achievement behind them, the women hoped that large-scale evacuation could at last commence. Ironically, their amazingly swift victory proved to be hollow and the mercy ships movement soon collapsed. One cause of failure was inability of the Women's Committee to find or form an organization which could manage arrangements for providing ships. A second problem involved safe-conduct guarantees. As the women themselves had feared, and as several people had predicted, Germany would not give the required assurance. Soon after the Senate passed the bill, the German government disclosed through unofficial sources that it could not guarantee safe-conduct because of the danger of uncharted mine fields. The *New York Times* editorial page joined the Women's Committee in their plea that the State Department ask Germany to agree only to refrain from attacking the ships; mines, they felt, were an unavoidable risk. But the Administration never had to face the problem of deciding exactly what safe-conduct assurances the new law required because arrangements for sending ships failed to reach an advanced stage. Joining the other obstacles in ruining the hopes of the Women's Committee was the British government's decided lack of enthusiasm for the project by late August. A London dispatch to the *New York Times* reported that "so far as the British are concerned, the American Congress has been wasting its time, because the entire question of evacuation has been shoved up to the attic for the duration of the war." [24]

A few hundred English children came to Canada and the United States during the late summer of 1940 in commercial shipping under nongovernmental sponsorship. Near the end of August a liner en route to Canada with 875 people, including 320 refugee children, was torpedoed in the North Atlantic. Fortunately, except for one of the crew, all were rescued. But less than three weeks later tragedy struck. Without warning, a submarine sank the *City of Benares,* 600 miles at sea on its way to Canada. Of the 90 children on board, 79 were among the 260 people lost. The British government reacted to this disaster by forbidding further evacuation of children. At that point, in early October, about 4,000 of 200,000 British children who had registered for removal overseas had reached North America. The United States Committee for the Care of European Children immediately cut its large staff and suspended a national fund-raising campaign. All the frenzied effort which had gone into development of the United States Committee and into the Women's Committee's drive, the thousands of offers of homes, and a vast amount of hope and concern had succeeded in bringing from England under the USC's corporate affidavit only 861 children.[25]

Officially, the plans of the United States Committee, the scope of the Mercy Ships Act, and the whole movement to evacuate children from the war zones were not limited to British boys and girls. Spokesmen for the United States Committee and the Women's Committee repeatedly mentioned that they were trying to help all European child victims of the war. But, as a matter of practical fact, the rush of American sympathy and effort in the summer of 1940 was almost entirely a response to the plight of the British. The monthly magazine of a Jewish fraternal labor organization caught the spirit accurately late that summer: "When we talk of refugees—and who doesn't these days—we think immediately of the children of England." A fund campaign memorandum written for the United States Committee noted that "the moving impulse beneath all these activities is the simple one: 'Bring England's children to America!'" The *New York Times* explained that the Mercy Ships Bill applied to all warring countries, "although it was primarily for the benefit of British children that it was proposed." As the measure neared enactment, the *Christian Century* pointed out that "actually, as everyone realizes, the benefits of the new legislation will be confined almost entirely to children from Great Britain."[26]

The British boys and girls were not refugees from Nazism in the sense of having to flee because of their political views or religious background. Discussion, then, of the movement for evacuation of English children appears to leave the main channel of this narrative for a side current. Yet, an account of the American effort to help British children, because it furnishes a meaningful contrast, has direct relevance to a study of the American response to political and religious fugitives from Nazism.[27]

The widely differing receptions given the Wagner-Rogers Bill and the mercy ships movement by the American public and by Congress cannot be evaded. Although support developed for admission of German children and homes opened to them, the sympathy they aroused was a trickle when compared with the deluge of popular feeling which went out to English boys and girls a year later. Unquestionably, one reason for the rush of concern for the British lay simply in the matter of communications. The plight of children in England, who were enduring bombing and who were thought to be in the path of imminent invasion, constantly gripped the attention of the American public. In contrast, the tragic conditions under which persecuted German children existed were much less widely or dramatically publicized. But this factor by no means explains fully the dissimilarity in the responses to the German and the British boys and girls. One wonders, for instance, why the restrictionist and patriotic groups failed to organize opposition to the Mercy Ships Bill. Strangely enough, the most insistent arguments voiced against the Wagner-Rogers Bill, both in Congress and among the public, were either missing or ineffective in the case of the Hennings Bill. Horror at the thought of separating families was conspicuously absent. Although a few restrictionists shed tears for poor American children, this time these appeals had almost no impact. One need only recall the anti-Semitism of these years to locate one important explanation for the contrasting responses to the Wagner-Rogers Bill and the movement to evacuate children from England: the British boys and girls were mostly Christian while the German children were mostly Jewish. A glimpse of the attractiveness of the Anglo-Saxon image appeared in a tabulation of letters offering homes for the young refugees. The type of child most often requested was "a blond English girl, 6 years old." [28]

In addition to the flood of sentiment for helping British children, a minor effort took shape in 1940 to extend the limits of concern to other victims of the storm.

THE RESPONSE TO THE PLIGHT OF CHILD REFUGEES
ON THE CONTINENT

Submerged in the clamor over mercy ships were a few American voices which asked if the United States might also find room for refugee children living under deplorable conditions in continental

Europe. Congressman Samuel Dickstein (D.) of New York wrote the *New York Times* that "the matter should not be treated as solely a British problem." The New York *Daily News* declared that non-English children also needed sanctuary. An editorial in *Collier's,* stressing that bombs were falling on England and that famine was stalking several areas of Europe, called for Congress to "get busy and slash the immigration quota and other red tape which . . . hampers and harries this child-rescue work." At an August press conference, President Roosevelt, questioned about complaint that American rescue plans included only British children, responded with an irrelevant comment on risks involved in transporting children through belligerent waters. Correspondence within the State Department disclosed that about 1,500 Polish children, some still with their mothers, were in extreme distress in Spain and Portugal. Almost no one was working to bring them to the United States, even though the Polish quota was not filled, because American efforts concentrated nearly exclusively on children actually under bombardment.[29]

Thousands of Polish and other refugees found themselves stranded in the Iberian Peninsula in August 1940 as a result of the Nazi drive through western Europe in the spring of that year. After the surrender of France, the vast tide of people who had fled south ahead of the German armies turned and began to flow homeward. But large numbers of refugees, mostly non-French, would have been unsafe under Nazi rule because of their religious or political backgrounds and so remained in Vichy France or south of the Pyrenees. Thousands congregated in and around Marseilles, hoping to obtain the visas that meant freedom. The Vichy government confined other thousands in wretched concentration camps.

The *Collier's* editorial predicting hunger and suffering was grimly accurate. German food levies on the vanquished countries combined with the British blockade to loose starvation, and the diseases which followed in its path, on Europe. In December 1940 a shocked Red Cross official described conditions at the crowded detention camp at Gurs in southern France. Twelve thousand people were attempting to subsist on rations intended for 9,000, shacks without windows or ventilation served as shelters, and mattresses and blankets were in short supply. That winter, mothers at Gurs wrapped babies in newspapers for lack of clothing. In the spring of 1941 a Quaker relief worker related that "the majority of camps are terribly overcrowded, filthy, without heat or light, without decent drainage or plumbing. The mortality in the camps is tremendous. In the camp of Gurs alone more than 800 persons died during the five winter months." The report went on to describe the plight of child refugees:

> The imprisonment of children in filthy, overcrowded barracks, without freedom of motion is a new unheard of phenomenon. Until February of this year these half-starved children were distributed, together with their parents, in various camps. In February came the order to place all the children [older than four years] in one camp of Rivesaltes. . . . Milk is distributed among the smaller children [that is, the ones allowed to stay with their mothers] very irregularly, children above four receive scant food only twice a day. . . . Famine, parasites, cold and diseases—this is the lot of the unfortunate children of Rivesaltes and of other camps erected in France for the refugees.[30]

Existence for refugees in the first months after France surrendered was far more endurable than in the winter that followed. Still, their suffering in the summer of 1940 was bad enough to arouse the concern of some Americans, including a few members of Congress. By mid-July six representatives and one senator had introduced bills to allow child war victims from continental Europe to come to the United States and stay until the end of the conflict. The Senate bill, submitted by Sheridan Downey (D.) of California, died without action.

On the mornings of August 7 and 8, the House Immigration Committee held hearings on the six House bills. At first, discussion centered on Polish children who had made their way across Europe. A fortunate thousand had reached England, but most were living under miserable conditions in France, Spain, and Portugal. Michigan Congressmen Rudolph G. Tenerowicz (D.) and John Lesinski (D.) testified that Americans of Polish background would readily supply shelter and financial support for these three or four thousand boys and girls. But James E. Van Zandt (R.) of Pennsylvania, not convinced that the young refugees would really go home after the war, was worried because they might grow up to add to the unemployment problem. For reasons which he did not disclose, Carl T. Curtis (R.) of Nebraska wanted to know whether Tenerowicz wished the legislation broadened to include "an arrangement to bring in Chinese children." Appearance of four members of the Women's Committee for Mercy Ships enlivened the proceedings more than it enlightened the lawmakers, for the ladies' testimony quickly revealed that they knew next to nothing about the legislation under consideration. As a result, talk about mercy ships dominated a large portion of the brief hearings.[31]

After the first morning of testimony, a subcommittee of four went over relevant problems with officials from the Immigration Service and the State and Justice Departments and then drafted a composite bill which William T. Schulte (D.) of Indiana submitted to the House that same day. The Schulte Bill provided that any European child under 16 who sought asylum from "the dangers or the effects of war" could apply for a special visitor's visa enabling him to stay in the United States until conditions allowed his safe return home. As the House Immigration Committee pointed out in its favorable report on the proposal, the Schulte Bill removed "the existing practical discrimination against children of certain nationalities" whose countries' quotas were full and who were ineligible for visitors' visas because they could not prove they had a homeland to which they could return. In essence, the measure would have given continental European child war victims the same privilege of entering the United States on visitors' visas that the Administration's new immigration regulations of July 13 had granted to British boys and girls.[32]

A few days after the Immigration Committee approved the Schulte Bill, the Rules Committee met to decide whether to permit the measure to come before the House. According to Representative Caroline O'Day, a supporter of the bill, members of the Rules Committee pigeonholed the legislation because they didn't want more aliens let in and because "we have American children who are in need and . . . charity begins at home." A week later Congressman Rudolph Tenerowicz introduced a resolution to call the Schulte Bill up for action on the House floor. Tenerowicz's proposal also went to the Rules Committee and, like the Schulte Bill, vanished.[33]

The near anonymity and failure of the Schulte Bill stand in sharp contrast to the great burst of support for the Mercy Ships Bill and the reluctance among congressmen to oppose it. Sponsors of the Schulte Bill, by bringing it out of committee when interest in the ships bill was at a high pitch, hoped the force of sentiment which had built up behind the Hennings measure would also propel their related proposal through Congress. These hopes were vain, for Congress, which tried to open the Red Sea for the children of England, did not attempt the miracle for the boys and girls of the Continent. The extremely different responses drawn by these two measures, along with the earlier failure of the Wagner-Rogers Bill, show clearly that, for a large part of the American people, sympathy for distressed children diminished considerably in crossing the English Channel.

Still, strenuous work by some American groups concerned about refugees brought a few children to the United States from Vichy France, Spain, and Portugal. In December 1940 a representative of the Unitarian Service Committee, in unoccupied France to supervise distribution of a shipment of canned milk, arranged to bring out a group of young refugees. With cooperation from the United States Committee for the Care of European Children, the Unitarian worker organized evacuation of 28 Czech, German, Austrian, and French boys and girls to the United States. The following month the director of the United States Committee reported "a scattered interest in bringing children in from the Continent," but pointed out that the heavy expense and complicated arrangements involved made removal of many boys and girls unlikely.[34]

Yet the deplorable conditions in the concentration camps of Vichy France continued to worsen. At Rivesaltes in the spring of 1941 children were dying of cholera from foraging in garbage cans. An American visitor to the camp at Gurs found inmates delighted at a delivery of clean straw to replace their lice-infested bedding. Responding to these pitiful circumstances, the United States Committee decided in early 1941 to add efforts to rescue continental children to its program of caring for British boys and girls who had arrived in the United States in 1940. Relying on Quaker relief workers in France to select the young immigrants and depending on European-Jewish Children's Aid for much of the care and placement work in the United States, the USC was able to bring 309 children over with quota visas in five shipments during the 18 months before August 1942. Even this small accomplishment required a tremendous amount of work. It took eight months to outlast the red tape connected with sending one group of 50 boys and girls. Another 100 of the fortunate few, collected from camps and orphan homes in unoccupied France, travelled by train from Marseilles to Lisbon on their way to the United States.

Since the railroad passed near the camp at Gurs, French authorities agreed to allow relatives held there to come to the station for a few minutes to bid the children farewell. The doctor in charge of the group wrote that even the gendarmes wept at the brief pathetic scene of parents and children trying to become reacquainted and then to absorb enough of each other's presence to last a lifetime.[35]

For many parents at the station near Gurs that lifetime was not protracted. In August 1942, responding to Nazi orders, the Vichy government began to pack non-French Jews into freight cars for deportation to Auschwitz. The first contingent comprised 3,600 and other trainloads brought the total to at least 10,000 by mid-October. Outraged protests from the Vatican and from leading French Catholic and Protestant churchmen, including the Archbishops of Lyon and Toulouse, were of little avail. Since most of those deported were adults, one result of this hideous project was that about 8,000 Jewish children in unoccupied France were left without parents and were in danger of deportation themselves.[36]

In the United States, refugee aid agencies and the President's Advisory Committee approached the government with urgent pleas for admission of a significant number of these boys and girls. The State Department in mid-September 1942 approved issuance of 1,000 quota visas for the children and in October agreed to increase the number to 5,000. In addition, most of the extensive red tape attached to the usual processing of quota visas was waived. Actually, these concessions were not extreme, for the quotas under which the children would come were at the time far undersubscribed and the simplified procedures were based on the special immigration regulations for refugee children which had been in effect since July 13, 1940. Still, the Administration was uneasy about the project and was very anxious to avoid publicity in order to steer clear of Congressional debate on the issue of admitting large groups of child refugees. The United States Committee made plans to receive the children and succeeded in finding contributors to underwrite the $400,000 needed for transportation and other costs. By late October relief workers in France had nearly completed arrangements for departure of the first 1,000. Negotiations by refugee agencies, supported by the American diplomatic mission, overcame weeks of stalling by the Vichy government and at the end of October produced a promise of exit permits for an initial 500 children. Then, on November 8, four days before the first of the young refugees were scheduled to leave Marseilles for Lisbon, Allied forces invaded North Africa. On November 11 the Germans occupied Vichy France and the doors swung shut on the waiting children. On the basis of offers by the United States and several other countries to accept the children, private agencies, with State Department assistance, negotiated for their release through the Swiss diplomatic mission in Vichy. Nothing came of these endeavors, for now the Nazis, who not long before had been most agreeable to emigration of Jews, had completed other arrangements for them.[37]

Frustrated in the effort to rescue children from France, the United States Committee turned its attention to refugee children who had escaped to Spain and Portugal. Most were existing in poverty; in Spain some were kept in prisons; and all lived under the realistic possibility of Nazi occupation of the Iberian Peninsula. The Administration granted permission to use some of the visas to bring these boys and girls to the United States, despite State Department anxiety about Congressional criticism that American visa policy was too generous. A contingent of 31 children came in January 1943, but fewer than 80 more crossed the ocean before hostilities ended. More successful after the war, the United States Committee helped nearly 3,000 homeless children to immigrate.[38]

After passage of the Mercy Ships Bill in the summer of 1940, no significant refugee measures obtained a hearing in Congress before the United States entered the war. People concerned about refugees reaped a lean legislative harvest in the years from the Austrian *Anschluss* until Pearl Harbor. Small appropriations for American participation in the Evian Conference and in the work of the Intergovernmental Committee on Refugees, 50 million dollars for food and supplies for refugees overseas, and a mercy ships measure which proved to be a dead letter were all Congress would yield. Unwillingness to modify the immigration laws meant that the quota restrictions established under the Act of 1924 marked the boundaries within which the American government's refugee policy operated. In the case of one category of refugees, though, the Administration devised an exceptional procedure which succeeded in saving 2,000 endangered people.

Part IV
# The Administration

# Chapter 7

# Visas for Political Refugees

Of the refugees who fled from the Nazis between 1933 and 1940, perhaps five percent emigrated because of political opposition to the Hitler regime. France, especially Paris, harbored many of these enemies of the Third Reich. When the German armies swept over France in June 1940, numbers of the political fugitives escaped to a precarious refuge in the unoccupied zone. Bottled up there, they confronted the same hardships of hunger, disease, and demoralization which were the lot of all refugees. In addition, because of their anti-Nazi activities in the past, political refugees faced particularly grave danger. The nineteenth article of the armistice terms imposed by Germany required the French government "to surrender upon demand all Germans named by the German Government." As interpreted, the term "Germans" included Austrians, Czechs, and, in practice, any others whom the Nazis chose to terrorize. Although confusion following the capitulation of France delayed the man hunt, no one doubted that the Gestapo would soon start tracking down these old enemies.[1]

Almost instantly some Americans voiced concern for the safety of the trapped antifascists. Groups formed to help rescue not only political fugitives, but also endangered intellectual and cultural leaders who were democrats. Accordingly, labor leaders, politicians, artists, musicians, writers, scientists, and clergymen were among those whom these organizations asked the United States government to try to save.[2]

On June 18 Hamilton Fish Armstrong, editor of *Foreign Affairs* and a member of the President's Advisory Committee on Political Refugees, telegraphed the White House to suggest that American diplomatic missions offer sanctuary to leading intellectual refugees caught in France. The following day a second telegram from Armstrong reported that the Gestapo was arresting suspected anti-Nazis and urged prompt American action to save as many of the imperiled men and women as possible. And on June 21 Armstrong wired to Washington a list of names of known democrats who needed to get out of France rapidly. The very next day the State Department cabled the list to its consulates in Lisbon, Marseilles, and Bordeaux with instructions for immediate steps toward issuance of visas for the specified persons. The Jewish Labor Committee, representing many labor unions and Jewish political groups in the American movement for defense of Jewish rights, compiled a list of several hundred endangered European labor leaders and intellectuals whom it wanted to bring out. On July 2 a delegation led by AFL president William Green took the list to Assistant Secretary of State Breckinridge Long who agreed to grant special emergency visitors' visas to the designated refugees and their families. These labor leaders and Jewish scholars included people fleeing eastern Europe and the Soviet GPU as well as refugees escaping the Gestapo. Long also met with a group of Orthodox rabbis and accepted their lists totaling over 700 names of Jewish theological students and rabbis in the Baltic area. Still another list, that of the American Jewish Congress, received favorable action by the State Department.[3]

Before the end of July, the President's Advisory Committee on Political Refugees (PAC) became concerned because "committees were springing up on every hand," each with its own list of refugees, "and already they were beginning to fight among themselves and accuse the Government of favoring one side or the other." One of the principal new groups proved unacceptable to some Catholics because its leadership included a reporter who had been involved with the Loyalist side in the Spanish Civil War. As a result, these Catholics set up a separate committee. An association to help Austrian fugitives was too leftist to satisfy Archduke Otto, so he endeavored to establish another organization. French, Czech, Italian, Spanish, Belgian, and Dutch committees formed and then split on political lines in kaleidoscopic fashion.[4]

To bring order to the situation, the President's Advisory Committee decided to take responsibility for coordinating efforts to obtain emergency visitors' visas for endangered political and intellectual refugees.

James G. McDonald, the chairman, and George L. Warren, the executive secretary, met on July 26 with leading officials of the Justice and State Departments and agreed on an arrangement by which the PAC would serve as a conduit between the private groups and the Federal authorities. Under the new procedure, all requests for special emergency visas went first to the President's Advisory Committee in New York City. The committee checked on every recommended person's character and his purpose for coming to the United States and relayed each approved name to the Department of Justice for clearance against its files. The application then moved to the State Department which consulted any records it had regarding the refugee and decided whether he had legitimate reason for entering the country and whether he presented danger of engaging in "activity inimical to the United States." If an applicant was acceptable, the State Department would immediately notify the consul closest to the refugee. Because the law placed responsibility for issuance of visas on the consuls, technically the State Department could not order consular officers to grant visas. But a circular telegram dispatched to diplomatic and consular officials directly after the meeting with McDonald and Warren conveyed, as Breckinridge Long later phrased it, "more or less mandatory instructions" to issue visas to these recommended refugees.[5]

Up until this time the President's Advisory Committee, cooperating closely with the Intergovernmental Committee on Refugees, had put its main energies into efforts to plan and develop refugee resettlement colonies such as the one in the Dominican Republic. In addition, the PAC had functioned as a liaison between the State Department and private American agencies interested in helping with colonization projects and with other aspects of the Intergovernmental Committee's program. Once the President's Advisory Committee assumed the task of screening visa applications for political refugees, its work mushroomed. But, because it was not a government agency, the PAC, as in the past, received no public funds. George Warren's salary and the costs of office help came from contributions to the President's Committee by private organizations.[6]

With most pertinent quotas already oversubscribed, the Administration had to turn to visitors' visas to translate its concern for endangered political refugees into realistic aid. The great advantage of visitors' visas lay in the absence of numerical limitations on their issuance. But assigning these temporary permits to the political refugees raised a thorny legal problem. The Immigration Act of 1924 specified almost nothing in regard to visitors' visas, thereby placing their administration nearly entirely within the area of executive regulations. Naturally, certain practices had evolved which, though subject to change by the executive, virtually had the force of law. Foremost among these practices was the logical requirement that temporary immigrants prove their ability to return to their home countries or to move on to some other nation. Otherwise the phrase "visiting the United States temporarily," which was in the Act, would tend to lose its meaning. Without such a requirement, moreover, the major purpose of Congress in enacting the quota system would be jeopardized. Still, the Administration legally could set whatever standards it desired for assignment of temporary visas provided it enforced the public charge, physical, mental, moral, and other qualifications of the Immigration Act of 1917.[7]

Obviously, the political refugees who received emergency visitors' visas did not have homes outside the United States to which they could return without facing death. But, since only visitors' visas were available, the Administration decided to stretch a point and to suspend the usual six-month limit for these "visits." To help justify this strained interpretation of a temporary visit, the emergency visa application included a clause stating that the immigrant agreed to depart from the United States as soon as possible and would start immediately to make efforts to do so. In addition, the President's Advisory Committee and the organizations originally recommending the refugees had to assure the State Department that they would do all they could to move the immigrants rapidly to other countries. In a December 1940 press release, the State Department declared that before granting the special visas it had taken care to ascertain that the refugees were able to leave for other destinations. But, less than two months later, Breckinridge Long informed Assistant Secretary of State Adolf A. Berle, Jr., that from the start the emergency program had been "a departure from long-established interpretation of the immigration law in order that visitors' visas . . . could be issued to refugees desiring to come here and who probably will remain in this country." In fact, most fugitives who entered with emergency visitors' visas stayed in the United States indefinitely. Many did leave, but only to go briefly to a neighboring country in order to re-enter the United States as permanent quota immigrants under a special arrangement.[8]

Besides showing that the refugee intended to leave the United States, an application for an emergency visa had to include the usual affidavit of financial support from a resident of the United States assuring that the immigrant would not become a public charge. Also required were a brief biographical sketch of the refugee and a "moral affidavit." The biography contained, among other information, a report on any past political activities, an assessment of the contribution which the alien would make to the United States, and a statement explaining why and to what degree he was in danger. The "moral affidavit," acceptable only from an American citizen who had knowledge of the refugee's character, testified that the newcomer's activities would not be inimical to the United States and that the signer would keep informed about the alien's actions after arrival.[9]

Use of special visitors' visas to give practical expression to the Administration's concern for endangered political refugees raises a question about the government's general policy toward admission of fugitives from Nazism. Undoubtedly the great immediate danger facing political opponents of Hitler's government was crucial in the thinking of American policy makers. Nonetheless, if the sojourn of the political refugees, who were unable to return home while the Nazi regime lasted, could be interpreted as a temporary visit, why could not the same reasoning have applied to all victims of Nazi persecution? Logically, it might have, but, realistically, if the Administration had attempted to allow large numbers of refugees to enter under this arrangement, Congress would certainly have moved swiftly to quash the entire program.[10]

By providing emergency visas, the United States government made escape possible for selected political refugees. In most cases, these people required help to turn the possibility of flight into actuality. Many recipients of special visas lacked essential information regarding the various arrangements involved in emigration. Need of financial aid for ship passage and other expenses was widespread. Some political refugees were hiding and either did not realize that American visas were available or did not dare make themselves known. In many cases assistance in moving antifascists to safety came from organizations long experienced in emigration work. Hundreds of others escaped with the aid of people who went to France especially for that purpose. Dr. Frank Bohn spent three months in Marseilles helping people on the AFL list to get out. The Emergency Rescue Committee

(ERC), led by Frank Kingdon, president of the University of Newark, formed in New York City in June 1940 with the objective of bringing out writers, artists, and other intellectual and political refugees trapped in southern France. In August 1940 Varian Fry undertook what he thought would be one month of work for the ERC in unoccupied France locating leading refugees and helping them to emigrate. Fry departed only when forced out by the Vichy authorities 13 months later. When necessary, Fry and his co-workers at the *Centre Américain de Secours,* as they named their operation in Marseilles, used forged documents and smuggled refugees across borders to send them toward points of embarkation, especially Lisbon. Their efforts moved over a thousand refugees out of France on the way to the United States or other destinations. In the Portuguese capital the Unitarian Service Committee helped many of the Emergency Rescue Committee's charges to continue their journeys to freedom.[11]

Within a few weeks of the start of the emergency visa program problems began to crop up. One complication centered on the State Department and concerned visa issuance. A second involved difficulty in obtaining exit permits from the Vichy government and transit permits to cross Spain and Portugal. A third problem was the shortage of ocean transportation.

The first trouble to arise over State Department control of special emergency visas was easily ironed out. In late August the Emergency Rescue Committee informed Eleanor Roosevelt that the American consulate in Marseilles, on instructions from the Visa Division, had stopped granting visas to refugees who did not have French exit permits. Under German pressure, the Vichy government would not issue exit permits to refugees. Accordingly, endangered antifascists had to slip out illegally, but needed first to obtain their American visas in order to gain entry to Portugal. In response to Mrs. Roosevelt's inquiry, Undersecretary of State Sumner Welles explained that the procedure of requiring an exit permit before issuing a visa had been ordered to avoid giving the appearance that the United States government was helping people to break French laws. But, reported Welles, the State Department had changed its instructions and would grant visas to non-French citizens even if they did not have exit permits.[12]

By late September a major conflict over visa policy neared the kindling point. Groups concerned with political refugees began to lose patience because of the slow flow of emergency visas. Enthusiasm for the special visa program was clearly lacking in some sectors of the

State Department and on the part of some American consuls abroad. The President's Advisory Committee reported to the Chief Executive that of 567 names submitted by it between August 1 and September 10, all but two had received approval from the Departments of State and Justice. Yet, by late September, two months after the program had begun, only about 40 visas had been issued to refugees recommended by the PAC.[13]

The dispute, which had only been smoldering, broke into flames late in September when a letter from the State Department to the President's Advisory Committee announced severe curtailment of the emergency visa program. The sequence of events which lay behind this letter is revealing. On September 10 the State Department received a message from the American Minister in Lisbon, Herbert C. Pell, advising that the program for political refugees was working out differently than had been planned. Pell reported that

it is resulting in visas being granted in many cases to the least desirable element and those against whom there is evident ground for doubt. Desirable individuals presenting themselves at the Consulate are often unable to qualify for visas since they do not have organizations to push their cases in America. Incidentally I regret to say that some of the most active organizations pushing immigration cases are racial.

Dissatisfied with the department's instructions of July 26 which had directed consuls to issue visas to approved political refugees, Pell recommended a return to instructions sent out in June which, because of the prevailing emergency, had ordered that consuls should refuse visas whenever there was "any doubt whatsoever concerning the alien." In Pell's view, there were "good reasons to have the greatest doubt" about some individuals, although proof was "not readily available." In other instances, he suspected the applicants were German agents. Pell complained that "in a number of cases" the Lisbon consulate had refused visas only to have the refugees arrange for groups in the United States to obtain special emergency visas for them. These occurrences had been "embarrassing" to the consuls and the situation could "become an open scandal" because of prevalent talk in Lisbon that the consulate could "be overruled by anyone able to use influence in the United States." [14]

Eight days after receipt of Pell's message, Assistant Secretary of

State Breckinridge Long wrote President Roosevelt spelling out a State Department proposal "to modify slightly the procedure" for emergency visas. Leaning heavily on Pell's communication, Long explained that tighter restrictions were necessary in view of "substantial evidence" showing that "a number of the persons" approved for emergency visas had "records of activity abroad" which indicated that, once in the United States, their conduct "would not be in entire accord with our policy." In a near quotation from Pell's letter, Long informed Roosevelt that

> it is reported to us that there are a number of persons who our
> officers abroad feel are not of the desirable element and against
> whom there is evident ground for doubt as to the propriety of
> their admissibility.

To illustrate, Long cited "two of a number of instances" that had come to the State Department's attention. One case was that of a German woman who, asked to show that she would be able to leave the United States after her emergency visitor's visa expired, presented a letter from the German diplomatic mission in Lisbon agreeing to allow her to return to Germany. The State Department reasoned that either she was not in imminent danger or she was working for the German authorities. The other example involved two French citizens approved by the PAC and backed by banking firms in the United States. The financial interests of these two refugees reportedly were in Pan-American holding companies which, according to Long, might have been formed "to avoid American legal requirements and control by the S.E.C." On the basis of this kind of evidence, the State Department concluded that consuls should check people recommended for special emergency visas more carefully in order to guard "against the penetration of German agents or the use of the courtesy and hospitality of the United States for ulterior purposes." [15]

In his letter to the President, Long also reported that 2,583 special visas had already been authorized, nearly half to people on the AFL list, more than a quarter to Jewish religious leaders on lists submitted by the Orthodox rabbis, and 561 to refugees named by the President's Advisory Committee. The State Department felt that enough time had passed for submission of the names of most outstanding political and intellectual refugees and proposed closing the lists except for limited recommendation of intellectual leaders in immediate danger. Further, the department wanted to cancel its mandatory instructions to consuls to issue visas to approved applicants so that "some latitude of judgment" would remain with the consuls. Could Long have been unaware that only about 40 of the 561 refugees recommended by the PAC and approved by the State Department had received visas? These figures suggest that consuls already had been exercising "some latitude of judgment." The numbers also indicate that refugees were not extracting visas from American officials in Lisbon as successfully as Pell's communication implied.[16]

To effect curtailment of the emergency visa program a letter to the President's Advisory Committee, prepared for Secretary Hull's signature, accompanied Long's communication to Roosevelt. The President approved the changed procedures and the letter went to the PAC. Almost simultaneously, on September 19, the State Department cabled instructions to diplomatic and consular officers in Europe to check carefully before issuing special emergency visas and to require refugees to present clearer evidence if any doubt existed regarding their past conduct or possible future activities in the United States.[17]

The letter to the President's Advisory Committee precipitated a sharp dispute between that group and the State Department. The communication stated that enough time had elapsed for recommendation of the most urgent cases, so the PAC should submit no more names except those of outstanding intellectual leaders in imminent peril. Moreover, consuls would in the future examine each case carefully to make sure that the applicant had not taken part in questionable actions in the past and would not, if admitted to the United States, undertake any activity hostile to the nation. Responding to the virtual termination of the special program for political refugees, McDonald and Warren of the PAC, after a heated session with Breckinridge Long, contacted Eleanor Roosevelt and, later, wrote the President to protest the small number of visas already issued and to assert their disbelief that entrance of the other 520 refugees whom they had investigated and approved would threaten the national interest. Mrs. Roosevelt brought the dispute to the attention of the President. He consulted Sumner Welles and then, on October 3, met with Breckinridge Long. Long reported that Roosevelt, who had decided to have a talk with McDonald, agreed fully with the State Department's position.[18]

After speaking with the President, Long returned to his office to find a telegram waiting for him from Laurence A. Steinhardt, American Ambassador to Russia. Steinhardt vehemently objected to recent instructions from the State Department to suspend the new restrictions on emergency visas for a group of AFL-sponsored refugees escaping eastern Europe via Moscow and the trans-Siberian route. Critical international conditions, warned the ambassador, did not permit "the slightest relaxation of vigilance." He asserted that experience in the Moscow consulate had shown clearly that American organizations sponsoring political and intellectual refugees had purposely "grossly misrepresented" the status and intentions of "virtually all" aliens recommended for special emergency visas. Furthermore, most applicants had been unable to convince the consuls in Moscow that they had any intention of ever departing from the United States. Steinhardt reported that many refugees named in the new list sponsored by the AFL had been "politically active" in such groups as the Zionist Labor Party and "might well transplant their entire political organization to the United States." Because of uncertainty about the "past and future activities of many of these applicants," the consular section had suspended consideration of all doubtful cases. Since Steinhardt's telegram corroborated his own point of view, Long immediately forwarded it to Roosevelt with a message suggesting that the President read it prior to his meeting with McDonald.[19]

Remarks recorded by Breckinridge Long in his diary after a lengthy conversation with Laurence Steinhardt in late 1941 help explain the actions of both men in the refugee crisis of 1940. Long set down his approval of Steinhardt's clear-cut opposition to

immigration in large numbers from Russia and Poland of the Eastern Europeans whom he characterizes as entirely unfit to become citizens of this country. He says they are lawless, scheming, defiant—and in many ways unassimilable. He said the general type of intending immigrant was just the same as the criminal Jews who crowd our police court dockets in New York and with whom he is acquainted. . . . I think he is right—not as regards the Russian and Polish Jew alone but the lower level of all that Slav population of Eastern Europe and Western Asia.[20]

The President's conference with James McDonald took place on October 9, 1940. At McDonald's request, George Warren, Solicitor

General Francis Biddle, and Biddle's assistant, Henry M. Hart, Jr., accompanied him. Hart recalls that at this meeting a very cordial Roosevelt spun a succession of stories. Whenever McDonald tried to confront the President with the refugee issue, Roosevelt would be reminded of something else and another anecdote would result. This entertainment continued until the half hour was up and "Pa" Watson came in to mention that the next appointment was due. Then followed a few rushed minutes of trying to present the problem before the group left.[21]

The day after the meeting, Long, Hull, and Welles conferred with the President. According to Long, Roosevelt told them

> that he hadn't had time to listen to McDonald and when he started condemning and criticizing me [Long] the President told him not to "pull any sob stuff" on him and said that he knew enough about the situation to know that the Consuls abroad were not in sympathy with the policy. . . . He said that he was sure the Consuls had to have, and he would insist upon their having, jurisdiction in these cases. . . . Further, he told McDonald to wait in town a few days until Mr. Biddle of the Department of Justice could confer with Mr. Welles and me and come to some understanding on the matter along the above lines.

The outcome of the meeting was that Roosevelt had left the PAC, its ally the Justice Department, and the State Department to fight the issue out among themselves.[22]

While the PAC and the two government departments inched toward agreement, the visa situation for political refugees was showing the effects of the State Department's September 19 instructions to its consuls to tighten issuance of special visitors' visas. In November a representative of the Emergency Rescue Committee reported to Eleanor Roosevelt that since mid-September almost no new visas had been granted under the program for political refugees. Several refugees whose visas had earlier been approved in Washington were unable to obtain them from the consuls. The problem was particularly difficult in Lisbon where the consulate was still turning down people whose visa authorizations had arrived from Washington more than two months before.[23]

Through much of the autumn of 1940, representatives of the Departments of State and Justice clashed over the future of the emergency visa program and the role in it of the President's Advisory Committee. Late in November the main compromise emerged. The committee could continue to submit names of endangered political and intellectual refugees, provided it had investigated their character, verified the reliability of their sponsors, and agreed to help the immigrants move on to other countries. An entirely new procedural step called for a committee composed of representatives of the State Department, the Justice Department, Army Intelligence, and Naval Intelligence to check on PAC-recommended refugees from the standpoint of national security. This interdepartmental committee would advise the State and Justice Departments of its findings. Names which those two departments approved would go to consuls overseas for immediate consideration and favorable action unless the latter had information indicating that an applicant should be excluded. Before refusing a visa, however, the consul was to cable full details to Washington so the interdepartmental committee might attempt to iron out the difficulty. In accordance with the law, the final decision remained with the consul.[24]

Near the end of 1940, a flurry of protest against State Department delays in granting visas to political refugees broke out in the liberal press. In response, Breckinridge Long prepared a news release justifying visa policy toward political refugees since the defeat of France. It outlined the new procedure, explained the role of the interdepartmental committee, and emphasized that all emergency visa applications received to date had been processed. The *Nation,* suspicious of the new system, viewed the interdepartmental committee as an added hurdle in the obstacle course which in its opinion comprised the State Department's refugee policy.[25]

The emergency visa program ended in July 1941, although rescue efforts continued for political refugees whose visas had been authorized but not yet issued. Fullest statistics on the number who came to the United States under the special arrangement derive from the State Department and extend only through the end of 1940. By then 3,268 emergency visas had been authorized, but only 1,236 of these had actually been granted. Among the 1,236 who had received special visas were 402 people recommended by the President's Advisory Committee, 413 from the AFL list, and 250 from lists submitted by Jewish groups. More than 800 PAC-approved refugees, nearly 300 from the AFL list, and almost 900 of those recommended by Jewish organizations had not obtained visas. The State Department supplied plausible reasons for nonissuance of the permits. Most refugees recommended by the Jewish organizations were in eastern Europe, under Russian control, and found travel almost impossible. Moreover, the only American visa consul in Russian territory was in Moscow and the Soviet government would not allow the consulate to go to other cities to issue visas. As for political refugees in southwestern Europe, many were living under false names, or were hiding, or had changed residence, and were either unable or afraid to approach an American consul to obtain visas. These explanations, while entirely valid, overlooked an important factor, the reluctance of some American foreign service personnel to issue State Department-approved visas. Taking Ambassador Steinhardt's reaction into account, one can hardly conceive of the Moscow consulate's having moved about to grant visas even if the Russians had permitted it. Nor does the evidence show that foreign service officers in Lisbon were intent on facilitating issuance of special visas to refugees.[26]

During 1941 approximately 800 additional refugees came to the United States under the emergency visa arrangement, bringing to about 2,000 the number of political and intellectual fugitives who reached safety through the Administration's special program. In view of the negative feeling toward the project which prevailed in some quarters of the State Department, as well as the real possibility that Congressional restrictionists would set up a howl at the use of visitors' visas to admit European liberals, including democratic Socialists, why was the Administration willing to go out on a limb to aid these particular refugees? Undoubtedly the prestige and power of William Green of the AFL were crucially important, and CIO support strengthened the Administration in this undertaking. Pressure from such distinguished men as Hamilton Fish Armstrong, Professor Joseph Chamberlain, James G. McDonald, and others on the President's Advisory Committee played an important role. Sponsors of the Emergency Rescue Committee, a group which included well-known news-analysts Elmer Davis, Raymond Gram Swing, and Dorothy Thompson, and academic leaders Robert Hutchins, Alvin Johnson, and William A. Neilson, also carried influence. But perhaps the most telling factor was the active concern for endangered antifascists shared by Eleanor Roosevelt, Solicitor General Francis Biddle, Interior Secretary Harold

L. Ickes, and others in the Administration. Certainly the operation also depended importantly on a sympathetic, though less apparent, interest on the part of a President who at the time was heavily preoccupied with Britain's fight for survival, America's defense plans, and his own test at the polls. The rather limited achievements of the emergency program for political refugees, and the struggle required to accomplish even those results, underscore the complications and obstacles which confronted the project.[27]

The problem of obtaining visas to the United States and other overseas countries was not the only hindrance faced by political refugees in their attempts to reach safety. By the summer of 1940 Lisbon had become almost the last escape hatch from western Europe. But departure from France, transit across Spain, and entrance into Portugal were not easily accomplished, and at times were practically impossible. To facilitate the Gestapo's work of capturing persons wanted by the German government, the Vichy authorities almost immediately upon taking power closed the borders to legal departure of refugees. This control took the form of refusing to issue exit permits. But, until the confusion attendant upon the fall of France abated, Vichy officials at the Spanish frontier rarely turned back refugees who had overseas visas, even though they lacked French exit permits. And, up to the end of September, Spain readily issued transit visas to people who had obtained permission to travel through Portugal. In these first months, Portugal followed a generous policy toward admission of refugees bound overseas, granting them transit visas on the basis of almost any evidence that they could proceed to another country. Even Chinese, Belgian Congo, and Siamese immigration visas opened the door to Lisbon, although apparently no way existed to reach Siam and, reportedly, the Chinese "visa" stamped in Chinese on the traveller's passport consisted of a statement that the bearer was under no circumstances to be admitted to China. Many refugees used such dubious credentials to reach the comparative safety of Portugal and there await American or other overseas visas. Of course, people with valid visas entered without trouble. Because of Portuguese liberality, approximately 100,000 refugees escaped via Lisbon during the war years, about half passing through in the year following the surrender of France.[28]

During the summer of 1940, because Portugal did not scrutinize the overseas visas of incoming fugitives, thousands of refugees without valid papers for departure began to pile up in the small nation. Difficulty in securing ocean transportation for those who did have usable overseas visas further complicated the situation. By the end of August 1940, 11,000 refugees were stalled in Portugal, and more were arriving daily. Consequently, at the end of September, Portuguese consuls in France stopped issuing transit visas except upon proof of ability to proceed from Lisbon, including evidence that passage had been reserved for a definite sailing. Spanish authorities would not let anyone pass through Spain without a Portuguese transit visa. By this time the Gestapo had commenced to tighten control of the French-Spanish border. And still the Vichy government withheld exit permits. This combination of factors made escape to Lisbon from southern France extremely difficult, either legally or illegally. As a result, many refugees in unoccupied France who held American visas could not get out during the last months of 1940.[29]

A major barrier gave way in January 1941 when the Vichy government started to issue exit permits, probably indicating that the Gestapo had completed its screening of refugees in southern France. But, in case they had missed any political enemies, the Nazis set up a final net in Madrid; Spain issued no transit visas without approval from Gestapo agents there. Despite this man trap, the first half of 1941 saw a small but steady stream of refugees flow across Spain and out through Lisbon. This favorable turn of events for refugees did not last. At the end of June 1941, issuance of American visas ceased briefly, then resumed under much stricter and slower-moving procedures. The emergency visa program came to a halt, and all refugee immigration into the United States diminished and remained small throughout the war. In addition to the difficulties involved in obtaining American visas and in reaching a port of embarkation, political fugitives who came under the Administration's special emergency arrangements also encountered the troublesome problem of finding transportation overseas.[30]

THE SHIPPING SITUATION

Scarcity of ocean passage was, of course, a concern common to all refugees and to other travellers as well. Nor was the transportation problem limited to the months between the surrender of France and the middle of 1941, although it reached its most acute stage during that period. How did the transportation situation develop from 1938 through mid-1941?

Until the war began in September 1939, refugees readily found space on passenger liners. Through the prewar period, the bulk of the exodus passed through German harbors, although other European ports carried a share of the traffic. During the first eight months of the war, the major hindrance to refugee transportation was financial. After hostilities opened, foreign lines would no longer accept German money. Since the American immigration law excluded aliens whose passage was paid by an organization, most refugees had to rely on friends or relatives outside Germany to buy their boat tickets. Thousands of Germans on the United States quota lists could not secure this help and as a result were bypassed when their numbers came up because they could not prove to American consuls that they had ship reservations. Despite the complications, ships were by no means unavailable, and, on account of the huge demand, the German quota was 95 percent filled in the fiscal year which ended in mid-1940.[31]

The Nazi drive through western Europe in the spring of 1940 aggravated the transportation problem in two ways. First, the call for passage climbed swiftly as thousands of Americans and citizens of other neutral countries hastened to quit the war areas. Second, and more telling, important shipping lanes dwindled or vanished. In April the Germans moved into Scandinavia and choked off the Baltic Sea routes. Italy entered the war in June and shut her ports, blocking a major path of exit from Central and East Europe. The Italian attack on France brought the western Mediterranean into the list of combat areas forbidden to American vessels by the Neutrality Act. By mid-June only the harbors of Ireland, Portugal, and the Atlantic coast of Spain remained open to United States ships. In a matter of weeks, points of departure from western Europe had narrowed almost to Lisbon and the British ports, and British passenger shipping was in short supply because of the lack of convoying vessels. Some refugees reached safety via Spanish ports, while others made their way across the Mediterranean in small boats and came out through Casablanca. But the vast bulk of emigration between mid-1940 and the end of 1941 passed through Lisbon. For those with money and perseverance, an ingenious eastern route developed in the spring of 1940. Refugees travelled by railroad across Russia and down through Manchuria, by boat to Japan, and on ocean liners to the Western Hemisphere. But, shortly before the German invasion of Russia in June 1941, the Soviet Union closed this road of escape.[32]

In spite of the pressure on ocean transportation facilities during 1940, wealth and position were able to find a way. In mid-July the royal family of Luxemburg had a simple remedy for avoiding the struggle for steamship reservations. The United States cruiser *Trenton* picked up seven of the royal persons along with some of their household staff at Lisbon and put them ashore at Annapolis amidst sounds of a 21-gun salute and the blare of trumpets. *Fortune* reported that an English duke located a haven for a thousand of his orchid plants in Florida and that about 80 Rolls-Royces had "landed in this country as refugees" along with their masters.[33]

Although the shipping situation was difficult in the second half of 1940, it reached its most acute phase in the late winter and spring of 1941. By March reports from England advised that refugees there would have to wait a year to obtain passage to the United States. Liners plying the routes from Lisbon were booked three to nine months ahead. Ships sailing directly from Marseilles to Martinique afforded some relief in these critical months, but only a few hundred refugees were able to take advantage of this avenue of escape before it closed in late May. The Vichy government cancelled further sailings after the British seized one of the vessels in the West Indies.[34]

In March 1941 refugee aid organizations and the President's Advisory Committee tried to arrange for addition of one or two liners to the Lisbon run. The President's Advisory Committee pressed the United States Maritime Commission to permit the United States Lines to assign the *Washington* and the *Manhattan* to the Lisbon route to help bring out refugees. Permission was refused. According to a high-ranking official in the State Department, the Maritime Commission mentioned three reasons for its unanimous decision not to make the *Washington* available for transporting refugees to the United States: insurance costs would triple, Hitler would be tempted to sink such an important vessel, and, somewhat cryptically, reasons of sentiment were involved regarding the number of people to be let into the United States. A week and a half later the State Department informed the President's Advisory Committee that the Army had chartered the *Washington* and that the *Manhattan* would be in dry dock for three months. A Unitarian Service Committee leader was troubled because few refugees could move from unoccupied France to Lisbon until those in Portugal had departed. In Vienna, the repercussions of the Maritime Commission's decision were more deadly. The Nazis had suspended mass expulsion of Viennese Jews to Poland while attempts were underway to have relatives in the United States arrange ocean passage for them. The deportations recommenced directly after the American government decided against increasing shipping capacity between Lisbon and New York.[35]

The transportation shortage undoubtedly had a bearing on the fact that the quotas of the refugee-producing countries were only 53 percent filled during the fiscal year that opened soon after the fall of France. But more important reasons for the sharp decline in refugee immigration which occurred after mid-1940 emerge from an overall analysis of American refugee policy as administered by the Department of State.

## Chapter 8

# The Department of State

Near the end of 1940 a State Department press release observed that "the refugee problem is inextricably involved with the question of visas." But the question of visas was inextricably involved with the State Department, both in Washington and abroad. Although general visa policies took shape in the upper levels of the department, the Visa Division interpreted these decisions to foreign service officials in the field. Yet, in the last analysis, the legal authority for issuance of visas belonged to the consuls abroad. They weighed the evidence and made the final decisions in immigration cases.[1]

## THE CONSULS

Until fifth column fears spread in 1940, the most crucial consular judgments involved evaluation of affidavits of financial support required to assure that prospective immigrants would not become public charges. The clause in the Immigration Act of 1917 which excluded any person likely to become a public charge (the LPC clause) permitted widely varying interpretations. Although in March 1938 the Administration officially stopped using the LPC clause to curb immigration, the Visa Division did not establish explicit standards regarding financial assurances. Consequently, the matter was left to each consulate and requirements differed depending on the interpretations of individual consuls. Because criteria for suitable affidavits of support were indefinite, an official had little trouble finding grounds to refuse a visa which he did not wish to grant. On the other hand, rigid standards did not necessarily stem from an uncooperative attitude and in many instances reflected only an honest, if strict, interpretation of the law. Besides the LPC test, the physical, mental, moral, political, and other requirements of the immigration laws were open to various degrees of severity in interpretation. When in 1940 concern grew about penetration by fifth columnists, additional restrictions developed as the Administration worked toward formulation of a policy to assure exclusion of subversive persons. Putting these safeguards into practice gave further play to the divergent judgments of the different consuls. But long before the spy issue came into prominence, refugees and refugee aid groups found through experience that the policies of certain consulates made procurement of an American visa difficult beyond reason.[2]

During the years of the Hitler regime, tens of thousands of victims of Nazi oppression escaped to Switzerland. Because the Swiss frowned on permanent immigration and generally barred refugees from employment, most fugitives planned to wait in the safety of the small mountain republic only until their turns arrived for American or other overseas visas. But many refugees soon discovered that obtaining an American visa from the Zurich consulate involved more than fulfilling the requirements which were in effect, for example, at the United States consulates in Vienna or Berlin.

In April 1938, a month after the Austrian *Anschluss* and nearly three weeks after President Roosevelt opened the German-Austrian quota to full use, an official of the Women's International League for Peace and Freedom (WIL), resident in Switzerland, wrote to American friends about the problems presented by United States consuls in Switzerland. In several instances refugees learned that their affidavits of support from relatives or friends were deemed insufficient. Each time an applicant returned with increased financial assurances or other requested changes, the consulate found some further detail out of order and again rejected the affidavit. Some non-Jewish political refugees, forbidden to leave the Reich and unable to acquire passports, had managed to enter Switzerland. Although American immigration regulations permitted substitution of whatever documents were available, lack of proper papers provided reason enough for these consuls to refuse visas. Dorothy Detzer, executive secretary of the American branch of the WIL, visited Avra M. Warren, chief of the Visa Division, in Washington and received his word that he would write the American consul, particularly in regard to aliens without passports. While this action may have helped in a few cases, the general viewpoint of the consulate at Zurich held firm.[3]

In Geneva for a conference in December 1939, Miss Detzer talked with a group of refugees each of whom had assembled all papers required for immigration to the United States. None had been able to obtain a visa from the Zurich consulate. One fugitive, a prominent Bavarian Catholic, had affidavits from several Americans, including Mayor Fiorello La Guardia of New York City. The resources of the man's sponsors totaled over a million dollars. Miss Detzer talked with the consul but could make no headway and was unable even to secure a tangible reason for the refusal. Nor was she more successful at Zurich in the case of an 18-year-old half-Jewish Viennese youth who also possessed affidavits and all other necessary papers. Since his passport would expire at the end of the year, he would soon face deportation to the Nazis. Dorothy Detzer obtained an extra month's stay for the youth from the Swiss authorities. Then, upon returning to Washington, she talked again with Avra Warren. A heated dispute broke out when Miss Detzer accused the Zurich consulate of being anti-Catholic and anti-Semitic. Although she could only rely on "all that I heard when I was in Europe" when Warren challenged her to produce evidence, the visa chief himself volunteered his knowledge that the Swiss government believed the consulate was anti-Catholic and anti-Semitic. Warren made no promises regarding the Viennese youth. After more than two weeks of waiting for news from the Visa Division, Miss Detzer in late January 1940 received word from Switzerland that the boy's deportation was four days away. The Visa Division then reported regretfully that regulations did not allow interference with consular rulings. At that point Dorothy Detzer lit some fires. In a one-hour conference she told the full Zurich story to Cordell Hull. Hull was sympathetic and arranged an interview for her with outgoing Assistant Secretary of State George S. Messersmith. After a good deal of moral suasion, Messersmith telegraphed the Zurich consulate asking immediate information regarding nonissuance of a visa to the endangered youth. The consulate granted the visa one day before the scheduled deportation.[4]

Anxious for a change at Zurich, Dorothy Detzer took the matter to Eleanor Roosevelt who stated that she would see Sumner Welles about it. Soon afterward Welles made a European trip during which he visited American officials at Zurich. While no causal relationship can be proven, within a very short time Consul General Arthur C. Frost was transferred from Zurich to a post in Spain.[5]

In the meantime, between April 1938 and January 1939, a long-suffering refugee in Switzerland and an insistent sponsor in the United States tenaciously worked their way through a maze of paper walls built by the Zurich consulate. The refugee, who will here be called x, had reached the highest ranks of his profession in Vienna and had attracted an international clientele. Directly after the *Anschluss,* x fled to Switzerland where he had arranged some time before to have part of his savings deposited. There he and his family awaited permission to move to a country of final settlement. One of x's American friends found that Laura Z. Hobson, then with Time, Incorporated, and later to become an outstanding novelist, was willing to provide an affidavit of support for x and his family. At this time x possessed the equivalent of 7,000 dollars in savings available to bring to the United States, an amount that surely would have sufficed to re-establish him in his profession. His sponsor, Mrs. Hobson, had an annual income extending into five figures. Economically, as well as in terms of personal qualities, x was unquestionably the type of person who would be an asset to the country.[6]

In April 1938 Mrs. Hobson arranged for a lawyer fully experienced in preparing immigration papers to draw up her affidavit of support. In this document she swore that she assumed complete responsibility for the members of the x family and guaranteed that they would never become public charges. Early in June x learned from the Zurich consulate that the affidavit was not fully acceptable. Although photostatic copies of cancelled income tax payment checks were sufficient proof of the sponsor's past salary to some consulates, the Zurich office required in addition a notarized copy of the income tax return. Within a week the tax forms were on the way to Switzerland. On September 20 the consul at Zurich announced rejection of the visa application, apparently because the American sponsor was not related to x. Mrs. Hobson then wrote to ask visa chief Avra Warren for his help, explaining that with x's savings, his connections in the United States, and her own concern for his family, there was no question of financial support. Warren replied that the State Department could not instruct consuls to issue visas, but that he would send to Zurich for a telegraphic report on the case. Three days later Warren relayed to Mrs. Hobson the two reasons stated by the consulate for refusal of the visas. First, x had not provided evidence to prove that he possessed 7,000 dollars. Second, the affidavit from Laura Hobson was not considered sufficient because it expressed only general interest in the x family and did not include any obligation to help support them.[7]

Mrs. Hobson promptly cabled the Zurich consulate that she felt "deeply responsible" for the x's and would "guarantee monthly support if necessary." The consul general replied that if she would provide a supplementary statement regarding her motives in agreeing to support the x family and the plans she had formed for them, the consulate would take it into consideration. Laura Hobson then sent the consul a formal statement incorporating the pledge given in her cablegram and assuring that she would "stand by them until they are completely on their own here." In mid-October x mailed a somewhat different version of the problem to his sponsor. He stated that he had been told his application had been rejected because Mrs. Hobson was not a relative and because his own savings were insufficient. Only following the recent cablegrams had the consulate requested more extensive proof of his possession of the money. Refugee x also reported his concern over another complication which he had not previously mentioned, but of which he had been aware since April. Although his wife and her parents had always been Austrian citizens, she had been born in Budapest. For that reason the consul insisted on assigning Mrs. x to the waiting list of the small Hungarian quota. As a result, if the x's should receive visas, the wife would, at the very least, have to wait several months before rejoining her husband and children. Immediately upon receiving this news, Laura Hobson sent a telegram about Mrs. x's predicament to Avra Warren. She also pointed out that x's Swiss visitor's permit would expire in two weeks and asked if Warren could somehow influence the Zurich consulate "to cease this apparently endless search for new red tape." Warren replied that the State Department had cabled to Zurich for a further report on the case.[8]

In the interval, the consulate had uncovered a new problem. Finally convinced that the savings in x's bank account were really his, the American officials next wanted to know why x had not declared the money when he first applied for a visa in April instead of delaying mention of it until late May. Mr. x explained that his departure from

Austria had been legalized only in May and that until then, under German law, his possession of funds outside Germany had been a capital crime. However, the complications about the bank account seem to have evaporated before the State Department's proddings. The department must also have emphasized to the Zurich consulate the fact that the Immigration Act of 1924 provided that if a visa applicant's wife came under a different, more crowded, quota than her husband, both could enter on the quota of the husband's country of birth. In any event, Avra Warren informed Mrs. Hobson in early November of Zurich's report that the only item still lacking was her supplementary statement of financial support which was already in the mail. The consulate had also decided that Mrs. x could join the others under the German quota.[9]

Approval of the visa applications late in November ended the ordeal, although quota numbers were not available for several weeks. Assured that the x's would actually be emigrating, the Swiss authorities extended the family's visitor's permit. Late in January 1939 the refugees at last set sail for the United States where x soon re-established himself in his work and commenced a successful and useful career. He was fortunate in that his own intelligence and the strong support of a persistent and able sponsor made it possible to outlast the piecemeal method by which the Zurich consulate presented its reasons for nonissuance of the visas. Unquestionably many other refugees met similar complications, but were unable to solve them, and failed to obtain the crucial permission to enter the United States.[10]

Arrival of James B. Stewart as consul general at Zurich early in 1940 did not end the problems there for refugees. A Quaker worker reported in July of that year that she had been able to accomplish almost nothing toward helping refugees to emigrate from Switzerland. A telephone conversation with a Zurich consular official had been very unsuccessful. The only concession she had secured was an appointment to talk with him the following week. That meeting was not much more effective than the phone call. Over a year later, an American woman outlined the difficulty she and her Yugoslav husband had encountered in obtaining his visa. While the Yugoslav was facing deportation, the Zurich consulate had allowed the couple to wait six weeks under the incorrect impression that the visa application was entirely in order. The woman asserted that the problem lay in the consulate's having mistakenly believed that she was Jewish. When the American officials discovered that she was not a Jew, she reported, the consulate went into rapid action, got hold of a visa, and interceded with the Swiss police at the last minute to stave off the deportation.[11]

Several other consulates presented complications in varying degrees. Lack of unity in the standards set for acceptable affidavits of support underlay many of the difficulties. American Friends Service Committee personnel sent early in 1939 to help with refugee emigration received a cordial welcome and close cooperation from American foreign service officials throughout Europe. Consuls in Germany and Vienna especially were open to Quaker suggestions and held their requirements for affidavits to reasonable levels. To the Friends, the situation in Stockholm was less satisfactory. They felt that vice-consul William P. Snow was an excellent and conscientious person, but he appeared overly concerned to avoid erring in the direction of leniency. They reported that literally no affidavit was sufficient to convince him that an immigrant would not become a public charge. Some refugees who had fled to Sweden to await overseas visas in safety held affidavits which American consuls in Germany had approved. But the documents were not adequate in Stockholm. Snow required that the alien have either a bank deposit of his own in the United States or sufficient cash with him in Sweden to prove he would be self-supporting in America. Since emigrants could take little money out of Germany, refugees who had escaped to Sweden were often unable to fulfill the specifications of the Stockholm consulate. Furthermore, the consul would not state how much cash was needed. The applicant would present his evidence of assets and the official would then advise him whether it was enough.[12]

The Quakers found the visa consul in Oslo a little less rigid. Still, he felt that an affidavit given by a stranger was unacceptable and that no American should make out more than one affidavit. He also required that refugees possess a certain amount of cash. While this consul would set a definite figure, the Friends noted that he placed it at a maximum in the hope of dissuading the alien from going to America. They reported that he believed it was not good to let too many Jews into the United States.[13]

American officials in Antwerp also proved difficult. Unsatisfied by affidavits of support, the Antwerp consulate wished the affiant to deposit in the United States an irrevocable trust fund restricted to the purpose of providing for the immigrant if need arose. A group of 52 refugees, who had begun visa proceedings in Austria and whose affidavits had been approved there, fled to the safety of Luxemburg to await the visas. When their quota numbers became current, the Antwerp consulate turned the Austrians down, suggesting that each person arrange for an irrevocable bank account of several thousand dollars. At least one refugee who faced this trust fund barrier went to England and secured a visa from the American consul there on the strength of his affidavit alone.[14]

After the fall of France, the difficulties presented by diverse interpretations of the public charge clause were augmented by the varying consular attitudes toward the threat of immigration of fifth columnists. Certain foreign service officers felt that refugees with a record of antifascist activity were suspect for that very reason. A leader of the Unitarian Service Committee, after a few weeks at work in Lisbon, felt that some consuls held "a definite prejudice against those who have been active politically on the democratic side." He further observed that "the best chance of getting an American visa is to have been an inconspicuous person, never having done anything good or bad, and to have wealthy relatives in America." In late 1940 the American visa consul at Nice asked a refugee what he would do if he were in the United States and someone solicited him to join in an effort against the German or Italian government. The applicant replied that he would do whatever seemed best for the United States. The consul refused the visa, saying that America did not want immigrants who were going to meddle in politics. The refugee had to go back to the camp at Gurs and his wife and child were also unable to secure American visas. The same consul at Nice followed the piecemeal approach to documentation which occurred in the case of x at Zurich. He replied to inquiries about visas with form letters referring to certain requirements which had not been satisfactorily fulfilled. Since he kept finding some additional element still missing, the process would be repeated again and again. Frequently refugees found it more feasible to travel to Marseilles to deal with the consulate there. Perhaps the height of suspicion was reached in a case handled by consular officials at Nice. Among credentials required for a visa was a police report stating that the applicant had not been in trouble with the law. A 78-year-old woman had obtained her document from the police in occupied France. Because the statement had been made out a month before, the Nice consulate held it to be too old! [15]

By the middle of 1941, the *New Republic* was charging openly that anti-Semitism within the State Department and on the part of some American officials abroad was hindering immigration of refugees. At the end of April it carried an article by Alfred Wagg who had been working on refugee matters for the State Department until his resignation on the first of March. Wagg stated that the American "refugee effort has been at best a stepchild in Washington, to be beaten and buffeted, and at worst a football for anti-Semitism and for petty bureaucrats, including those who take delight in sabotaging the President's program just because it is his." (Wagg's published report was privately confirmed by an American Friends Service Committee staff member who had reliable contacts with people in and close to the State Department.) In June the *New Republic* declared that some Department of State personnel had "been charged, with formidable evidence, of anti-Semitism, of deliberately making more difficult the removal of refugees from Europe." A month later the same magazine asserted that it was "common gossip in Washington" that there was "widespread anti-Semitism in the foreign service." Varian Fry related that in his work in unoccupied France for the Emergency Rescue Committee he had found some consuls who opposed immigration generally and others who made no pretense about their reluctance to allow Jewish refugees to enter the United States. In November 1940 a French woman engaged in relief work for an American organization told Fry of her encounter with an official in the American Embassy at Vichy who hoped she was not helping Jews to emigrate to the United States. When the relief worker asked the official what he thought ought to be done about Jewish refugees, "he hunched his shoulders in the position of a man holding a submachine gun" and said: " 'Ptt-ptt-ptt-ptt-ptt.' " [16]

Conceivably the official at the Vichy Embassy was not expressing an actual viewpoint, but was simply indulging a macabre, warped sense of humor. Nonetheless, at about the same time, an antialien attitude shading over into anti-Semitism had grown into a critical problem at Lisbon. As noted earlier, the Portuguese capital became the only major point of embarkation from the Continent after France surrendered in June 1940. The American consulate there was crucially important. A cooperative approach on its part could do much to facilitate a smooth flow of refugees away from the Nazis. Rigid or slow-moving procedures would hamper departure from Portugal and result in blocking escape of more refugees into that nation from

France and other countries. When the deluge of fleeing people reached Lisbon, facilities at the American consulate proved inadequate and considerable confusion resulted. Though the staff was increased, a Unitarian Service Committee worker reported in mid-August that the consulate was still "altogether swamped," a situation which, in combination with the high humidity, gave rise to "short and snappy" tempers. In addition to these troubles, which were inherent in the circumstances, it soon became apparent that the consular attitude toward refugees was essentially negative. The Unitarian representative found American officials at Lisbon "very difficult to deal with" as well as generally unable to view the problem except in terms of

> paper work—registration dates, . . . affidavit forms, seals and signatures and all the dreary necessary bureaucratic details of the Immigration Law of 1924. (That year was when history stopped for most of these birds in the consulates—Sinai was last time afire on that date.)

The frustrations met by refugees who initiated immigration applications at Lisbon were shared by others who held expired visas from American consulates elsewhere. Under the Immigration Act of 1924, visas became invalid if not used within four months. Normally that length of time was ample, but after mid-1940 long delays in reaching a port and in obtaining ocean passage were not unusual. If the alien had unavoidably exceeded the four-month time limit, the consul at the port might reasonably have accepted the judgment of the previous consul and have issued a new visa. In fact, the State Department had ruled that consuls could grant "replace visas" to these people immediately if they succeeded in securing transportation. A major difficulty faced by refugees in Lisbon was that American officials there treated renewal cases in the same manner as new ones. They undertook a full review and, as a Quaker worker reported, since the Lisbon consulate was strict, problems resulted.[17]

By early November 1940 representatives of Jewish refugee agencies in Lisbon found their emigration work hampered by inability to establish cooperative contacts with some American foreign service officials. Consequently, the Jewish agencies in New York approached the American Friends Service Committee (AFSC) regarding possible assignment of a non-Jewish representative to Lisbon to try to encourage a more positive attitude in the consulate. An AFSC staff member,

Mrs. Marjorie P. Schauffler, arrived in Lisbon in mid-February 1941 and remained until the beginning of April to study the situation there and to develop favorable contacts with American officials. Early in March Mrs. Schauffler reported that the consulate was issuing visas with a sparing hand and that she was conferring with the consul general and the vice-consul in charge of visas. By the middle of the month she noted gradual progress in establishment of cordial relationships. Although this short visit brought positive gains, the AFSC decided upon a long-term effort. A detailed report on the situation in Portugal, prepared as an aid in determining whether to set up a Friends' office there, summarized the need as follows:

> An important function to be served is a favorable contact on behalf of refugees with the American Consulate and Legation. This is not being adequately performed by any existing agency in Lisbon, and its importance cannot be overestimated. Particularly in the Consulate there is a strong antialien feeling. It is useful to have a quiet friendly insistence on the need to keep the humanitarian emphasis traditional to America, and the need to view cases as individuals rather than as an "undesirable group." This emphasis, to be most acceptable, should grow out of a friendly social "American" non-Jewish relationship.

In May 1941 the AFSC established an office in Lisbon under the leadership of Dr. Philip A. Conard, long a representative of the YMCA in South America.[18]

The State Department may have placed some pressure on the Lisbon consulate. According to a report in March, a cablegram from Washington had suggested a more lenient policy in regard to renewing expired visas. And in late April Harry M. Donaldson, the vice-consul in charge of visas, was transferred to Marseilles. The Friends' Lisbon office continued the work begun in February by Mrs. Schauffler. In October Philip Conard wrote that "relations with the American Consulate have been excellent" and "on the whole . . . we get very fair treatment" from the new visa consul, although "at times we have felt that there was insufficient consideration of the individuals and human values involved." By the end of the summer a leader of the American Jewish Joint Distribution Committee concluded that Lisbon no longer presented an acute problem.[19]

While the aforementioned consular practices were not entirely representative of the foreign service as a whole, nevertheless, refugees frequently encountered negative attitudes among American officials in Europe. Furthermore, the practical effects of these attitudes were enhanced by the fact that they came to bear on the refugee problem at the crucial point of visa issuance. Various factors lay behind the severe requirements imposed by some consulates. A foreign service official was naturally concerned to advance in his profession, or at least to hold his position. A sympathetic approach to refugee problems would hardly increase his chances of promotion. Indeed, the sternest policy was the safest policy. The more rigid the requirements, the more certain the consul would be that he would not be held responsible for some immigrant who might become a public charge or turn out to be a subversive. The fewer visas issued, the fewer risks to the consul. Leaving the personal level for a broader outlook, officials could understandably feel that admission of refugees did not sufficiently advance the interests of the United States to justify the risk of letting in people who might become public charges or engage in political agitation or subversive activities. Although these hardheaded, practical viewpoints were rationally grounded, three comments are in order. First, the fact that the consul had final judgment in assigning visas did not mean that he should have taken upon himself responsibility for deciding what American refugee policy should have been. Second, the viewpoint which places its heaviest emphasis on avoiding blame and mistakes, though perhaps indigenous to a bureaucratic environment, reflects only the negative aspect of responsibility. While avoiding mistakes is important, responsible administration includes more than minimal action. Third, the need for precautions regarding the public charge problem and the possible entry of subversives too often opened the way for exercise of personal antialien and anti-Jewish prejudices.

Some foreign service officers did see beyond the narrow confines of negative responsibility and grasped the importance of humanitarian considerations. Herbert S. Goold, consul general at Casablanca in early 1941, was very concerned about refugees held in nearby concentration camps. He visited the camps, pressed for amelioration of conditions, and insisted on immediate release of anyone to whom he could issue a visa. A person reporting from Casablanca pointed out that this attitude did not, however, preclude "very strict" requirements and refusal of "a goodly number" of visas. Responding to the huge increase in work caused by the influx of refugees, consular officials in Casablanca spent most of their free hours processing applications. A consul in Lisbon willingly put in 12 to 14 hours a day in the summer and fall of 1940 to speed up visa applications and to interview refugees. The wife of an official there opened two rooms of her apartment for the use of refugees and contributed half-time work to the office of a refugee agency. Another American official in Portugal received a letter from a 13-year-old refugee girl asking help for her parents who had been imprisoned in Spain after fleeing France. He checked on the family's background and then proceeded to obtain their release. During the rush to escape Germany after the Night of Broken Glass, refugees who had proof they could move on within three months were accepted into Luxemburg. Official American statements regarding the probable date when the refugees' quota numbers would come up were acceptable evidence to Luxemburg authorities. Consequently, the American diplomatic mission in Luxemburg devoted a large amount of time to verifying the status of refugee visa applications in process at the American consulate in Stuttgart. George P. Waller, American chargé in Luxemburg, reported that "it is a comfort to realize that through such cooperation it has been possible for a great many helpless and persecuted people to receive shelter and a waiting place in Luxemburg." Obviously this helpfulness depended on a similar concern at the Stuttgart consulate. When the Nazis invaded Norway in April 1940, the American consulate at Oslo gave sanctuary to many of Norway's German-Jewish refugees until they were able to flee to Sweden. American Friends Service Committee workers who went to Europe in early 1939 to facilitate refugee emigration found a cooperative attitude quite general at the consulates in Germany. Particularly close relationships between the Friends and American officials developed at Vienna and Berlin with the result that mutual assistance and exchange of information were valuable assets to the work of both the Quakers and the consulates.[20]

Until the late spring of 1941 the consulate at Marseilles was especially cooperative in helping refugees to leave for the United States, a most fortunate circumstance for many political and intellectual fugitives in southern France who qualified for American emergency visas. The Emergency Rescue Committee found that Marseilles consuls "minimized formalities instead of creating barriers to the departure of refugees, and did everything in their power to help those ready to go." This attitude was particularly useful because of the unpredictable schedules for ships leaving Marseilles. Since short notice preceded the sailing of most vessels, frantic efforts were necessary to prepare emigrants. If the consulate had stalled, many refugees would have lost the chance to escape. A central figure in a bizarre rescue scene was Hiram Bingham, Jr., the visa consul at Marseilles. Soon after the surrender of France, Bingham, son of the former United States senator from Connecticut, drove to a location near a concentration camp where the interned men were permitted to swim. By prearrangement the German novelist Lion Feuchtwanger was waiting there for the consul's arrival. Dressing in clothes brought by Bingham, Feuchtwanger disguised himself as an old lady and rode back to Bingham's villa at Marseilles. There the writer hid until his visa was approved and it seemed safe to attempt the trip across Spain. In September 1940 a Unitarian Service Committee staff member took Feuchtwanger through to Portugal and on to the United States.[21]

Although visa consuls were technically free to exercise their own judgment in each case, in practice they operated within guidelines drawn in Washington. Since the Administration's visa policy was a crucial aspect of the American response to the refugee problem, it is important to bring it into closer focus.

A CHANGING VISA POLICY

From early 1938 through 1941 in actuality a series of American visa policies unfolded. While the causes for the shifts cannot be determined with accuracy in each instance, the policies themselves can be traced rather distinctly. It will be recalled that the Hoover Administration in 1930 reinterpreted the "likely to become a public charge" clause in such a strict manner that immigration dropped sharply. The Roosevelt Administration continued this plan, although the flow of refugees out of Germany worked some slow erosion on it through 1936. In 1937 the pressure of people fleeing Hitler cut quite deeply into the LPC policy. Then, after the Austrian *Anschluss* of March 1938, President Roosevelt opened the German-Austrian quota to full use.[22]

The first visa policy of immediate concern extended from March 1938 into September 1939. During these 18 months American immigration policy was more liberal than at any other time between 1931 and 1946. Despite the unemployment situation and pressures from restrictionist groups, the Administration stood by its pledge made at the Evian Conference to accept refugees up to the quota limits. In addition, following the Night of Broken Glass, President Roosevelt announced that the government would not force refugees already in the United States on visitors' visas to return home. Even though some consuls imposed extremely rigid standards, and pivotal consulates lacked sufficient staff to handle the rush, virtually all the quota numbers of countries where refugee pressure had developed were used. In line with the policy of full quotas, Avra Warren, chief of the Visa Division, visited the consulates in Central Europe early in 1939 and added 15 clerks at Vienna, 10 at Berlin, and five at Prague. He wanted to double those increases, but could not find available Americans and did not dare hire more Germans in view of the strong temptation to bribery. Warren accepted an offer made by Clarence Pickett of the American Friends Service Committee to recruit and help pay the expenses of up to 20 young Americans, fluent in German, to assist in the consulates in Europe. The first dissonant note in the Administration's visa policy sounded in the State Department when Assistant Secretary George S. Messersmith spiked the plan.[23]

Although these months in 1938 and 1939 marked the high point of American generosity toward refugees, aliens were by no means flooding the country. The obviously relevant quotas, those of Germany-Austria and Czechoslovakia, totaled 30,244. Since many Jews and antifascists in some of Germany's neighbors felt the Nazi threat, one may add the 7,393 quota places assigned to Poland and Hungary. Even including the allotments of Danzig, the three Baltic states, Rumania, Bulgaria, and Yugoslavia, a grand total of less than 40,000 quota refugees could enter the United States in one year, thus 60,000 in these 18 months. Allowing for about 5,000 nonquota immigrants, and for the 20,000, at most, who arrived on visitors' visas and did not leave, an outside estimate would point to immigration of under 85,000 refugees in the 18-month period. At this time the population of the United States was about 130 million.

The second visa policy came into effect soon after the outbreak of hostilities in September 1939 and continued until July 1940, thus covering most of the fiscal year 1940. Contrary to expectations, the coming of war did not cut immigration from Europe drastically. The influx of refugees decreased during the first two months of the conflict, but soon rose again. As it turned out, for fiscal 1940 the Hungarian allotment was taken up entirely and the main refugee quota, that of Germany, was 95 percent filled. Use of the Czech and Polish quotas dropped to 69 and 67 percent respectively, undoubtedly reflecting the difficulties in getting out of those subject nations and the complications in obtaining ocean transportation. Taken together, these factors give the impression that during this ten-month period the Administration continued its earlier policy of keeping the quotas open to full use. Actually, a more careful look at the emigration situation in Germany and a more thorough analysis of United States immigration statistics show a different American visa policy in this period than in the 18 months before the war.[24]

By November 1939 immigration directly from Germany was falling seriously. One major cause was that foreign ship lines would no longer accept German currency. Numerous refugees in the Reich were able to call on friends or relatives in the United States to pay their way; most were not. When this problem arose, American consuls began to require evidence of paid ship passage before granting visas. In addition to the transportation snag, an equally important factor in the decrease of immigration from Germany was imposition of stricter affidavit requirements, this time from Washington. In general, consuls no longer accepted affidavits from nonrelatives unless they had substantial means, and even then, in many cases, they had to place cash deposits for the refugees in American banks. The State Department informed refugee agencies of this change, explaining that it had found evidence of fraud in making affidavits. Because of the severe new affidavit standards and the difficulty in paying for ship passage, only about ten percent of the people on the waiting lists in Germany were able to qualify for visas when their quota numbers came up.[25]

Large-scale rejection of visa applicants in the Reich began to cut into the huge waiting list for the German quota. Late in 1939 the State Department predicted that the list might become entirely caught up within 18 months. Many of the thousands of refugees who had earlier found safety as temporary migrants in England, France, and other countries replaced applicants turned down in Germany. By November the State Department had transferred a large block of German quota numbers from Germany to England and a smaller amount to Cuba. Refugees in those countries consequently came up for visa consideration long before anticipated. Because of war devastation and unsanitary conditions, the American consul in Warsaw moved his office to Oslo and distributed much of the Polish quota to other consulates. Immigration statistics for fiscal 1940 reflect these several factors.[26]

The classification "Hebrew" in Immigration and Naturalization Service records provides a convenient indicator for trends in refugee immigration. True, this category does not include all refugees or even all Jews who came to the United States. However, evidence for the validity of "Hebrew" immigration as a gauge for the general refugee flow into the country lies in the fact that from 1938 through 1941 a consistent nine tenths or more of the aliens who entered from Germany were recorded as "Hebrews." Comparison of statistics for "Hebrew" immigration in fiscal 1940 with the figures for fiscal 1939 brings out an interesting migration pattern. The number of "Hebrews" coming from a residence in Germany dropped by one third, as did all immigration directly from Germany. Yet usage of the German quota, which was assigned according to country of birth, declined only five percent. Obviously, increasing numbers of German-born refugees were moving to the United States from countries to which they had previously fled to escape the Nazis. In the case of Poland the same trend appears but is more extreme because of the great obstacles which stood in the way of leaving that land after the war started. Immigration of "Hebrews" from Poland in fiscal 1940 fell a drastic 79 percent compared with the previous year, while the use made of the Polish quota declined 33 percent.

The other side of the picture emerges from analysis of "Hebrew" immigration from some transit countries in fiscal 1940 as measured against fiscal 1939. The number of "Hebrews" from Belgium tripled. Those from France nearly doubled and the Netherlands sent one and three fourths as many. The most striking change occurred in the case of Great Britain. More than 4,000 "Hebrews" moved from there to the United States, an increase of over five times the number in fiscal 1939. Without doubt, most of these people were charged to the German quota. To summarize, "Hebrew" immigration from Germany fell from 30,000 to 20,000. Yet the German quota was almost filled. The facts that 3,300 more "Hebrews" entered from Great Britain than had the year before and that an increase of 2,300 came from France and the Low Countries show that the slack in the German quota was being taken up by removal of refugees from transit countries to the United States.[27]

At least three causes explain this shift in the pattern of refugee immigration. For one thing, fugitives in the border countries, especially England, found arrangements for sea passage easier to make than did people in the Reich. Secondly, because the date of first application determined priority on the quota waiting list, the numbers of some refugees who had registered for visas in Germany and had then moved to transit countries became current. Rejection of thousands of applicants in Germany speeded this process. The third factor, stiffening of affidavit requirements by American consulates in Germany in the fall of 1939, played a telling role.

The reasons for increasing the financial assurances needed by refugees in Germany are not fully clear. Although the State Department explained that discovery of fraudulent and deceptive affidavit practices had forced the change, the problem could hardly have been extensive enough to require such a drastic remedy. The State Department's concern about Congressional pressures working against entry of refugees may have played a part in bringing on the stricter policy. Still an additional factor might have been involved, namely that soon after the war began the State Department may have agreed to an English request that German refugees in England receive priority for entry into the United States. Increasing anti-Semitism in England and the burden on the English Jewish community in supporting unemployed refugees were thought to be major contributing influences. Since affidavit requirements were not standardized, the State Department might have chosen to tighten them in Germany as a means of facilitating immigration of refugees from England. Whatever the causes behind extensive rejection of visa applications in Germany, pressure to get away from the Nazis was immense. In spite of stringent affidavit requirements and the transportation problem, more than 21,000 people managed to immigrate directly from Germany in fiscal 1940.[28]

The early summer of 1940 brought a new visa policy which continued into June 1941. While a decreasing trend in the flow of refugees from the Reich had characterized the second phase, the year of the third visa policy saw immigration from Germany plummet. During this time pressure to escape the Nazis remained strong and the Hitler government continued to encourage Jews to leave Germany, although it did raise obstacles to exit of refugees from some occupied countries and from Vichy France. In fact, still hoping to diminish the "Jewish problem" in Germany by emigration, the Nazis arranged special sealed refugee trains to carry Jews to Lisbon and to Spanish ports. Shortage of ocean transportation certainly constituted an important hindrance to emigration from all parts of Europe. But the main barrier which confronted refugees in Germany after mid-1940 was the paper wall raised around Central Europe by the United States in the summer and fall of that year.[29]

By early May, even before Germany invaded the Low Countries, visa chief Avra Warren was at work on proposed legislation for stricter immigration controls to protect the country from subversive aliens. Surprisingly, nothing in the immigration code closed the door to applicants for permanent residence because they might present a threat to national security. As Breckinridge Long explained in late May 1940, "we can exclude a temporary visitor because he has subversive connections or intentions, but we cannot exclude for those reasons one who comes here permanently to live." Long wanted early Congressional action to remedy the problem, but President Roosevelt and his Cabinet held back, apparently fearing that Congress might pass an excessively restrictive law. As a possible alternative, Long reported on May 29 that he and Attorney General Robert H. Jackson had "discussed power to act without additional legislation and admitted it probably existed but that if assumed without specific legislative authority it might subject the President to unnecessary criticism." [30]

Lacking a clear basis in law, the State Department had misgivings about openly imposing new and stringent controls on permanent visas. But, before June ended, Avra Warren and Breckinridge Long had devised a *modus operandi* which effectively walled out any applicants the State Department wished to exclude. Long spelled out the method in a June 26 memorandum addressed to Adolf A. Berle, Jr., and James C. Dunn:

> We can delay and effectively stop for a temporary period of indefinite length the number of immigrants into the United States. We could do this by simply advising our consuls to put every obstacle in the way and to require additional evidence and to resort to various administrative advices which would postpone and postpone and postpone the granting of the visas. However, this could only be temporary.

In fact, Long's method worked effectively for almost a year until legislation was secured excluding aliens who might endanger the national security.[31]

On June 29 the State Department instructed its diplomatic and consular officers to examine applications for permanent visas extremely carefully and to withhold visas from aliens about whom they had "any doubt whatsoever." The circular cablegram carrying the new orders pointed out that,

> although a drastic reduction in the number of quota and nonquota immigration visas issued will result therefrom and quotas against which there is a heavy demand will be underissued, it is essential to take every precaution at this time to safeguard the best interests of the United States.

Summarizing the sweeping innovation, Breckinridge Long tersely recorded in his diary: "The cables practically stopping immigration went!" [32]

Early in July Avra Warren set out on a four-month journey which took him through all of Europe except the Low Countries, Norway, and the British Isles. Ranging as far east as Russia and Turkey, the visa chief spent seven weeks in Germany and about ten days in each other nation on his itinerary. Arriving in Lisbon in mid-July, Warren increased the overburdened consular staff and carefully explained the new visa policy, stressing the State Department's recent orders to deny visas to aliens whose cases were at all doubtful. One afternoon in mid-August, during his stop in Vienna, Warren arranged to talk with an American emigration worker to whom he spelled out his mission and the effect of the new instructions. The visa chief stated that immigration from Germany was being terminated. The emigration worker asked whether the move was aimed at heading off Congressional pressure to eliminate all the quotas. Warren replied that Congress was not involved, but the President wanted to stop the flow of aliens into the United States, particularly those coming from Germany. He explained that the change was necessary because some refugees had been connected with fifth column activities, because anti-Semitism was rising in the United States, and because of the need to use German visas to move refugees out of England and Shanghai. The Stuttgart consulate, said Warren, had issued only three visas in July, and, while about 100 had been granted in Vienna, that rate would be sharply decreased. The emigration worker reported that the gist of the discussion was that immigration of Jewish refugees proceeding from Germany had just about ended.[33]

Indication that the State Department did not want the severity of the new restrictions generally known soon appeared in Vienna. Following Warren's visit, the consulate continued to permit refugees to nurture hopes of obtaining visas and let them spend weeks and money assembling documents and affidavits, fulfilling all the other American and German requirements, and arranging ship passage, only to reject them after the final interview as likely to become public charges. In one case, following a long and apparently satisfactory interview, an applicant was told to obtain a report from an x-ray specialist. The man complied, at some expense, and then learned that his application was rejected, but not because of poor health. Under the new system, the Vienna consulate was issuing three or four visas a week.[34]

A clear picture of the sequence of events at the Vienna consulate emerges from the case of a 63-year-old woman, living alone and under difficult conditions in Austria. Her son, who had reached the United States and had re-established himself in medical practice, was endeavoring to bring his mother out to safety. After an initial wait of a year and a half, the woman's turn to receive a visa came in March 1940. But the German authorities held up her passport and when she was able to take it to the American consulate a month later she learned that no more quota numbers would be available until the new fiscal year began in July. In May 1940 the Vienna consulate reported that the woman's affidavits of support were satisfactory, but that it could not grant a visa for several months. In August the consulate informed the lady that everything was in order and that the only remaining requirement was a medical examination scheduled for late in the month. To the dismay of herself, her son, and her two other affiants, one of them a wealthy American woman, the applicant learned in September that her visa was refused because her evidence of support was inadequate and her physical condition was not good enough to assure her earning a living in the United States. Her sponsors of course had no way of knowing about Avra Warren's visit to Vienna which occurred in the interval between the scheduling of the medical examination and the date on which it took place. At length, pressure put on the State Department by the woman's friends in the United States brought results. The Vienna consulate approved her papers again in March 1941 and this time raised no question about her physical condition. She received the precious visa and rejoined her son.[35]

As Avra Warren worked his way across Europe, evidence that he was making his points clear to the consulates sprouted in other places than Vienna. In Zurich an applicant was denied a visa in September 1940 because her presence was not necessary in the United States. A report from the Swiss city in October stated that in some cases people with four adequate affidavits received refusal notices. By the beginning of November the Zurich consulate had commenced to send form letters explaining that it had rejected visa applications because of the "state of emergency" in the United States. In October the Stockholm consulate was turning down refugees with affidavits and American bank accounts which would previously have been adequate. By early December the National Refugee Service learned that Stockholm also required proof that the immigrant would "be an asset to the United States." As late as March 1941 a Quaker representative found the attitudes that had appeared in various consulates following Warren's visits still much in evidence in Lisbon and Madrid.[36]

Immigration statistics reflect the results of the visa policy initiated in mid-1940. Since the period of the third visa policy generally coincided with the fiscal year 1941, comparison of statistics for fiscal 1941 with those of the previous fiscal year brings the effects of the third phase into focus. Immigration from Germany dropped by 81 percent, from Hungary by 83 percent, and from Czechoslovakia by 71 percent. During the same year, the numbers who came to the United States under the German quota (namely, all immigrants born in Germany) fell also, but at the substantially smaller rate of 50 percent. Use of the Hungarian quota lessened by 59 percent and that of the Czechoslovak allotment by only ten percent. Clearly, the bulk of the refugees who immigrated in fiscal 1941 came from transit countries. As an indicator, only 4,000 of the 13,000 people who entered under the German quota left directly from a residence in Germany. Figures show that, while immigration from Central Europe plunged, entry of refugees into the United States from countries not under the Nazi yoke increased, though not greatly. "Hebrews" coming from Great Britain rose from 4,100 to 4,700. "Hebrew" immigration from Portugal shot up from nine to 599; from Canada the numbers increased from below 1,000 to almost 1,400. From South America came 987 in contrast to 238 the year before. Most dramatic was the surge in immigration of "Hebrews" from the West Indies, virtually all arriving from Cuba. The 558 of fiscal 1940 jumped to 2,642. In fact, over one fifth of the people who entered the United States under the German quota proceeded from residences in Canada or Latin America. More than one fourth of the nearly 1,800 natives of Czechoslovakia who immigrated in fiscal 1941 had also previously reached the safety of the Western Hemisphere. In February 1941 Avra Warren informed a House subcommittee that the Czech quota was assigned almost entirely to Czechoslovakian nationals in Portugal and Cuba. A different source showed that as a result during March 1941 Czechs in danger in Vienna could not obtain visas because the quota numbers had all been distributed to other consulates.[37]

Well before the immigration statistics which reflected the new visa policy were compiled and generally available, some people perceived the change in the Administration's attitude toward refugee immigration. An early hint appeared in an Associated Press dispatch from Berlin on July 16, 1940. Several refugees who had secured ship tickets and were about to receive visas had been turned down. The rejected applicants stated that they had met "a new line of questioning [which] was evidently based on fears in America of 'fifth column' operations. Reliable sources said recent instructions from the State Department advised 'special care' to pass only applicants capable of becoming true Americans." In late September a New York travel agent reported that refugees in Germany, previously informed by American consuls that their documentation was fully in order, had seen their visa applications reexamined and rejected despite their compliance with requests for additional information, stronger guarantees of support, and proof of reserved ship passage. By September the National Refugee Service observed that immigration had fallen off and in November the American Committee for Christian Refugees noted an "increasing reluctance to giving visas." By November 1940 the United States Committee for the Care of European Children, the National Refugee Service, the International Migration Service, and the American Friends Service Committee were quite concerned about the situation. Leaders of these groups met to pool their information and, according to one of them, concluded that "the basic difficulty is an attitude on the part of most of the State Department which is determined to reduce immigration to a minimum." A delegation of three from the United States Committee took the problem to President Roosevelt and felt "that they had made some considerable impression" on him, although they were not hopeful about an early change in policy.[38]

An interesting feature of the third visa policy is that the Administration never made the change public. In October 1940 refugee workers present at a conference of HIAS, a foremost Jewish emigration agency, reported that "while the American Consuls abroad and the State Department say officially that no new visa instructions or procedure are in effect, actually everyone knows that such is the case." Near the end of 1940 the State Department declared that "a maximum number of persons who can fulfill the requirements is being received in this country under the present quotas." As a matter of fact, during that fiscal year the quotas of the countries of refugee origin were 53 percent filled. In 1943, as knowledge of systematic extermination of Jews by the Nazis spread, voices rose in the United States for stronger governmental action to rescue refugees. Responding to this pressure, Assistant Secretary Breckinridge Long, summarizing State Department efforts on behalf of refugees, maintained that "we did, within the territory of Germany, take all kinds of steps that were possible to take while we had diplomatic representatives and consular representatives within German territory." The record shows that American consular officials were forced to leave the Nazi-controlled areas of Europe in July 1941. The preceding several paragraphs have given some indication of the "kinds of steps" taken by the State Department within German territory in the year before withdrawal of the consulates.[39]

Despite the effectiveness of the State Department's informal means of cutting immigration, Breckinridge Long persistently sought a solid legislative foundation for excluding prospective permanent immigrants whose presence in the United States might endanger the public safety. But approval by the Department of Justice was necessary before the State Department could initiate such legislation. Although Attorney General Robert Jackson was cooperative, others in the Department of Justice thought "public safety" too vague a basis for the requested power and tied up the proposal for a year.[40]

Over the months, Long revealed the ambiguity of his position as he recorded his frustrations regarding the proposed legislation. In early October 1940:

Long conference with the Attorney General again on the question of immigration, and particularly about a draft of a bill to exclude permanent immigrants on the basis that their activities in the United States would be against the public safety. Such persons are excludable now as temporary visitors but not as permanent [immigrants]. . . . Jackson himself is in entire accord. He said that he would take the matter up with his people over there and get them in line. They are preparing an adverse report to him on the proposed bill.

On November 27, 1940:

Six months ago we submitted to the Department of Justice the text of a proposed law which would place [permanent] immigrants on the same basis as visitors. . . . In the case of visitors we are authorized by law to withhold visas if the person applying for a visa intends to engage in political activity in the United States which might be against the interests of the United States. We wanted that same authority to refuse a visa to a person who was coming to the United States to live permanently. The Department of Justice blocked it. . . . We tried to agree upon a compromise in phraseology. The text of the compromise has remained in a pigeon hole in the Department of Justice, and we are unable to get any agreement on it.

Yet, in January 1941 Long clearly indicated that the State Department had been acting as though it held the very authority which he had been seeking for so long:

Consuls have been instructed to be as liberal as the law allows and to expedite action in the cases of qualified applicants when satisfied that they will not engage in activities inimical to the interests of the United States.

In February:

Lunch with Senator Russell of Georgia. He will introduce bill to exclude immigrants who are considered to be inimical to our welfare. Now they are not excludable if they come for permanent residence—only if visitors or in transit. We have tried to get the bill agreed to by Justice for six months—just succeeded.

Enactment finally came in June 1941 in time to clear the way for a fourth and even more stringent visa policy.[41]

Meanwhile, during the latter part of 1940, the State Department had modified the procedures for utilization of the quotas. The innovation, called "unblocking," liberalized the overall refugee program somewhat, yet did no violence to the policy of keeping immigration from Germany and Central Europe at a very low rate. Directly after returning from his European trip in November 1940, Avra Warren told an Interior Department official that he anticipated most quotas would catch up with their waiting lists inside of a few months. One cause, which went unmentioned, involved the instructions the visa chief had recently finished delivering to the consulates. The other was "unblocking." Under this arrangement, as Warren himself explained to a House subcommittee, the State Department directed its consuls in Germany to contact visa applicants in order of priority on the quota lists. Those who had exit permits and could show evidence of available transportation "were invited to be examined, to see whether they were safe risks to enter the United States." The quota numbers of people unable to obtain travel reservations or to meet consular standards were set aside and their places opened or "unblocked" for the use of applicants who had registered later but who could gain consular clearance and secure transportation. To make visas available to refugees who could more readily utilize them, "unblocking" included allocation of a large share of the monthly allotments of quota numbers to the consulates most accessible to facilities for transportation to the United States. Formerly, American consuls in each foreign nation had reserved most quota numbers for distribution within that country. For example, under the previous system the bulk of the German quota went to the consuls in Germany. The new procedure meant that consulates in Canada, Cuba, Portugal, France, and other places where refugees were awaiting visas received sizable amounts of German quota numbers. The Polish, Czechoslovak, Hungarian, and other quotas were similarly distributed.[42]

The effects of "unblocking" appeared rapidly. Refugees commenced to flow to the United States, especially from Lisbon and points in the Western Hemisphere. Waiting lists in many areas began to shrink and by the end of February 1941 all European quotas were up to date except those of Latvia, Rumania, and Hungary. Still, although the new burst of visa activity enlarged refugee immigration, the increase was not great. During the first six months following "unblocking," immigration charged to the quotas of Germany and the other countries of refugee origin exceeded that of the previous six months by about 3,500.[43]

Among people helped by "unblocking" the quotas were refugees already in the United States on visitors' visas. When the quotas of their native lands opened, they were able to change their status to that of permanent immigrants. By an arrangement made with Canada in the fall of 1940, temporary visitors to the United States could enter Canada to obtain permanent quota visas from American consulates there. The Canadian government agreed to the procedure on condition that the United States government guarantee to accept the aliens back. Consequently, a pre-examination system was used under which both the Immigration and Naturalization Service in this country and an American consul in Canada made preliminary decisions on the refugee's qualifications for a permanent visa. Approved applicants then travelled to Canada to receive their visas and returned shortly to the United States as quota immigrants. Departure from the United States was necessary because only consuls could issue visas. Canada, then involved in the war, excluded refugees of German and Italian background as enemy aliens, so these people had to take the more costly trip to Cuba or Mexico.[44]

Despite the liberalization of visa policy brought about by "unblocking" the quotas, the earlier decision to cut refugee immigration from Central Europe to a low rate seems to have continued. One indication to the contrary came from Vienna in early 1941. A Quaker working there as a vice-consul stated that most refugees who were able to secure reservations for ocean passage were receiving visas. But the overall statistical picture shows that only 927 more natives of Germany and Austria immigrated in the initial six months following "unblocking" than had in the previous half year. Even this small increase was probably more than accounted for by German- and Austrian-born refugees who, because of "unblocking," were able to enter the United States from France, Portugal, Latin America, and other countries to which they had previously fled. Also numbered in the German quota were temporary visitors in the United States who underwent the pre-examination procedure and succeeded in changing their status to that of permanent immigrants.[45]

The causes behind the decision made in mid-1940 to decrease immigration from Central Europe do not emerge with full clarity. Probably the most important factor was apprehensiveness within the Administration concerning entry of subversives. The government knew that Nazi agents were attempting to infiltrate various countries in the guise of refugees. The more subtle technique of forcing genuine refugees to act as spies by holding the threat of torture or death over close relatives who remained behind was thought to be another part of the Nazi pattern of operation. Because the Hitler government could easily scrutinize potential emigrants in Germany, Austria, and Czechoslovakia, the Administration may have seen them as particularly susceptible to extortion of pledges to spy for Germany. Breckinridge Long, for instance, believed the Nazis granted exit permits only to people whom they wanted to enter the United States. Accordingly, he looked on arrangements for special trains to carry Jewish refugees from Germany to Portugal as "sinister" and "a perfect opening for Germany to load the United States with agents." [46]

Whether or not this reasoning explains the tight restrictions placed on immigration from Central Europe, concern about subversives certainly weighed on President Roosevelt's mind by early May 1940. On May 8 Roosevelt put the State Department to work on methods of preventing further infiltration of Nazi and Russian agents into the United States. On May 16, reacting to the rapid disintegration of Allied resistance in the Low Countries, the Chief Executive went before Congress to call for sharply increased defense spending. His remarks included a passing reference to "the treacherous use of the 'fifth column' by which persons supposed to be peaceful visitors were actually a part of an enemy unit of occupation." Ten days later, as the Nazi drive across northern France reached the English Channel, Roosevelt in a "fireside chat" on national defense warned more emphatically of "the fifth column that betrays a nation unprepared for treachery." At a press conference with the American Youth Congress on June 5, the President pointed out that other countries had discovered spies among refugees, including a number forced to carry out espionage under threat of reprisal against their relatives. He stated that although the problem applied to only a tiny percentage of refugees, the situation required vigilance. In the autumn of 1940 the Department of State pressed the president of Haiti to cancel a plan for entry of 100 refugee families into his country. The State Department maintained that Haiti lacked effective means for controlling the subversive elements which would undoubtedly enter with the refugees. Among arguments the American chargé marshalled to persuade the Haitian president were these:

One, all refugees from Germany are at most only anti-Hitler; two, pressure can be exerted on those still having property in Germany to do the bidding of the German Government; three, further pressure can be brought to bear on them through acts or threats against their relatives still in Germany; four, German agents have been sent out in the guise of refugees.

Uneasiness about fifth columnists among refugees continued and increased within the Administration, culminating in mid-1941 in establishment of an intricate system for screening potential immigrants.[47]

Reasons other than the problem of subversives may have been involved in limiting immigration from Central Europe. The State Department worried from early 1938 at least into late 1942 that Congress might reduce the quotas drastically if immigration seemed to flow too freely. Imposition of tight restrictions in 1940 may in part have reflected an effort to head off such Congressional action. Another object of the third visa policy could have been, as Avra Warren hinted, to free enough quota numbers to enable a sizeable amount of German refugees in England to move on to the United States.

From 1938 into the middle of 1941 a series of three visa policies characterized the Administration's response to the refugee problem. The first extended from the Austrian *Anschluss* into the early weeks of the war. The second lasted from then until the defeat of France. The third was in force during the months between the summer of 1940 and June of 1941. A fourth and tighter phase followed.

## Chapter 9

# The Door Is Nearly Closed

## THE FEAR OF FIFTH COLUMNISTS

As western Europe crumbled before the German onslaught in the spring months of 1940, a startled world saw in the operation of the Nazi fifth column a major cause for Hitler's success. That the fifth column could be a decisive factor in modern warfare emerged from the Spanish Civil War and both haunted the public mind and worried government officials of non-Axis countries. Although seldom clearly projected, the common image of the fifth column included saboteurs and spies as well as propagandists who aimed to divide the populace and undermine the government by convincing masses of people of the fruitlessness of resisting the enemy. Aliens were of course prime suspects.

Soon after the start of the war, France interned all adult male Germans, but within a few months released most of them. Then, when the blitzkrieg struck, the French government placed thousands of refugees in concentration camps as a precaution against pro-German activities. In mid-May 1940 Great Britain also began to confine aliens. By summer the government had taken more than 20,000 into custody and had sent 9,000 to the Dominions. Strong public indignation at the policy of detaining anti-Nazi refugees forced an end to Britain's general internment of aliens. Still, by late 1941, 9,000 foreigners remained in custody, perhaps one half of them Axis sympathizers.[1]

In 1940 and 1941 anxieties about aliens grew and spread in the United States. Resulting pressures moved toward two goals: to arrange controls on aliens already in the country and to bolt the door against entry of more possible "Trojan Horses." Nativists, unable in the depression years to ride the unemployment argument to total success, found that the fifth column threat rapidly swept the government and the public nearer to their long-standing views that foreigners should be kept under close surveillance and that immigration should end. Growing support for legislation to cut off immigration, to deport aliens, and to fingerprint foreigners assured restrictionists that the public was at last awakening to "the dangers in our midst right here at home." A leader of the Junior Order United American Mechanics summarized the successful merger of nativist thought and public opinion: "For years we carried on in the face of great odds and difficulties. We did not falter or quit. Now we see the fruition, the happy reaction at hand." At the same time that expansion of the European conflict began to stimulate the American economy, blunting the edge of the unemployment argument against immigration, the war brought into play a force which helped swing the gates nearly shut. After mid-1940 the older currents of resistance to refugee entry—unemployment, nativism, and anti-Semitism—were joined by the flood tide of fifth column fear.[2]

Almost as soon as the war broke out, Senator Robert R. Reynolds (D.) of North Carolina commenced to translate traditional nativist suspicion of foreigners into more sinister terms of national danger. In October 1939 he warned that thousands of alien enemies were spying in the United States. Early in 1940 Reynolds disclosed to the Senate that "today our country is honeycombed with saboteurs and spies," and in late May, after sounding the alarm that "we are surrounded by the enemy," he announced his fear of "an attack by the enemy from within." One year before, such statements would have been attributed to electioneering and exaggerated antialienism. But in mid-1940 the North Carolinian was rowing in the mainstream, though on the more panicky edge of it. A Roper poll, published in *Fortune* in July 1940, found 71 percent of the respondents convinced that Germany had "already started to organize a 'Fifth Column' in this country." In reply to another question, 46 percent agreed that the United States government should deport or imprison Nazi sympathizers. *Fortune* warned of a potentially dangerous situation because many people interviewed had volunteered that they were watching certain neighbors they suspected were fifth columnists.[3]

The periodical press reflected, and undoubtedly intensified, public concern about the fifth column danger. Some magazines worked to exploit the drama inherent in the issue, others sought to alert the country to the subversive menace, and a few tried to inject an element of calm into the near-hysteria. In nine monthly issues beginning with August 1940, the *American Magazine* presented six pieces on the fifth column threat under such titles as "Enemies within Our Gates," "Treachery in the Air," and "Hitler's Slave Spies in America." The *Reader's Digest* printed articles in each of the last three issues of 1940 on the dangers of subversion. The *Nation* reported on Nazi and native-grown fifth column activities in a continuing feature entitled "Within the Gates." *Fortune* undertook a short series of studies on Fascist and Communist activities in the United States. Among the earliest articles urging sense and restraint regarding fifth column fears were three in July and September 1940 in the Catholic weekly *America*. A year later, writing in the *American Magazine* for August 1941, FBI director J. Edgar Hoover cautioned the public against assuming that people were spies and asked Americans to restrict their antififth column actions to reporting suspicious individuals to the government.[4]

Secretary of the Interior Harold Ickes observed as early as May 1940 that Attorney General Robert Jackson was "plainly worried about the disposition, in various parts of the country, of local authorities, and even irresponsible groups, to go out on a 'spy hunt.' " At a Cabinet meeting three weeks later, according to Ickes' *Secret Diary*, Jackson reported further on

> the hysteria that is sweeping the country against aliens and fifth columnists. . . . People are breaking into other people's houses and confronting them with a flag demanding that they salute it. Down in Georgia, Governor Rivers has promptly declared war on all aliens. . . . Jackson . . . indicated that it might be necessary for the Government actually to indict some prominent local or state officials in order to make it known to the country that we were not being ruled by disorderly mobs.[5]

One characteristic of the fifth column was its obscurity. Consequently, almost any groups to the left or right of center to some degree, as well as some which were not, were tarred with the same brush. *Fortune* drew a seriocomic picture that was not wide of the mark:

It is important to know if such a "fifth column" exists in the U.S., and if so, where. It has seemed to be everywhere. The fifth column is being led, said Writer Clarence Budington Kelland, by no less a personage than President Roosevelt; his view was upheld by many. Joseph P. Kamp, of the Constitutional Educational League, preferred to believe that the President is the unwitting dupe of columnites in the government, among whom he listed Secretary Perkins, Attorney General Jackson [and others]. These people, said Mr. Kamp, were Communists. But the Communists, through the *Daily Worker,* announced that columnites in the U.S. were really under the command of J. P. Morgan. . . . The German American Bund put the finger instead on the Pilgrim Society, the English Speaking Union, and the Carnegie Endowment for International Peace. When members of Jehovah's Witnesses were manhandled in various parts of the country as columnites, their leader, Judge Rutherford, wrote a pamphlet proving that the real column was Catholic Action. . . . In any case, whatever and wherever it was, Americans determined to root it out. The FBI reported that tips from loyal citizens concerning espionage, sabotage, and subversive activities had increased from thirty-five a year in 1937 to over 2,800 in one day of 1940. Jeff Davis, self-styled King of the Hobos, organized an anti-fifth-column squad of Jungle Bulls. . . . Volunteer firemen at their national convention in Philadelphia swore to fight the column. . . . Mayor Hague of Jersey City and the Associated Farmers of California announced that they were in hot pursuit of the column. Fifty women members of the National Legion of Mothers of America organized a rifle club to shoot down parachutists.[6]

While the general public may have been confused about the fifth column, President Roosevelt was not. The German advance of April and May 1940 convinced the Chief Executive of the need to tighten controls against possible entry of Nazi agents. On May 22 the President sent Congress a plan for transfer of the Immigration and Naturalization Service from the Labor Department to the Justice Department to ensure "more effective control over aliens." At his press conference the previous day, Roosevelt had explained that the move was necessary for reasons of national defense and had acknowledged that it was part of the overall effort to curb sabotage and spying. In

1941 the President stated the transfer had come about because of "a dangerous threat from abroad in the form of the fifth column and other activities." Under the Reorganization Act of 1939, the President's recommendation would have gone into effect automatically in 60 days unless Congress in the interval had passed a concurrent resolution against it. A cooperative Congress instead rushed through a resolution to effect the change in mid-June. Congress also doubled the size of the Border Patrol. In his statement accepting jurisdiction over the Immigration Service, Attorney General Robert Jackson reflected the third visa policy toward entry of refugees from Central Europe which was then just emerging. Jackson announced on June 14, 1940, that from then on the idea that an alien might immigrate unless he would endanger this country "must at least temporarily yield to the policy that none shall be admitted unless it affirmatively appears to be for the American interest." [7]

Not to be outdistanced by the President in controlling subversive activities, Congress completed action in June on the Alien Registration Act of 1940. Nearly a year earlier the bill had passed the House without a record vote. Its strength was obvious, however, from the 272 to 48 defeat suffered by a motion made at that time to recommit it. Then, in June 1940, after the Senate had passed its version, the House accepted the conference report 382 to four. The new law, commonly known as the Smith Act, dealt with three issues. The first title outlawed certain subversive activities. Included were promotion of disloyalty among the military forces, advocacy of the overthrow of any government in the United States by force, and affiliation with a group advocating forcible overthrow of the government. This first title was to become the best known feature of the Smith Act because of its postwar use in suppressing domestic Communism. Title II expanded grounds for deportation and provided for suspension of deportation in certain cases. The third title, the most striking aspect of the measure, represented a long sought victory for restrictionists. It required all aliens in the United States 14 years of age or older to register and be fingerprinted. [8]

During the summer of 1940, the fifth column threat became associated with refugees fleeing Nazism. As August opened, the War Department fed spy fears with a sensational report that 81 foreign agents had been rounded up in the Panama Canal Zone. Those detained turned out to be refugees whose papers were not fully in order. Some had been stranded in the Canal Zone for over a year while awaiting permanent entry elsewhere. But an unequivocal warning about risks involved in allowing entry of refugees was not long in coming. William C. Bullitt, former Ambassador to France and witness to its fall, spoke in Philadelphia on August 18. Although Bullitt dwelt mainly on the danger which Hitler posed to the United States and on the need for preparedness, he included a statement which hurt the chances of refugee immigration. Against the background of rising tensions about fifth column activities, Bullitt declared:

> The French had been more hospitable than are even we Americans to refugees from Germany. More than one half the spies captured doing actual military spy work against the French Army were refugees from Germany. Do you believe that there are no Nazi and Communist agents of this sort in America? [9]

Sharp disagreement with Bullitt appeared in the *Nation,* both in an editorial and in an article by Heinz Pol, a German refugee journalist recently arrived from France. There over several years time he had developed contacts with French officials, army personnel, and journalists. Pol asserted that Nazi fifth columnists in France had been German citizens, sent by the Nazi government. They had operated relatively openly until the war began. According to Pol, some spies, when arrested, insisted they were refugees, but French authorities, frequently with the help of refugee organizations, had been able to ascertain the falsity of their claims. Despite several investigations by the French government, Pol stressed that he knew of no German refugee involved in espionage. Pol explained that Nazi leaders had better sense than to try to use refugees as spies. Most were not fluent in French and consequently were marked people. Furthermore, refugees tended to watch each other "far more vigilantly than would the most suspicious police agent." Bullitt brushed aside this challenge, for when his speech came out later in book form the passage on refugees was unchanged. Generally, groups concerned with refugees agreed that German spies had entered France and perhaps England by pretending to be escaping the Nazis. But they felt it unfair to label German refugees as Nazi spies without making clear that the German agents were not genuine refugees.[10]

Reports that actual refugees were serving as Nazi spies and that German agents were posing as refugees arose from several quarters. In October 1940 a Belgian newspaperman, writing about the fifth column in the *New York Herald Tribune,* declared that Belgian state police had detected 42 Nazi spies, some "camouflaged as Jewish refugees," others "recruited among 'half' and 'quarter' Jews, who had been promised an 'Aryan' passport for their work." The spring of 1941 brought forth two striking magazine articles on the problem. Samuel Lubell related in the *Saturday Evening Post* that "disguised as refugees, Nazi agents have penetrated all over the world, as spies, fifth columnists, propagandists or secret commercial agents." He disclosed that "an unofficial report" told of a Gestapo school in Prague where spies, in order to pass as Jews, learned "to speak Yiddish, to read Hebrew, to pray." And they were "supposed to submit to circumcision." Shortly afterward the *American Magazine* carried an article entitled "Hitler's Slave Spies in America" which asserted that "several agents of the Vichy-Nazi system" had been found among refugees coming to the United States. The writers, Donald Keyhoe and John Daly, reported that the Nazis were building a "network of unwilling spies and saboteurs" in the United States by forcing people who had relatives in Nazi territory to serve as German agents under threat of harm to their loved ones, thereby forming "the foundation for a super-Gestapo." From the Senate floor, Robert R. Reynolds continued to warn the nation that "with every 25 or 50 refugees who come there are agents of Hitler and Stalin." [11]

Late in May 1941, 200 spectators were drawn to a session of the House Committee on Un-American Activities. The attraction, Richard Krebs, was a reformed Comintern agent, veteran of Nazi prisons, and author, under the pen name of Jan Valtin, of *Out of the Night.* Speaking from his knowledge of Gestapo operations, Krebs described Nazi methods of espionage in the United States. Asked whether the Gestapo had dispatched agents to this country disguised as political refugees, Krebs answered:

> Yes; this group forms a very large group of people used by the Gestapo. Some are trained Nazis posing as political refugees, but many are actually former political prisoners from Germany whose families are kept as hostages and who were sent out to work for the Gestapo.

Krebs explained that these people had to forward monthly reports to the Gestapo in order to keep their relatives from harm. Because they are clearly anti-Nazis, Krebs continued, these refugees "find it particularly easy to be accepted by the public of democratic countries." He declared that

> it has gone so far that to my experience it was impossible for anyone to be released from a Nazi concentration camp unless he signed a pledge that he would serve the Gestapo. . . . Anyone who would not sign the pledge had no chance of being released at all.[12]

Several groups took a dim view of Krebs's testimony. The *Nation* derided his statement that no one could get out of a Nazi concentration camp without agreeing to work for the Gestapo as "reckless and ridiculous." The German American Congress for Democracy, an anti-Nazi association, protested it as "slander of numerous honorable, decent, sincere anti-Nazis, former prisoners in Nazi concentration camps." Dr. Frank Kingdon, speaking for five refugee rescue organizations, questioned Krebs's testimony that Nazi agents had arrived in the United States in the guise of refugees. Kingdon stated that these organizations, having recognized the danger long before, had carefully investigated each of their charges before immigration and were certain that none was "a Gestapo emissary, a Communist, or a fifth columnist of any kind." But, carried on the tide of fifth column fear, Krebs's remarks undoubtedly coursed far ahead of the criticisms sent after them. Within this milieu of apprehensiveness the Administration developed a new refugee policy based on extremely tight screening of immigrants.[13]

THE FOURTH VISA POLICY

During the summer of 1940 concern with subversion figured large in the Administration's decision to impose stringent controls on immigration, particularly from Germany and countries east of it. Through late 1940 and on into 1941, official anxiety about entry of foreign agents intensified. From Moscow, Ambassador Laurence A. Steinhardt flashed a series of danger signals to the State Department regarding admission of aliens from Soviet-held territory. Early in

November 1940 he advised Washington that a visa applicant from Russian-occupied Poland had told him Soviet authorities would not issue exit permits to potential emigrants to the United States unless they pledged to serve as espionage agents. The ambassador pointed out that since most visa applicants had relatives remaining in Russian-held territory, the Soviet government could press emigrants to uphold their agreements. Two months later, Steinhardt reported that a refugee recommended by the President's Advisory Committee had notified him that 10 to 20 percent of the many people he knew in Lithuania who were on the PAC list of approved political fugitives had been solicited by the GPU to engage in espionage in the United States. According to the informant, many refugees had accepted the GPU's overtures in order to secure exit permits. Summarizing the situation in late May 1941, Steinhardt declared it "dangerous not to say reckless, to continue to grant American visas indiscriminately to applicants recently residing in or who are now residing in the Soviet Union or Soviet-occupied territories." [14]

But long before May 1941 the State Department had concluded that most immigration from Axis- or Soviet-held territory endangered American security. In January 1941 the department notified the President that "in view of reports indicating that Nazi and other totalitarian agents are endeavoring to enter the United States in the guise of refugees, it has been considered essential in the national interest to scrutinize all applications carefully." A month before, American refugee agencies had noticed a stiffening in requirements. Many United States consuls had begun asking sponsors of refugees to submit "loyalty" or "moral" affidavits in the form of letters guaranteeing that the visa applicants were persons of high character and integrity who would not engage in subversive activities. To qualify as character reference for a refugee, one had to be an American citizen of responsible standing in his community and to be personally acquainted with the alien or his family. [15]

By April 1941 the faint outlines of a new visa policy then in the making commenced to appear. Assistant Secretary of State Breckinridge Long, in a conversation with Clarence Pickett of the American Friends Service Committee, explained the cancellation of visas already granted to 38 Polish rabbinical students, then in Yokohama. Long pointed out that recall of the students' visas came in response to a general order requiring reexamination of visas issued to aliens with relatives in Russia, Poland, or Germany. The assistant secretary stated the action had become necessary because of discovery that Soviet and Nazi agents in the United States were pressing refugees from Russia, Poland, and Germany to engage in espionage under threat of harm to relatives still in the home countries. Long said that although very few such cases had come to view, enough had appeared to warrant the general order.[16]

Another aspect of the new visa policy which would crystallize in June had been under consideration since early 1941. Reacting to reports of attempted infiltration of foreign agents, the State Department had initiated steps by late February to channel all visa applications through its offices in Washington before they went to the consuls for final decision. In mid-March the *New York Times* reported that the projected change aimed to use the department's superior facilities for securing information about the aliens' contacts in the United States, including their sponsors, "as a means of making less probable the entrance of spies or saboteurs into the country." Early in May Breckinridge Long went before a House Subcommittee on Appropriations to outline the need for increased expenditures to get the new system underway. He explained that, "in view of information received from our officers abroad regarding the known activities of certain foreign governments in endeavoring to introduce agents into the United States," the Administration planned to centralize control of visas in the State Department. Under the proposed new set up, an expanded Visa Division would carry out initial processing of immigration applications. It would operate on information secured from each alien's sponsors in the United States regarding the foreigner's character, his purposes for emigrating, his attitude toward the American type of government, and the validity of his assurances of support. Moreover, Long pointed out, the arrangement would facilitate careful investigation of the sponsors themselves to see whether they were "good citizens" or whether they were "engaged in activities inimical to the Government." Another feature of the new plan provided for establishment of five interdepartmental committees to check on applicants "from the viewpoint of national defense." The committees' findings and advice would go to the Visa Division which would sift the evidence and forward its recommendations to the consuls. Final decisions remained with the consuls who were to suspend action in uncertain cases and report them back to the department for further consideration. The interdepartmental committees would include representatives from the Visa Division, the Immigration and Naturalization Service, the Federal Bureau of Investigation, the Military Intelligence Division of the War Department, and the Navy Department's Office of Naval Intelligence. Clearly, the system operating since November 1940 to screen political refugees under the special emergency visa program had served as model for the projected new procedure for all immigration cases.[17]

The arrangement outlined by Breckinridge Long took effect on July 1, 1941. But before that date, while completing preparations for the change, the State Department stopped issuing visas to a large category of refugees. On June 5 instructions went to diplomatic and consular officers to withhold visas from all applicants who had parents, children, husband, wife, brothers, or sisters resident in territory under the control of Germany, Italy, or Russia. Nearly two weeks later the State Department, forced by accidental leakage of the news, informed the press of the move. The *New York Times* reported that State Department officials thought the decision absolutely essential because of extensive evidence that Germany had been using threats of harm to near relatives of immigrants to force the fugitives to become spies. Officials cited one case, that of a German-Jewish refugee in Cuba who was trying to get into the United States. His family was in Germany and apparently the Nazis were putting pressure on him for he was reportedly in daily contact with the German Embassy in Havana.[18]

In a memorandum to President Roosevelt in August, the State Department outlined the background and effects of its instructions of June 5, 1941, and noted that this suspension of visa issuance had been in the nature of a holding operation until Congress could complete action on legislation to bar subversive elements from the nation. Actually, for about a year the State Department had followed a policy of excluding foreigners whose presence in the United States might endanger national security, although nothing in the immigration laws specifically provided for such a move. Throughout that year Breckinridge Long had worked steadily to obtain explicit legislative authorization for this policy. But negotiations with the Department of Justice on the form the legislation should take had been incredibly protracted and only in June 1941 did a draft reach Congress. By then the State Department also wanted an unequivocal legal foundation for its stringent visa policy scheduled to take effect on July 1. Congress hastened to pass two bills to clarify the situation.[19]

One measure, submitted by Senator Richard B. Russell (D.) of Georgia, empowered American consuls to refuse visas to aliens who they believed were trying to enter this country to engage in activities which would "endanger the public safety of the United States." The legislation required the consul to refer such cases of visa denial to the State Department for review. The Senate Committee on Immigration unanimously approved the bill on June 4. The next day Russell explained the measure to the Senate, stating that it conferred a power on consuls "which I already thought they had." By unanimous consent the proposal then came up for consideration and passed without debate. A week later the House took similar action, pausing only to register astonishment that consuls did not already possess the authority given by the Russell Bill.[20]

The other measure, introduced by Congressman Sol Bloom (D.) of New York, amended a law enacted in May 1918 which had granted the President broad control over entry and departure of both citizens and aliens when the United States was at war. The main effect of the Bloom legislation was to bring this control into operation at once by making it applicable not only when the United States was at war, but also during the national emergency which the President had proclaimed in late May 1941. Bloom's original bill authorized the President to invoke the powers of the Act of 1918 whenever any countries were at war. On June 11 the proposal cleared the House without difficulty, but a week later the Senate modified it at the insistence of Robert A. Taft (R.) of Ohio. Taft agreed the step was needed, but opposed such sweeping executive power. A compromise resulted which permitted control over American citizens when the United States itself was at war or during the recently declared national emergency. But the President could impose travel restrictions on aliens whenever hostilities existed between any countries. Executive regulations based on this legislation included the provision that "no alien shall be permitted to enter the United States if it appears to the satisfaction of the Secretary of State that such entry would be prejudicial to the interests of the United States." [21]

On June 24, 1941, a few days after the Russell and Bloom measures had sped through Congress, the State Department announced new visa regulations to begin on July 1. The major innovation was the system of centralized immigration control in Washington which Breckinridge Long had outlined to the House Subcommittee on Appropriations in early May. All visa applications in process were voided, including those of people who had received tentative consular approval but had not secured the actual permit. Documentation had to be re-initiated on forms supplied from Washington by the Visa Division. The new procedures required a biographical sketch of the alien and two affidavits combining "political-moral" sponsorship and financial guarantees. Sponsors of refugees completed these papers in the United States, signed them under oath, and returned them to Washington for consideration by the State Department and the interdepartmental committees. Information in the files of all five agencies represented on these committees went into the decision-making process. Approved cases were forwarded to consuls overseas for final determination. This arrangement, combined with the general rule already operating to exclude most aliens who had close relatives in Axis or Soviet territory, brought the fourth visa policy into full effect.[22]

Many fugitives from Nazism, almost on the point of escaping Europe, were turned back by the shift in policy. The *Centre Américain de Secours* in Marseilles related that only a few of about 100 people who had previously been promised visas were finally able to obtain them. Some refugees found themselves in predicaments similar to that of a husband and wife in Lisbon. Three days before they were scheduled to receive their visa, the regulation regarding close relatives cut them off because the man's mother was in Berlin. Rapid work by their affiant, a lawyer in New York, made it appear they might secure the permit after all, but centralization of procedures in Washington on July 1 meant they had to start the application all over again. After more than another year of work by their affiant and the Unitarian Service Committee, they obtained the visa. The antifascist credentials of the man, a Social Democrat, were unimpeachable. He had twice been in Nazi prisons. In another case handled by the Unitarians, a German refugee and his wife, who had originally fled to England, went to France in early 1940 to help their married daughter through a serious illness. England would not take them back, but they made their way to Lisbon and there obtained affidavits from the United States. The affidavits were in order, but the consul refused the visa on grounds that the refugees had been dishonest in some respect. Unitarian workers thought the problem lay in a language misunderstanding and tried to get the application reviewed. While this effort was underway, the policy about close relatives came into effect and the presence of their daughter in France disqualified the couple. Ultimately the Unitarian Service Committee succeeded in helping them to reach Mexico.[23]

Set in motion on July 1, 1941, the new machinery for processing applications in Washington turned out visas at a distressingly slow rate. By the latter part of July, the State Department's printed forms for affidavits and biographical statements were still unavailable and the interim mimeographed ones were in "very limited" supply. Of five projected interdepartmental committees, only two had been formed. Together they could handle 100 cases per day. By mid-September 4,500 applications had backed up. Early in October the American Committee for Christian Refugees noted that immigration had dwindled to a trickle, but reported that the Visa Division expected the flow to rise rapidly by the middle of the month as the new processing system gained speed. On October 10 the chief of the Visa Division, conferring with American Friends Service Committee personnel, maintained that delay in handling cases did not stem from his department, but from another agency, and would probably end soon. Yet, meeting in New York in late November, representatives of most major American refugee aid agencies agreed that the slow pace of the new arrangement for processing applications had all but shut off immigration and that, despite assurances from the Visa Division, little change toward speedier action had occurred.[24]

Another obstacle to refugee entry arose out of worsening German-American diplomatic relations in the late spring of 1941. In mid-June the United States government ordered the closing of all German consulates by July 10 on the presumption that they provided an umbrella for Nazi fifth column activities. Three days later the Nazis retaliated by demanding withdrawal of American consular forces from Germany and German-occupied countries. Consequently, after mid-July, persons in Nazi-held territory could not secure American visas unless they first left Nazi jurisdiction. This turn of events destroyed the hopes of thousands of refugees.[25]

In June, soon after the State Department announced its new visa policy, protests began to mount. Much of the outburst came from

Jewish publications, although previously Jewish organizations had directed little criticism at American refugee policy. *Congress Weekly,* speaking for the American Jewish Congress, approved precautions against espionage, but believed the decision to refuse visas to refugees with close relatives in Nazi territory was "much too severe even at this time" because it would bring suffering to "large numbers of innocent people . . . in order to ensure safety against a single involuntary criminal that may be among them." *Jewish Frontier,* a periodical reflecting a Zionist labor outlook, suggested investigation of individual refugees whom the FBI suspected, but asserted that the regulation regarding close relatives would bring tragedy to thousands without really inconveniencing "the Gestapo's work in this country through the medium of a fifth column that is frequently American-born." *Opinion,* "A Journal of Jewish Life and Letters," concurred in the need to guard against subversive activities, but asked if it did not seem "unnecessarily harsh" to hold thousands responsible for "the crime of the smallest minority of their fellow-sufferers." Declaring that "we are cruel and unimaginative," *Workmen's Circle Call,* voice of a Jewish fraternal labor association, maintained that "it is wrong for our immigration laws to add to the anguish of the anti-fascist refugee." Under the caption "Keep Your Tired, Your Poor," B'nai B'rith's *National Jewish Monthly* in December stated that since "July 1 the immigration quota law, which still remains on the books, has really been a dead letter, nullified in effect by administrative action by the State Department." [26]

Criticism of the stringent new visa policy came from many distinguished individuals. Albert Einstein, in a letter to Eleanor Roosevelt, asserted that the State Department had made entry of refugees nearly impossible "by erecting a wall of bureaucratic measures alleged to be necessary to protect America against subversive, dangerous elements." In mid-July a strong public protest against the regulation regarding relatives was signed by Roger Baldwin, Marshall Field, Max Lerner, Reinhold Niebuhr, Dorothy Thompson, William Allen White, and several other prominent persons. Their statement recognized the importance of controlling spying and sabotage, but declared the method too sweeping as well as unnecessary. They held that the few potentially dangerous refugees could be detected without great difficulty.[27]

The most strident attacks on the new visa policy came from the *New Republic* and the *Nation.* The *New Republic* asserted that "a man under such compulsion makes a bad spy," maintained that Hitler had plenty of recent nonrefugee German immigrants in the United States who would be very willing to work for him, and charged that

> there will be many people all over the world who will believe that the motive for this action comes not from genuine concern about Nazi spies but from the same little nest of anti-Semites and anti-democrats in the State Department who have in the past done so much to muddy the waters of our democratic efforts.

The *Nation,* equally angry, termed the State Department's explanation that refugees' relatives would be used as hostages an "excuse concocted by the Visa Division," and "a good story with which to win popular support for a brutal and unjust restriction." In the editor's view, the State Department's real concern was to keep out refugees and its ruling regarding close relatives had been devised for that purpose on the basis of little or no evidence of forced espionage.[28]

No distinct picture emerges of the manner in which the policy concerning near relatives was actually applied. From the beginning the State Department maintained the instruction did not automatically exclude all people with close relatives in Nazi areas and claimed each case would receive individual consideration. Two weeks after the regulation went into effect, the department vaguely announced that following careful study it had already approved "a substantial number of meritorious cases" in this category. In early July representatives of refugee aid agencies negotiating with the State Department for relaxation of the ruling detected some progress. Still, immigration remained at a trickle through the summer and autumn of 1941. When the close relatives policy at last solidified into formal Federal regulations in November, it had taken on a slightly more liberal character. In the final version, presence of relatives "in certain foreign countries" unfriendly to the United States could supplement other evidence pointing toward visa denial. But, by clear implication, visa refusal required grounds other than simply the problem of the relatives. In practice, however, this modification seems to have brought little liberalization.[29]

Utilizing its close connection with the Administration, the President's Advisory Committee on Political Refugees registered the most effective protest against the fourth visa policy. In August the PAC requested an interview with the President regarding the new immigration procedures. Asked for advice, the State Department approved such a conference on grounds that it "would take care of a possible bad outcome a little later." Breckinridge Long sent a six-page memorandum to Roosevelt explaining the policy about close relatives and Cordell Hull dispatched a note stressing the "absolute importance" of having Long personally review the situation with the President before the meeting. The six-page memorandum stated that some "foreign agents posing as refugees" had "already been apprehended in the United States" and others had been "apprehended after they left Europe but before they reached the United States." Nonetheless, the department felt that the President's Advisory Committee and others who had protested the new visa policy had probably been justly critical in view of their lack of access to all the information available to the State Department. One week before the conference, Long talked the refugee problem over with Roosevelt and departed from the White House convinced the President was "thoroughly in accord with our policies and practices." [30]

On September 4, 1941, James G. McDonald and seven other distinguished members of the President's Advisory Committee met with Roosevelt and delivered a one-page summary of their viewpoint. The group declared its deep concern for national security, but suggested that four changes could safely be made in visa policy. First, McDonald's committee recommended cancellation or substantial modification of the ruling concerning close relatives. It explained that "experience with refugees has convinced us that it is unnecessary, illogical, ill adapted to the purposes claimed for it, and cruelly burdensome on the refugees affected by it." Secondly, the PAC wanted the interdepartmental committees reconstituted to include only representatives of the Departments of State and Justice. The streamlined committees would utilize information provided by the FBI and Army and Navy Intelligence agencies. Third, the group suggested immediate establishment of a board of review to hear appeals in cases rejected by the interdepartmental committees. Finally, the PAC asked permission for sponsors of refugees to appear before the proposed board of review.[31]

Breckinridge Long and Attorney General Francis Biddle attended the conference. The hostility existing between the President's Advisory Committee and Long shows vividly in Long's reaction to the meeting. He believed that

> each one of these men hate[s] me. . . . The exclusion of any person is objectionable to these eminent gentlemen and my system of selection is anathema to them. They . . . will try in the future as they have in the past to ruin my political status.[32]

The President's Advisory Committee did not gain all the objectives it asked of the President. Although Biddle and the Justice Department fought for nearly three months for the PAC viewpoint, the FBI, Army, and Navy representatives remained on the interdepartmental committees. And the change in the relatives rule which finally emerged made little practical difference. Yet, one concession extracted from the State Department threw a tiny shaft of light into the thick gloom rapidly enveloping refugee hopes as 1941 neared its end.[33]

Executive regulations issued in November established a complex arrangement for appeal of rejected visa applications. The new system, which went into effect on December 1, 1941, included three Review Committees and a Board of Appeals. The Review Committees consisted of officials from the same five agencies represented on the original interdepartmental committees (thereafter called Primary Committees). On the Board of Appeals were two men appointed by the President. Visa applications first went to the Primary Committees where decisions rested on majority vote. For each case approved on this level and cleared by the State Department, a favorable advisory opinion was relayed to the consul. If the Primary Committee or the State Department decided against the applicant, or if any member of the Primary Committee specifically requested it, the case went to a Review Committee. On this second level, the alien's American sponsors or their attorney or other representative could testify. Testimony was under oath and witnesses had to answer "any material interrogatories" from committee members. As with the Primary Committees, a Review Committee's decision, if favorable to the alien and acceptable to the State Department, was forwarded to the consul as an advisory opinion. Cases disapproved by the Review Committees or by the State Department went to the Board of Appeals. Its decisions were made on the written record sent by the committees. If the

Appeals Board divided on a judgment, or if the State Department disagreed with the board, the department's viewpoint prevailed. Otherwise the decision of the Board of Appeals was sent to the consul as an advisory opinion. Sponsor and applicant learned only of the judgment made, never the reasons. Cases rejected by the Board of Appeals were eligible for reconsideration six months after the decision. If a favorable advisory opinion went to a consul and he believed entry of the alien would be against the interests of the United States, he suspended action and sent a complete report to the State Department for further consideration and advice.[34]

Refugee aid workers, attempting to assess the probable effects of the new arrangement, referred to it as the "endless" appeals system. They predicted even longer delays than before because, they reasoned, the Primary Committees would tend to disapprove all doubtful cases; the committees knew they would be reviewed. Actually, despite its slowing influence, the appeal procedure brought a slight liberalizing tendency into the program for screening potential immigrants. But the limited relaxation which took place had little connection with the Review Committees. Those bodies consistently sustained the findings of the Primary Committees, overturning only 10 to 15 percent of the adverse decisions appealed from the lower level. During the spring of 1942 refugee aid agencies were disturbed about attitudes shown by some Review Committees at hearings where sponsors of refugees appeared. Several kinds of inquiries directed to sponsors reflected concern to scrutinize *them* as well as the refugees. Supposedly in search of subversive influences, these Review Committees raised such questions as:

Are you Jewish by race and faith?
Do you belong to any political group or organization in this country?
Have you read Tolstoy?
Are you still a pacifist?
Did the Social Democratic Party want to change the government? [35]

The approach of the Board of Appeals was markedly different. Ex-Senator Robert J. Bulkley of Ohio and Dr. Frederick P. Keppel, president of the Carnegie Corporation, served as members. Dean

F.D.G. Ribble of the University of Virginia Law School was alternate. Indicative of the board's viewpoint was its treatment of the problem concerning applicants who were natives of enemy countries. Almost as soon as the board started its work, the United States entered the war. Executive regulations regarding visas then changed in two ways. First, applications from persons born in enemy territory had to move through all three levels of screening. Second, no enemy alien could secure a visa without proof that he would be a benefit to the United States. The Appeals Board saw "benefit in maintaining the traditional American policy of providing a haven of refuge for decent people who are in distress and peril." Under this interpretation, any decent refugee could clear the "benefit" hurdle. The Appeals Board also declared itself unafraid of refugees who had been connected with controversial movements in Europe, even though they might become politically active in the United States. Twenty to 25 percent of the cases sent from the Review Committees to the Board of Appeals were changed from disapproved to acceptable.[36]

Undoubtedly most Americans who troubled themselves with the issue recognized and agreed with the need to check refugees carefully in order to protect the country from foreign agents. But the reasoning behind the severity of the State Department's screening program did not go unquestioned, even within the Administration. Notes taken on a speech delivered in October 1941 show that Assistant Secretary of State Adolf A. Berle, Jr., believed the danger of fifth columnists entering as refugees vastly overrated. Berle thought American refugee policy should not revolve around fear of infiltration of subversives. Three men importantly involved in the immigration filtering system argued against the theory that refugees with close relatives in Nazi territory were likely to become useful tools of the Gestapo. In their report to the President on the first 11 months of operation of the Board of Appeals, Robert Bulkley, Frederick Keppel, and F.D.G. Ribble agreed that

> it does not seem likely that hostage pressure can be used as
> an effective means of compelling anti-Nazis in the United States
> actively to serve the Nazi cause. The reason lies in the simple
> fact that such service ordinarily would necessitate collaboration
> on the part of Nazi agents. That collaboration, even though it
> might not completely reveal the identity of a Nazi agent, would

necessarily give a clue to his identity. The anti-Nazi subjected to pressure and necessarily filled with hate of the Nazi power might readily turn his knowledge over to the proper American authorities. In other words, the chance that Nazi agents will disclose themselves by their use of hostage pressure to make persons in the United States cooperate in Nazi plans seem [sic] so great that a realistic appraisal indicates such methods would scarcely be used.[37]

The fine mesh set up by the fourth visa policy reduced refugee immigration sharply. But the precise effects of the stringent screening procedure cannot be determined. Immigration figures for the fiscal year 1942 include nearly seven months during which the United States was at war, a situation which brought new factors to bear on the refugee problem. Even for the months from July until Pearl Harbor, the results of the fourth visa policy do not emerge clearly because no way exists for finding out how much of the decline in immigration was due to the closing of American consulates in Nazi territory in mid-July 1941. Still, statistics for the last half of 1941, although including three wartime weeks, provide some indication of the effects of the Administration's complex screening program. Comparison of quota immigration for July through December 1941 with that of the first six months of the same calendar year shows a drop from 18,734 to 9,158. Entry of Germans fell from 7,000 to 4,150, of Poles from 2,700 to 1,050, of Czechs from 1,200 to 400, and of Hungarians from 445 to 215. This shrinkage of immigration, though striking, reflects only part of the decrease. According to visa chief Avra Warren, only 3,000 quota visas were issued between July 1 and December 1. Obviously, a large proportion of foreigners who entered under the quotas in the last half of 1941 received visas before the system was centralized in Washington on July 1. But they arrived in the United States during the months after that date. The extreme shortage of ship passage in the spring of 1941 and the fact that visas, once actually secured, were valid for four months explain this delay in immigration.[38]

One consequence of the sharp decline in visa issuance was rapid evaporation of the transportation problem so critical in the earlier months of 1941. By late August liners were sailing from Portugal to the United States half empty. A month later a refugee worker in

Lisbon reported American visa issuance almost at a standstill. He noted that Portuguese ship lines were transferring some vessels to the South American run.[39]

In an insignificant corner on the back page of its news bulletin for December 1941, the American Committee for Christian Refugees observed that

> constant reports are being received from Germany by the ACCR and other refugee agencies, to the effect that no exit permits are being granted to anyone in Germany or occupied territory, regardless of age, sex, or creed. . . . The fact that no agency has any record of a person receiving an exit permit from Germany or occupied territory during the past month or so, gives added credence to the reports.

These rumors from Germany were accurate. In October legal exit from Nazi territory had ended. Escapes took place throughout the war, but for most victims of Nazi terror the closed borders formed an almost insuperable barrier.[40]

Events from late spring through the end of 1941 crushed the hopes of thousands who had looked to the United States for asylum. In June the State Department all but excluded refugees with close relatives in Nazi areas. The next month brought stringent visa screening in Washington and the forced closing of American consulates in German territory. In the fall legal flight from Nazi Europe came to a halt. And in December the United States entered the war. Bitter as these circumstances were for victims of Nazi persecution, the worst was yet to come for those who had not found a way out of German-controlled territory. American refugee agencies had discovered that the Nazis had sealed the walls. But they had no way then of knowing the terrible implications of that step. Not successful in pushing the unwanted people onto an unwilling world, Hitler and his advisers had initiated plans for eradicating them completely.

# Conclusion

# Conclusion

The 40 months between the Austrian *Anschluss* and the departure of American consular forces from German territory stand out as a vast lost chance. After the *Anschluss* and the Night of Broken Glass, the need for rescue was painfully clear. The world was fully aware, yet relatively little was done.

Estimates show that the American contribution, though limited, went beyond that of any other country, both for the Nazi period as a whole and for the crucial years from 1938 through 1941. From 1933 through 1945, something like 250,000 refugees from Nazism reached safety in the United States. Only Palestine, which received approximately 150,000, approached the American record. During the critical months from early 1938 through mid-1941, some 150,000 refugees entered the United States. About 55,000 found their way into Palestine in that period.[1]

Although the United States led the nations as a refugee haven, American ability to absorb immigration was vastly greater than that of the small European countries or the little-industrialized, though spacious and less populated, areas of Latin America and Africa. Viewed in relation to capacity, the English, Dutch, French, and others in western Europe were far more generous than the United States.[2]

Why did the United States fall short of its potential as a haven for refugees? The outstanding reason was the solidity of the national origins quota system. Had the relevant quotas been completely filled from the *Anschluss* through Pearl Harbor, some 206,000 persons could have entered the United States, only 50,000 more than the approximate number of refugees who did immigrate in those years.

The quota limitations formed by far the most significant bulwark against large-scale American rescue of refugees.[3]

Why, then, were the quotas not widened? The chances for driving liberalized immigration legislation through Congress in the 1930's and early 1940's were virtually nonexistent. Groups which favored a liberal refugee policy believed such efforts would not only be fruitless, but actually might risk greater restriction by Congress. Nevertheless, they launched one major attempt, the Wagner-Rogers Children's Bill, which Congress strangled without allowing it to reach the floor of either house.

Although responsibility for unwillingness to modify the quota system must lie in the first instance with Congress, one has to ask the more basic question of why Congress failed to act. A Gallup poll in early 1939 found only 26 percent approval for possible legislation for entry of 10,000 German refugee children (66 percent opposed; eight percent had no opinion). Certainly Congress had no need to fear that an aroused public would press the issue of rescuing child victims of Nazism. Popular support was still smaller for liberalizing immigration without reference to age. An Opinion Research Corporation poll in March 1938, the month of the Austrian *Anschluss,* found only 17 percent agreeable to admission of "a larger number of Jewish exiles from Germany" (75 percent opposed; eight percent had no opinion). Repeated in November 1938, in the midst of American and world protest against events of the week of Broken Glass, the question drew a slightly increased favorable response of 21 percent (71 percent opposed; eight percent had no opinion). In December 1938, while the November pogroms were still in the news, a Roper poll recorded an even more negative popular attitude. Only 8.7 percent favored entry of "a larger number of European refugees than now admitted under our immigration quotas" (83 percent opposed; 8.3 percent had no opinion).[4]

These polls, with their consistently small findings of "no opinion" and their consistently huge majorities against refugee immigration, indicate that more than apathy underlay the American public's attitude toward refugee immigration. Popular hostility toward enlarging the quotas was firmly rooted in social and economic conditions in the United States in the late 1930's and early 1940's. The Great Depression rekindled antialien emotions which had run very high in the 1920's. Anti-Semitism, hanging heavy in the atmosphere of the period, intensified resistance to admission of refugees. A decade of economic insecurity coupled with the common belief that each newcomer might put an American out of work generated strong pressures against increased immigration and even posed a threat to existing quotas. By the time unemployment ceased to be a convincing argument against immigration, widespread fear of a fifth column had arisen and buttressed the case against entry of foreigners. These forces, which played upon large segments of the American public, simultaneously flowed through Congress.

The national legislature suffered no shortage of active alien-baiters and harbored many quieter but staunchly dependable nativists. Anti-Semitism surfaced only infrequently on Capitol Hill, but it was certainly present. Congressmen, supersensitive to the unemployment problem, looked askance at any proposal that might possibly worsen that situation. And no group in the nation could hope to outdo Congress on the issue of safeguarding the United States from fifth columnists. The Congressional response to the refugee problem paralleled that of a majority of the American people.

The Roosevelt Administration did not attempt to bypass the law to rescue any sizable number of refugees. Such a move undoubtedly would have been both futile and dangerous; futile because Congress would have moved immediately to block the opening, and dangerous because the restrictionist backlash might well have cut deeply into the quotas themselves. When Roosevelt refused in late 1938 to expel 15,000 refugees who were in the United States on visitors' visas, he was treading the outer limits of Congressional toleration.

Constrained to operate within the quota system, the President did make the quotas fully available to refugee immigration from early 1938 until mid-1940—a period during which approximately 120,000 refugees arrived in the United States. But in June 1940 the State Department halved the refugee flow by shutting off most immigration proceeding directly from Germany and the rest of central and eastern Europe. This move meant that the quotas no longer defined the limits of American policy.

The half-filled quotas of mid-1940 to mid-1941, when refugee rescue remained entirely feasible, symbolize 20,000 to 25,000 lives lost because of the changed American policy.[5] In terms of the need, this is not a large number; it is minute in relation to the five to six million lost in the holocaust. It is tiny compared with what the

United States could have done had the quotas been mutable. It is even small when measured against the 250,000 who found a haven from Nazism in the United States. But the value of one life cannot be discounted because it is only one. Nor are 20,000 lives any less important because the number is comparatively small.

Why did Franklin Roosevelt, who definitely was aware of the new policy, permit it to stand? There is no direct evidence of the President's thinking on the matter. Fear of subversion certainly was involved. Furthermore, the months which were crucial in the reformulation of refugee policy were also months when Roosevelt's attention was primarily occupied by the collapse of France and the ordeal of Great Britain. Whether for this or for some other reason, Roosevelt left refugee policy almost entirely to the State Department, which in effect meant to Assistant Secretary Breckinridge Long. With such a responsibility, a skilled administrator possessed of deep sensibilities for human values would have been sorely tested to strike a balance between those values and essential national interests. Long was not a man of that caliber. Generally suspicious of foreigners, he was determined to exclude immigrants who might conceivably turn out to be spies or to be subject to pressure from the German or Russian governments. He may have succeeded in keeping infiltration of foreign agents to a minimum—but if he did, his accomplishment came at a high price.

The actual seriousness of the threat posed to American security by refugee immigration must remain unknown for the time being because relevant government files are closed. Time and again Long alluded to knowledge of numerous cases of spies disguised as refugees. But the few specific examples which appear in available records are not convincing and indicate that the Administration could have controlled the problem by much less severe means than it employed.[6]

In the overall picture, the State Department compiled a dismal record. It discouraged or actively opposed virtually all efforts for a more generous American policy, from the Wagner-Rogers Bill to proposals to settle refugees in Alaska and the Virgin Islands. It obstructed the emergency visa program for political refugees. And it tolerated consuls whose antialien, anti-Semitic, and politically conservative attitudes influenced their decisions in visa cases.

But again, what can be said of the President who accorded the State Department nearly free rein in refugee affairs? Franklin D.

Roosevelt played an ambiguous role in the refugee crisis. Sympathetic toward victims of Nazi terror, he opened the quotas to full use in 1938, reversing a depression policy of minimum immigration inherited from the Hoover Administration. Later in the year he granted long-term asylum to 15,000 fugitives then in the country on temporary visas. These moves substantially helped refugees. But they drew sharp fire from restrictionists and Roosevelt did not venture forth again. He consistently disclaimed any plans for widening the quotas, preferring to shift the issue to the politically safe level of encouraging tropical or semitropical settlements for refugees. He refused in 1939 to take a stand on the bill to admit 20,000 German children. Convinced by May 1940 that Nazi fifth column tactics threatened the nation, he accepted the State Department's stringent tightening of immigration that summer and concurred in its nearly prohibitive screening procedures of July 1941.

One may level the finger of accusation at Franklin Roosevelt for having done so little and at Congress for having done nothing. But the accuser will find himself simultaneously pointing at the society which gave American refugee policy its fundamental shape. Like the President, the majority of Americans condemned Nazi persecution. But most opposed widening the gates for Europe's oppressed. Viewed within the context of its times, United States refugee policy from 1938 to the end of 1941 was essentially what the American people wanted.

# Appendices

# Appendix I

# How Many Refugees Found Asylum in the United States?

Because records of the United States Immigration and Naturalization Service do not differentiate between refugees and other immigrants, statistics on refugees must be compiled by indirect means and can never be more than close approximations. Estimates have varied widely as to the number of fugitives from Nazism taken into the United States from the time of Hitler's accession to power until the end of World War II. At one end of the scale stand the assertions of some contemporary restrictionists and anti-Semites that aliens were flooding the country by the millions, partly by evading the Border Patrol, partly with the connivance of the Department of Labor. These claims may be dismissed as absurd.

Largest estimates from responsible sources originated in the Department of State. In his *Memoirs,* Cordell Hull set the number of immigrants from Nazi territory at "approximately 600,000 persons, mostly refugees." Earlier, in testimony before the House Foreign Affairs Committee in November 1943, Assistant Secretary of State Breckinridge Long claimed that until that time about 580,000 refugees had entered the United States. Analyses of Long's statement by organizations concerned about refugees showed he had been overzealous in picturing the State Department's accomplishments in the area of refugee rescue.[1]

Perhaps the lowest reasonable estimate appeared in the booklet *Refugees at Work,* published at Columbia University in 1942. For the fiscal years 1933 through 1941 a figure of about 150,000 refugees was calculated. By applying the system used in the booklet to the years 1942 through 1945, another 20,000 fugitives would be added, rendering a total of approximately 170,000.[2]

In a carefully drawn analysis, Maurice R. Davie in *Refugees in America* concluded that about 266,000 refugees had reached the United States by the autumn of 1944. Because of the author's method, which assigned all doubtful groups to the refugee category, this estimate has to be a maximum. Davie assumed all permanent immigrants from Germany for the fiscal years 1933 through 1944 were refugees. For the rest of Europe, all permanent immigrants from July 1937 through June 1944 from all countries except Great Britain, Ireland, Portugal, Sweden, Switzerland, Iceland, and Turkey also were considered to be refugees. Davie, then, numbered as refugees all permanent immigrants for the fiscal years 1938 through 1944 from all European countries except the seven which entirely escaped fascist rule. This tabulation produced a figure of 243,862.[3]

Applying the same method to temporary immigration, Davie found 196,432 visitors had come to the United States from Germany and the other European nations under fascist domination. While one can assume that permanent immigrants remained in the United States, no way exists for determining how many of the visitors came to escape persecution and stayed on by one means or another, and how many were simply on vacation or conducting business and soon returned home. However, the annual report of the Immigration and Naturalization Service for 1944 numbered at almost 15,000 those aliens who had entered the United States since July 1, 1938, on visitors' visas and had remained in the country by means of successive renewals of these permits. Assuming they were mostly refugees, Davie accepted 15,000 as his estimate for refugees who had found asylum in the United States through the use of temporary visas. Combining these 15,000 on visitors' permits with the approximately 250,000 who entered as permanent immigrants and another special group of 1,000 interned at a camp near Oswego, New York, in 1944, Davie reached his total estimate of 266,000 refugees in the United States by the autumn of 1944.[4]

To adapt Davie's figures specifically to refugees from Nazism only minor modifications are necessary. First, since fugitives from the fascism of Franco do not fit this category, the 2,826 permanent immigrants from Spain should be subtracted. Secondly, few of the 21,672 immigrants from Italy from 1938 through 1944 could have been refugees from Nazism. Probably not many of them were refugees at all. Since those who emigrated because of Italy's anti-Semitic decrees of 1938 might be thought of as indirect victims of Nazism, it is plausible to accept Davie's statement that about 4,000 of the Italian immigrants to the United States actually were refugees.[5] Accordingly, 17,672 Italians should be deducted from Davie's total. In the third place, since Davie omitted immigration for fiscal 1945, the 5,016 natives of Nazi-held territory who came to the United States in that year should be included. These adjustments bring the estimated number of refugees from Nazism to 250,518.

This is a maximum figure because it is based on Davie's method of counting as refugees all immigrants after June 1937 from all countries that eventually came under Nazi domination. Although allowance should be made for the foresight of those people who anticipated Nazi expansion into their homelands, this date is still premature for all European countries except Germany and Austria. Most of the exodus from Czechoslovakia came after the Munich settlement of late September 1938. Even assuming a year's leeway before the German invasion, the flight of Poles from Nazism would not have begun before autumn 1938. Denmark, Norway, the Low Countries, and France were receivers rather than exporters of refugees until the invasions of the spring of 1940. Finally, German control did not extend to the Balkans and the Baltic States until later in 1940 or until 1941

# Some Notes on the Immigration Laws and the Quotas

Since American refugee policy was closely related to the quota system established under the Immigration Act of 1924, a few points about immigration classification may be useful. Basically, aliens entering the United States fell into one of two categories: "nonimmigrants" (those in the country temporarily) and "immigrants" (those planning to settle permanently). Nonimmigrants included foreign government officials with their families and staffs, temporary visitors for business or pleasure, people in continuous transit through the country, persons in the United States to conduct trade under treaties, and students 15 years of age or older. All these groups were required to obtain nonimmigrant visas. In the case of an alien in transit, the visa usually allowed no more than a 60-day stay. A student visa was valid as long as the holder continued his course of study at an accredited institution. Visas for visitors in the United States on business or pleasure were generally of six months duration and could be extended by the Immigration and Naturalization Service. To receive visas, transit aliens had to show proof of a destination other than the United States. Students and visitors for pleasure or business needed to verify that they could return to a homeland. Admission of nonimmigrants was subject to no numerical restriction. But, like all entering aliens, nonimmigrants had to meet the physical, mental, moral, and political qualifications of the Immigration Act of 1917 and had to show proof of financial backing sufficient to keep them from becoming public charges.[1]

Immigrants (permanent settlers) were divided into two classes: nonquota and quota. Nonquota immigrants were not subject to numerical limits. This class included wives and unmarried minor children of American citizens, husbands of American citizens if the marriage occurred before July 1932, college professors and ministers of religious denominations with their wives and children, and natives of independent countries of the Western Hemisphere.

Although some refugees entered as nonimmigrant visitors or as nonquota immigrants, the great majority of them were subject to the quota limitations of the Immigration Act of 1924 as well as to the personal qualifications of the Act of 1917. The total number of quota immigrants allowed per year for all countries was 153,774. Virtually the entire amount, 150,501, was allotted to European nations, while the remainder was apportioned in tiny quantities to countries in Asia, Africa, and the Pacific area. The British and Irish share of the total was 83,574. Yet, between 1933 and 1945 quota immigration from Great Britain and Ireland together did not rise higher than 4,300 in any one year. Consequently, over 79,000, or more than one half, of the total quota places were inoperative. In actuality, what might be called the overall "effective" quota never exceeded 75,000 per year.

A close-up of utilization of the German-Austrian quota not only mirrors refugee demand on the quotas, but also indirectly reflects some of the problems victims of persecution faced in attempting to emigrate. This quota allowed entry of 27,370 persons per year. It was by far the largest allotment assigned to any of the countries of refugee emigration, accounting for approximately 50 percent of the total for such countries. The following figures show the extent to which the German-Austrian quota was filled during the years of the Hitler regime.

| Fiscal year | 1933 | 1934 | 1935 | 1936 | 1937 | 1938 | 1939 |
|---|---|---|---|---|---|---|---|
| Percent | 5.3 | 13.7 | 20.2 | 24.3 | 42.1 | 65.3 | 119.7[2] |

| Fiscal year | 1940 | 1941 | 1942 | 1943 | 1944 | 1945 |
|---|---|---|---|---|---|---|
| Percent | 95.3 | 47.7 | 17.8 | 4.7 | 4.8 | 4.3 |

Over the 13-year period 35.8 percent of this quota was used. These statistics emphasize the acute pressure on the German-Austrian quota from 1938 to 1941, a period when Nazi persecution was increasing. The decline after fiscal 1941 was not the result of any abatement in Nazi oppression. Indeed, in late 1941 the policy of extermination was initiated. What this decrease did reflect was a shrinkage of available shipping, Nazi restrictions on legal exit from German-controlled territories, and especially an American policy of very tight screening of visa applicants to assure exclusion of possible spies and saboteurs.

# Notes

Abbreviations used to cite published sources
are as follows:

| | |
|---|---|
| *AJYB* | *American Jewish Year Book* |
| *CJR* | *Contemporary Jewish Record* |
| *CR* | *Congressional Record* |
| *FR* | *Foreign Relations of the United States* |
| *NYT* | *New York Times* |

Abbreviated forms used to cite archival sources are
listed below. The locations of all archival collections
used in this work may be found in the Bibliography.

| | |
|---|---|
| AFSC | American Friends Service Committee Archives |
| GF | General Files |
| Minutes | Minutes Files |
| RS | Refugee Services Files |
| | Requests for more specific information on the location of documents in the American Friends Service Committee Archives may be addressed to the author or to the publisher. |
| AJC | American Jewish Committee Archives |
| | All material cited is in the Immigration Series. |
| BL Diary | Breckinridge Long Diary |
| BL Papers | Breckinridge Long Papers |
| FDR | Franklin D. Roosevelt Papers |
| OF | Official File |
| PPF | President's Personal File |
| NA | National Archives |
| WILPF | Women's International League for Peace and Freedom |

*Note on the use of †: Since the completion of the research for this study, much of the material in the American Friends Service Committee Archives, previously stored in the form in which it arrived from the offices, has been consolidated and reclassified into a more logical and systematic filing arrangement. In a careful check made late in the spring of 1968, the author located in the new files all but 24 of the documents cited in this book. (The author has in his possession photocopies of six of the unlocated documents.) A few of these missing documents may be in files that are still being processed. Others may actually be in the new files and may have eluded the search. But it must be presumed that most of the 24 are lost. In the Notes, the missing documents are indicated by the symbol † following the archival citation.*

## Preface

1. From the final resolution of the Evian Conference, July 1938, as reproduced in *FR, 1938* (Washington, 1955), I, 755–756.

2. John Hope Simpson, *The Refugee Problem: Report of a Survey* (London, 1939), 128–129, 130.

3. As late as 1946 a national survey by the Opinion Research Corporation found that 42 percent of the respondents thought of Jews as a race. (Charles Herbert Stember and others, *Jews in the Mind of America* [New York, 1966], 50.)

## Chapter 1

1. Read Lewis and Marian Schibsby, "Status of the Refugee Under American Immigration Laws," *Annals of the American Academy of Political and Social Science,* CCIII (May,1939), 78; Department of State, *Press Releases,* No. 50 (September 13, 1930), 176, No. 62 (December 6, 1930), 423

2. Ibid., No. 50 (September 13, 1930), 177, No. 62 (December 6, 1930), 422, No. 64 (December 20, 1930), 457.

3. Ibid., No. 50 (September 13, 1930), 177; Robert A. Divine, *American Immigration Policy, 1924–1952* (New Haven, 1957), 79–86.

4. Franklin D. Roosevelt to Herbert H. Lehman, November 13, 1935, Lehman to Roosevelt, June 15, 1936, with enclosures, Roosevelt to Lehman, July 2, 1936, FDR, OF 133; statement by Avra Warren, chief of the Visa Division, in "Deportation of Aliens," *Hearings before a Subcommittee of the Committee on Immigration, United States Senate,* 76 Cong., 1 sess. (March 21, 22, and 23, 1939), 71. Immigration from Germany in fiscal 1935 was 5,436; in fiscal 1936, 6,538; in fiscal 1937, 11, 648.

5. *NYT,* March 26, 1938, p. 1; U.S. Bureau of the Census, *Historical Statistics of the United States, Colonial Times to 1957* (Washington, 1960), 73.

6. *Junior American,* XIV (March, 1939), 5; Arthur Derounian [John Roy Carlson, pseud.], *Under Cover: My Four Years in the Nazi Underworld of America* (Philadelphia, 1943), 66; "Memorandum on the Street Disturbances in New York City," mimeographed [late 1938 or early 1939], p. 1, copy in American Jewish Committee Library; *National Jewish Monthly,* LIV (May, 1940), 295; "Deportation of Aliens," *Hearings before a Subcommittee,* 61–64, 72.

7. Henry W. Levy to Frank Trager, March 29, 1939, AJC, Refugees, 1938–44; *Tablet,* XXX (May 21, 1938), 11, XXX (November 5, 1938), 15; David M. Bockenek to George Fredman, December 22, 1939, AJC, Immigration, 1944–40; Isabel Lundberg, "Who Are These Refugees?" *Harper's Magazine,* CLXXXII (January, 1941), 170; "Deportation of Aliens," *Hearings before a Subcommittee,* 153–154; Maurice R. Davie, *Refugees in America* (New York, 1947), 373–374; *Philadelphia Evening Bulletin,* April 7, 1939, p. 3; National Board, YWCA, *Meet the Refugees* (New York, 1940), 17; *Congress Bulletin,* V (June 2, 1939), 1; Henry Smith Leiper, "Those German Refugees," *Current History,* L (May, 1939), 20.

8. National Board, YWCA, *Meet the Refugees,* 18; *National Jewish Monthly,* LV (November, 1940), 90; "Refugees Build U.S. Industries," *Business Week,* No. 556 (April 27, 1940), 18, 20; David Dempsey, "The Jericho Road," *Christian Science Monitor,* Weekly Magazine Section, February 10, 1940, p. 3.

9. This view was clearly set forth by Henry Smith Leiper, associate secretary of the Federal Council of Churches, in "Those German Refugees," 19–22. Other sources include Maxwell S. Stewart, "The Immigrant as a Worker," *Social Work Today,* VII (December, 1939), 39; Bernard W. Levmore, "A Stimulus for American Industry: Nonprofessional Refugees," *Annals,* CCIII (May, 1939), 162–163; *Refugee Facts* (Philadelphia, 1939), 7–9; National Board, YWCA, *Meet the Refugees,* 8–10, 15–16; Frank Ritchie, "America Needs Them," *Forum,* CI (June, 1939), 319.

10. Stewart, "The Immigrant as a Worker," 39; National Board, YWCA, *Meet the Refugees,* 15–16; *AJYB,* XLIII (1941), 743; Louis Adamic, *America and the Refugees,* Public Affairs Pamphlet No. 29 (New York, 1939), 24; "The American Way," an editorial, *Collier's,* CII (December 31, 1938), 50; *New Republic,* XCV (July 20, 1938), 292; *Refugee Facts,* 15; Levmore, "A Stimulus for American Industry," 163; James L. Houghteling to the Immigration Committee of the United States Senate, April 10, 1939, NA, Legislative Branch, File SEN 76A-E1; "Deportation of Aliens," *Hearings before a Subcommittee,* 148.

11. Leiper, "Those German Refugees," 21–22; *Refugee Facts,* 16–20, 22; National Board, YWCA, *Meet the Refugees,* 18–19; Ritchie, "America Needs Them," 320; Levmore, "A Stimulus for American Industry," 164; "Data on Refugee Enterprises for Speech Material," n.d., AFSC, GF; National Refugee Service, *Dividends from New Americans* (New York, 1941), 1–3; "Refugees Build U.S. Industries," 20.

12. Bernhard Ostrolenk, "The Economics of an Imprisoned World —A Brief for the Removal of Immigration Restrictions," *Annals,* CCIII (May, 1939), 196–197; Felix S. Cohen, "Exclusionary Immigration Laws—Their Social and Economic Consequences," *CJR,* III (March–April, 1940), 148–150. Similar viewpoints were expressed by Dorothy Thompson in *Refugees: Anarchy or Organization?* (New York, 1938), 81; and by Henry Goddard Leach, editor of *Forum,* in an editorial "Whither Refugees?" in that periodical, C (November, 1938), 210.

13. "Report on Refugee Program," April 7, 1939, "Refugee Campaign Report," April 19, 1939, a four-page undated report beginning "In its attempt to create a healthy public attitude toward refugees," Henry W. Levy to Frank N. Trager, September, 1939, AJC, Refugees, Facts and Figures; *Refugee Facts*; Clarence E. Pickett, *For*

*More Than Bread* (Boston, 1953), 148. The Leiper article in *Current History* went to the 75,000 circulation of that periodical as well as being distributed in 30,000 reprint copies. Leiper made a radio address on the subject in New York City and stories or editorials based on the article appeared in at least 35 newspapers. Two thousand reprints of Ostrolenk's article in the May 1939 *Annals* were sent out. Articles stressing the economic contribution which refugees were making appeared in such varied publications as *American Magazine* (S.F. Porter, "Refugee Gold Rush," CXXXIV [October, 1942]) and *Business Week* ("Refugees Build U.S. Industries," No. 556 [April 27, 1940]).

14. "Deportation of Aliens," *Hearings before a Subcommittee,* 65–66; Stephen F. Chadwick, "We Dare Be Free," *American Legion Magazine,* XXVI (May, 1939), 12.

15. *Defender Magazine,* XIII (May, 1938), 2; *Junior American,* XIII (May, 1938), 2, XIV (March, 1939), 5.

16. Harry H. Laughlin, *Conquest by Immigration* (New York, 1939), front cover, chapter 4, and pages 91–93, 104; *NYT,* June 8, 1939, p. 9; Henry W. Levy to Frank N. Trager, June 26, 1939, AJC, Immigration, 1939–.

17. "Deportation of Aliens," *Hearings before a Subcommittee,* 64.

18. Ibid., 21, 68.

19. J.H. Patten, *The "Immigration Crew" on the New Deal "Railroad"* ([Chicago], 1935), 10–13.

20. *Vital Speeches of the Day,* V (December 15, 1938), 159; *Defender Magazine,* XIII (January, 1939), 16; *CR,* LXXXIV, Part 4, 76 Cong., 1 sess., 3629; *Social Justice,* IIIA (February 27, 1939), 2.

21. *Twenty-Seventh Annual Report of the Secretary of Labor, for the Fiscal Year Ended June 30, 1939* (Washington, 1939), 90; *Twenty-Eighth Annual Report of the Secretary of Labor, for the Fiscal Year Ended June 30, 1940* (Washington, 1940), 102–103; *Collier's,* CV (January 27, 1940), 70.

22. Charles Herbert Stember and others, *Jews in the Mind of America* (New York, 1966), shows, especially in chapters 3, 5, and 10, the large extent of anti-Semitic feeling from 1938 through 1945. McWilliams' statement is from a street corner speech of July 13, 1940, as reported by Mike Landon [pseud.], "Is There a Führer in the House?" *New Republic,* CIII (August 12, 1940), 212 and corroborated independently by Leo Lowenthal and Norbert Guterman,

*Prophets of Deceit* (New York, 1949), 145. *CR,* LXXXIV, Part 14, 76 Cong., 1 sess., A3694-A3695, LXXXVI, Part 5, 76 Cong., 3 sess., 5631, LXXXVI, Part 15, 76 Cong., 3 sess., A2442-A2444, XC, Part 1, 78 Cong., 2 sess., 752.

23. Donald S. Strong, *Organized Anti-Semitism in America: The Rise of Group Prejudice During the Decade 1930–1940* (Washington, 1941), 30–34, 36–37; Stanley High, "Star-Spangled Fascists," *Saturday Evening Post,* CCXI (May 27, 1939), 6; *CJR,* III (January–February, 1940), 55.

24. *Free America!: Six Addresses on the Aims and Purposes of the German-American Bund: Delivered at Madison Square Garden, New York City, February 20, 1939* (New York, 1939); *AJYB,* XLI (1939), 215; *CJR,* II (March–April, 1939), 53; *NYT,* February 8, 1938, p. 9, February 11, 1938, p. 15, February 14, 1938, p. 18, April 21, 1938, p. 1. The *New York Times* on April 22, 1938, p. 12, reported a statement from American Legion officials explaining that the American Legion had not authorized this action and asserting that several of the anti-Nazi participants were probably not Legionnaires.

25. *AJYB,* XLI (1939), 213–215; Strong, *Organized Anti-Semitism,* 38–39.

26. Ibid., 41–45, 51–54; Harold Lavine, "Fifth Column 'Literature,' " *Saturday Review of Literature,* XXII (September 14, 1940), 4; Harold Lavine, *Fifth Column in America* (New York, 1940), 171–172; William Dudley Pelley, "Seven Minutes in Eternity," *American Magazine,* CVII (March, 1929), 7–9, 39–44; *Liberation,* VIII (January 21, 1938), 3; Norton Belth, "Problems of Anti-Semitism in the United States," *CJR,* II (May–June, 1939), 17, 51; High, "Star-Spangled Fascists," 70.

27. Lavine, "Fifth Column 'Literature,' " 3; [William Dudley Pelley], *What Every Congressman Should Know* (Asheville, N.C. [1938]), 1, 2, 5–39; *Liberation,* VIII (January 28, 1938), 3, 6–7, VIII (February 28, 1938), 8.

28. Strong, *Organized Anti-Semitism,* 156; *Liberation,* VIII (March 7, 1938), 2.

29. *AJYB,* XLII (1940), 291, XLIV (1942), 158; "Voices of Defeat: Dissident Groups Sow Lies and Hate within U.S.," *Life,* XII (April 13, 1942), 97.

30. Ibid., 93; "Nazi Agents in the U.S.," *Fortune,* XXII (October,

1940), 144; Lavine, "Fifth Column 'Literature,' " 3; *NYT*, April 3, 1938, IV, p. 7; High, "Star-Spangled Fascists," 72; American Institute of Public Opinion release of January 8, 1939.

31. *Social Justice*, IIA (July 18, 1938, through August 29, 1938), page 5 of each issue, and (November 21, 1938), 10–11.

32. *AJYB*, XLI (1939), 209–210; General Jewish Council, *Father Coughlin: His "Facts" and Arguments* ([New York], 1939), 32–35; *Social Justice*, IIA (November 28, 1938), 7, 10–11; Alfred M. Lee and Elizabeth B. Lee (eds.), *The Fine Art of Propaganda* (New York, 1939), 86–91.

33. Strong, *Organized Anti-Semitism*, 64–65, 67–68; *AJYB*, XLI (1939), 211–212; "Memorandum on the Street Disturbances in New York City," mimeographed [late 1938 or early 1939], pp. 1–4, copy in American Jewish Committee Library; Dale Kramer, "The American Fascists," *Harper's Magazine*, CLXXXI (September, 1940), 384; Theodore Irwin, "Inside the 'Christian Front,' " *Forum*, CIII (March, 1940), 102–105, 107.

34. Strong, *Organized Anti-Semitism*, 66; " 'Christian American' Jew Baiting," by the editors and staff of *Christian Social Action*, IV (September, 1939), 105; *AJYB*, XLII (1940), 287–289; *CJR*, IV (April, 1941), 180.

35. *Tablet*, XXX (December 3, 1938), 11, XXX (December 10, 1938), 13, XXX (December 24, 1938), 11, XXXI (March 11, 1939), 1; George N. Shuster, "The Conflict Among Catholics," *American Scholar*, X (Winter, 1940–41), 6.

36. *AJYB*, XLI (1939), 210–211, XLIII (1941), 107, XLIV (1942), 158–159; *CJR*, II (January, 1939), 52, 89, V (June, 1942), 296, 302; "Voices of Defeat," 93.

37. *Defender Magazine*, XIV (April, 1940), 1; "Voices of Defeat," 97; High, "Star-Spangled Fascists," 72; Belth, "Problems of Anti-Semitism," 17.

38. *Defender Magazine*, XIII (August, 1938), 16, XIII (September, 1938), 17–18, XIII (November, 1938), 10, XIII (January, 1939), 6, XIII (March, 1939), 5–6, XIV (May, 1939), 4, XIV (December, 1939), 4, XV (September, 1940), 3, XV (November, 1940), 5.

39. High, "Star-Spangled Fascists," 5, 7, 70–71; Strong, *Organized Anti-Semitism*, 125, 138–143; American Jewish Congress, Research Department, "Anti-Semitic Propaganda in the United States," mimeographed, 1939, p. 31, copy in American Jewish Committee

Library; Lewis W. Bondy, *Racketeers of Hatred* (London [1946]), 239, asserted that True had Patent No. 2,026,077 for the "Kike Killer."

40. Strong, *Organized Anti-Semitism,* 136–137.

41. Ibid., 134; *AJYB,* XL (1938), 120, XLI (1939), 213, XLIII (1941), 106; *NYT,* June 1, 1939, pp. 1, 4, June 2, 1939, p. 8; William L. White, "A Voice from Main Street, U.S.A.," *Survey Graphic,* XXVIII (February, 1939), 134; High, "Star-Spangled Fascists," 70.

42. Stember and others, *Jews in the Mind of America,* 53–55.

43. Ibid., 121, 123–124, 127–128.

44. Ibid., 84–85, 130–133, 208–210, 214.

45. *Refugee Facts,* 13; National Board, YWCA, *Meet the Refugees,* 12–13; *FR, 1939* (Washington, 1956), II, 147; Davie, *Refugees in America,* xvii, 33–36.

46. Carbon copy of a nine-page typed report beginning "During recent months a good deal of attention," dated March 6, 1940, Henry W. Levy to Executive Committee, "re REFUGEES," March 5, 1940, Alan Cranston to Sidney Freifeld, "Re: Refugees," n.d., AJC, Refugees, Facts and Figures; Levy to David Bernstein, "Subject: Refugee Publicity," July 3, 1940, AJC, Immigration, Refugees, High Commissioner.

47. *Newscast* (American Committee for Christian Refugees), II (January, 1942), 3; Mr. Schneiderman to Mr. Waldman, "Proposed immigration legislation," April 5, 1938, AJC, Immigration, 1939–; FBT to SW, December 29, 1938, AJC, Refugees, 1938–44.

48. *National Jewish Monthly,* LIV (March, 1940), 217, LIV (April, 1940), 249, LIV (July–August, 1940), 330, LV (January, 1941), 137, 141, LV (February, 1941), 173, LV (March, 1941), 203, LVI (April, 1942), 251

49. *Opinion,* XI (March, 1941), 22.

50. *Congress Bulletin,* V (May 12, 1939), 4.

51. "Suggested Program for Combatting Refugee Misconceptions," March 17, 1939, "Report on Refugee Program," April 7, 1939, "Refugee Campaign Report," April 19, 1939, carbon copy of an undated four-page typescript which begins "In its attempt to create a healthy public attitude toward refugees," AJC, Refugees, Facts and Figures.

52. Lyman Cromwell White, *300,000 New Americans* (New York, 1957), 13, 24, 40; Gerhart Saenger, "The Refugees Here," *Survey*

*Graphic,* XXIX (November, 1940), 581; Eli Ginzberg, *Report to American Jews* (New York, 1942), 29, 31–32.

53. Clarence E. Pickett to William Haber, December 26, 1939, telegram Paul Baerwald to Pickett, January 25, 1939, Pickett to Rufus Jones, April 3, 1939, Pickett to Eleanor Roosevelt, July 6, 1939, Pickett to Frank N. Trager, April 5, 1939, E.A. Caplin to A. Di Tullio, January 15, 1940, Di Tullio to Caplin, February 1, 1940, Lillian Traugott to Samuel L. Scheiner, April 29, 1940, AFSC, GF; Minutes of Board of Directors, April 5, 1939, AFSC, Minutes; "Report on Refugee Program," April 7, 1939, "Refugee Campaign Report," April 19, 1939, carbon copy of an undated four-page typescript which begins "In its attempt to create a healthy public attitude toward refugees," AJC, Refugees, Facts and Figures.

## Chapter 2

1. Of necessity this percentage is an estimate because no reliable figure exists for the number of "non-Aryans." Indications are that there were fewer "non-Aryans" than religious Jews. (John Hope Simpson, *The Refugee Problem: Report of a Survey* [London, 1939], 130n.) Since the 500,000 religious Jews in Germany in 1933 comprised less than one percent of the population, probably both groups combined accounted for between one and two percent of the German people. (John Hope Simpson, *Refugees: Preliminary Report of a Survey* [New York, 1938], 61; Maurice R. Davie, *Refugees in America* [New York, 1947], 6.)

2. Ibid., 6–7

3. Simpson, *The Refugee Problem,* 131–133, 140, 153; "The Jewish Catastrophe and Its Aftermath," in Institute of Jewish Affairs, *The Institute Anniversary Volume* (New York, 1962), 57–58; James G. McDonald, *Letter of Resignation: Addressed to the Secretary General of the League of Nations: with an Annex* (London, 1935), 6–9; Simpson, *Refugees: Preliminary Report of a Survey,* 60; Davie, *Refugees in America,* 7; Theodor H. Gaster, *A Digest of Nazi Legislation Against the Jews* ( New York, 1940), 4.

4. Simpson, *The Refugee Problem,* 135, 146; David H. Popper, "International Aid to German Refugees," *Foreign Policy Reports,* XIV (November 1, 1938), 188.

5. "The Jewish Catastrophe and Its Aftermath," 58–59; Simpson, *The Refugee Problem,* 130, 135, 142; Gaster, *A Digest of Nazi Legislation,* 3, 10.

6. *CJR,* I (September, 1938), 42–44; "The Jewish Catastrophe and Its Aftermath," 60–61; John Hope Simpson, *Refugees: A Review of the Situation Since September 1938* (London, 1939), 111, 113; Gaster, *A Digest of Nazi Legislation,* 5, 6.

7. Simpson, *The Refugee Problem,* 126, 136; *NYT,* March 23, 1938, p. 8, April 3, 1938, pp. 1, 36, April 20, 1938, p. 1, April 21, 1938, pp. 10, 18, April 28, 1938, p. 8; Joseph Tenenbaum, "The Crucial Year 1938," *Yad Washem Studies* (Jerusalem, 1958), II, 52; *CJR,* II (September–October, 1939), 91; *AJYB,* XLI (1939), 266.

8. John Hope Simpson, *The Refugee Question,* No. 13 of Oxford Pamphlets on World Affairs (2d ed.; London, 1940), 7–13; Simpson, *The Refugee Problem,* 200, 207; Simpson, *Refugees: Preliminary Report of a Survey,* 104; Louise W. Holborn, "The League of Nations and the Refugee Problem," *Annals of the American Academy of Political and Social Science,* CCIII (May, 1939), 124, 126, 131; Countess Waldeck, "The Great New Migration," *Foreign Affairs,* XV (April, 1937), 539–541; Dorothy Thompson, *Refugees: Anarchy or Organization?* (New York, 1938), 16–17.

9. Holborn, "The League of Nations," 133; Norman Bentwich, "The International Problem of Refugees," *Foreign Policy Reports,* XI (February 12, 1936), 312–313.

10. McDonald, *Letter of Resignation,* v–ix, 31, 33; Simpson, *The Refugee Problem,* 217; Holborn, "The League of Nations," 133–134.

11. Simpson, *The Refugee Problem,* 218–221; Simpson, *Refugees: Preliminary Report of a Survey,* 87; Holborn, "The League of Nations," 134; Louise W. Holborn, *The International Refugee Organization* (London, 1956), 8–9.

12. Simpson, *The Refugee Problem,* 297–298, 322–323, 473, 562–563.

13. Until July 1937, immigration into Palestine was unlimited for persons of independent means, for orphans with guaranteed support, and for others with "a definite prospect of employment" in numbers up to the "absorptive capacity" of the country. The "absorptive ca-

pacity" was recalculated every six months by the office of the British High Commissioner, supposedly on the basis of prevailing economic conditions. (Simpson, *The Refugee Problem,* 432–433.) However, in 1937 the "absorptive capacity" began to be affected by political factors and as a result immigration limits were sharply reduced. (Kurt R. Grossmann, "Refugees, DP's, and Migrants," in Institute of Jewish Affairs, *The Institute Anniversary Volume* [New York, 1962], 121, 123; Simpson, *The Refugee Problem,* 434–435; *1938 Britannica Book of the Year* [Chicago, 1938], 503.)

14. Simpson, *The Refugee Question,* 18; *NYT,* April 27, 1938, p. 11; Grossmann, "Refugees, DP's, and Migrants," 142, 148; Simpson, *Refugees: A Review of the Situation,* 24; Arthur Prinz, "The Role of the Gestapo in Obstructing and Promoting Jewish Emigration," *Yad Washem Studies* (Jerusalem, 1958), II, 208; *Documents on German Foreign Policy, 1918–1945* (Washington, 1953), series D, V, 927; "Informal Report on Immigration from Germany to the United States and Other Countries," mimeographed, November 21, 1939, p. 1, AFSC, RS; *CJR,* IV (August, 1941), 424, 426, IV (December, 1941), 661; *AJYB,* XLIV (1942), 296–297; Gerald Reitlinger, *The Final Solution: The Attempt to Exterminate the Jews of Europe 1939–1945* (New York, 1953), 28, 85, 87.

15. This general pattern is the subject of an article by Shaul Esh, "Between Discrimination and Extermination," *Yad Washem Studies* (Jerusalem, 1958), II, 79–93.

16. Gerhart Saenger, *Today's Refugees, Tomorrow's Citizens* (New York, 1941), 25; Bruno Bettelheim, "Freedom from Ghetto Thinking," *Midstream,* VIII (Spring, 1962), 16–20.

17. Kurt R. Grossmann, *Ten Years: American Federation of Jews from Central Europe, Inc., 1941–1951* (New York, 1952), 44, estimated 215,000. Davie, *Refugees in America,* 9, stated that 330,000 Jews were still in Greater Germany when the war began. Since over half of Austria's 180,000 Jews had escaped by then, Grossmann's figure is not far from Davie's. The *American Jewish Year Book,* LXIII (1941), 329, stated that from 1933 through the end of 1939 about 260,000 Jews left Germany. Since the German census of 1933 reported 500,000 Jews, Grossmann's estimate again is reasonably well borne out.

18. *AJYB,* XL (1938), 185, XLI (1939), 383, 386–387; Simpson, *Refugees: A Review of the Situation,* 52, 64–65, 67, 69, 79, 83–89,

96–98; *1940 Britannica Book of the Year* (Chicago, 1940), 518, 576; Simpson, *The Refugee Problem*, 347, 397; "Informal Report on Immigration from Germany to the United States and Other Countries," mimeographed, November 21, 1939, pp. 3–4, AFSC, RS; Read Lewis and Marian Schibsby, "Status of the Refugee Under American Immigration Laws," *Annals*, CCIII (May, 1939), 76; James G. Vail to Clarence E. Pickett, March 6, 1939, AFSC, GF; *CJR*, III (March–April, 1940), 163, III (July–August, 1940), 420.

19. H.P. Smolka, "Pimpernel Ltd.," *Living Age*, CCCLV (December, 1938), 306–309; James G. Vail to Clarence E. Pickett, March 6, 1939, "Immigration to Cuba" [spring, 1939], AFSC, GF; Prinz, "The Role of the Gestapo," 215–216; Grossmann, "Refugees, DP's, and Migrants," 124–125.

20. [Anna Ginsbourg], *Jewish Refugees in Shanghai* (Shanghai, 1940), 5–7, 14, 19, 20–22, 24; Bruno Lasker, "An Atlas of Hope," *Survey Graphic*, XXIX (November, 1940), 584.

21. *1940 Britannica Book of the Year*, 576; *FR, 1939* (Washington, 1956), II, 92–94, 96–97. A graphic summary of the refugee ships tragedy is in Grossmann, "Refugees, DP's, and Migrants," 142–143. *AJYB*, XLI (1939), 389, XLIII (1941), 333.

22. On the *St. Louis*: *AJYB*, XLI (1939), 387–388; James N. Rosenberg to Dear Friend, June 15, 1939, AFSC, RS; "RE: SS ST. LOUIS" [June, 1939], AFSC, GF; *New Republic*, XCIX (June 28, 1939), 197. On the *Struma*: *CJR*, V (April, 1942), 199, V (June, 1942), 316.


# Chapter 3

1. Department of State, *Press Releases,* XVIII (March 26, 1938), 411, XVIII (April 30, 1938), 514–517, XIX (October 8, 1938), 246, XX (January 21, 1939), 39; "Second Deficiency Appropriation Bill for 1938," *Hearings before a Subcommittee of the Committee on Appropriations, House of Representatives,* 75 Cong., 3 sess. (May 25, 1938), 697; *NYT*, March 25, 1938, p. 1, March 26, 1938, p. 1; "The Press Conferences of President Franklin D. Roosevelt," XI, Press Conference

No. 445 (March 25, 1938), 248–250, Franklin D. Roosevelt Library. Undersecretary of State Sumner Welles referred to the opening of the German and Austrian quotas to full use as "a distinctly abnormal relaxation." (Welles to Roosevelt, April 11, 1938, FDR, OF 3186.)

2. *Time*, XXXI (April 4, 1938), 11; *Newsweek*, XI (April 4, 1938), 11; interview on May 11, 1965, with George L. Warren, formerly executive secretary of the President's Advisory Committee on Political Refugees. *Time*, XXXII (August 8, 1938), 15, Oswald Garrison Villard in the *Nation*, CXLVII (September 3, 1938), 226, and Hamilton Fish Armstrong in the introduction to Dorothy Thompson's book *Refugees: Anarchy or Organization?* (New York, 1938) named Miss Thompson as the stimulator of Roosevelt's action in calling the conference. Dorothy Thompson, "Refugees, A World Problem," *Foreign Affairs*, XVI (April, 1938), 375–387; TCA [chilles], "REFUGEE PROGRAM," n.d. [late 1938], under cover of memorandum from Butler to Duggan and Drew, November 15, 1938, NA, State Department Records, File 840.48 Refugees/900½.

3. Department of State, *Press Releases*, XVIII (April 2, 1938), 426–432, XVIII (April 9, 1938), 475–476, XVIII (April 16, 1938), 480–482; *FR, 1938* (Washington, 1955), I, 742, 743.

4. *Time*, XXXI (April 4, 1938), 12; *AJYB*, XL (1938), 97; *NYT*, March 26, 1938, pp. 1, 4, 5; Mabel Brown Ellis, *Refugees* (New York, 1938), 1; *Commonweal*, XXVII (April 8, 1938), 647; a 17-page typewritten tabulation of replies with this penciled marginal note: "Digest of opinions on Increasing Quotas—compiled from letters received by . . . Editor of Brooklyn Jewish Examiner" [May, 1938], p. 14, AJC, Immigration, 1939–.

5. *NYT*, July 3, 1938, p. 8; *Interpreter Releases*, XV (April 18, 1938), 160; *America*, LIX (July 30, 1938), 388; *Tablet*, XXX (April 2, 1938), 10.

6. "Second Deficiency Appropriation Bill for 1938," *Hearings before a Subcommittee*, 697; *CR*, LXXXIII, Part 10, 75 Cong., 3 sess., A1207.

7. Ibid., LXXXIII, Part 4, 75 Cong., 3 sess., 4227–4228.

8. *Fortune*, XVIII (July, 1938), 80, quotations by courtesy of *Fortune*.

9. Louis T. Gross to John L. Bernstein, April 21, 1938, "Digest of opinions on Increasing Quotas . . ." [May, 1938], AJC, Immigration, 1939–.

10. *NYT*, April 9, 1938, p. 5; *Interpreter Releases*, xv (April 18, 1938), 160; Sumner Welles to Franklin D. Roosevelt, April 11, 1938, FDR, OF 3186; "Memorandum on White House Conference on Refugees," April 13, 1938, AFSC, GF; Department of State, *Press Releases*, xviii (May 21, 1938), 585–586.

11. Ibid., 586; David H. Popper, "International Aid to German Refugees," *Foreign Policy Reports*, xiv (November 1, 1938), 191; Kurt R. Grossmann, "Refugees, DP's, and Migrants," in Institute of Jewish Affairs, *The Institute Anniversary Volume* (New York, 1962), 152; Norman Bentwich, "The Evian Conference and After," *Fortnightly*, CL (September, 1938), 288; *Proceedings of the Intergovernmental Committee, Evian, July 6th to 15th, 1938, Verbatim Record of the Plenary Meetings of the Committee* (n.p., 1938), 17, 24, and Annex I; *Congress Bulletin*, v (May 19, 1939), 4, v (June 16, 1939), 4; the *Day* was quoted in *CJR*, I (September, 1938), 56; "Inter-Governmental Conference on Refugees Held at Evian," mimeographed, July 6, 1938, p. 2, and A.G. Brotman to Mr. Laski, copy of undated letter sent from the Evian Conference, AJC, Refugees, Evian Conference.

12. Department of State, *Press Releases*, xix (July 9, 1938), 21; *Proceedings of the Intergovernmental Committee*, 14–17, 19–22, 25, 27–28, 30–33, 36, 38, 42; *Newsweek*, xii (July 18, 1938), 13.

13. Department of State, *Press Releases*, xix (July 16, 1938), 34, xix (October 8, 1938), 247–249; *FR, 1938*, I, 755–756.

14. *Nation*, CXLVII (July 23, 1938), 78, CXLVII (August 6, 1938), 126; *New Republic*, xcv (July 20, 1938), 291–292; Popper, "International Aid to German Refugees," 194; *CJR*, I (September, 1938), 3–4, 47–56; Samuel I. Rosenman (ed.), *The Public Papers and Addresses of Franklin D. Roosevelt* (New York, 1941), vii, 171.

15. Sumner Welles, *Where Are We Heading?* (New York, 1946), 280, quoted by permission of Harper and Row, Publishers, Incorporated; Louise W. Holborn, *The International Refugee Organization* (London, 1956), 39; "Remarks on Testimony of Breckinridge Long, Assistant Secretary of State," December 21, 1943, p. 3, AJC, Immigration, Refugees, Rescue of, 1943–47. The budget for the ICR's first year was set at $50,000! (*FR, 1938*, I, 782.)

16. Ibid., I, 764, 769–770, 772, 780–781.

17. Ibid., I, 785, 791–792, 794–798, 799–801.

18. *Documents on German Foreign Policy, 1918–1945* (Washington, 1953), series D, V, 900–903; *FR, 1938,* I, 814–816, 819–820.

19. Ibid., I, 871, 873–874; *Documents on British Foreign Policy, 1919–1939* (London, 1950), 3d series, III, 675–677.

20. Ibid.; telegram Herschel Johnson (for George Rublee) to Cordell Hull, December 16, 1938, NA, State Department Records, File 840.48 Refugees/1125; *Documents on German Foreign Policy, 1918–1945* (Washington, 1951), series D, IV, 351; Hjalmar H.G. Schacht, *Confessions of "The Old Wizard"* (Boston, 1956), 351–352; *FR, 1938,* I, 874.

21. Ibid., I, 877; *Documents on British Foreign Policy, 1919–1939,* 3d series, III, 676–677.

22. *FR, 1938,* I, 875–877; *Congress Bulletin,* V (December 16, 1938), 1, V (December 23, 1938), 1, V (January 20, 1939), 1; *New Republic,* XCVII (December 21, 1938), 189; *Nation,* CXLVII (December 24, 1938), 681–682.

23. *FR, 1939* (Washington, 1956), II, 77–83, 87; John Hope Simpson, *Refugees: A Review of the Situation Since September 1938* (London, 1939), 20–22; Richard J. Whalen, *The Founding Father: The Story of Joseph P. Kennedy* (New York, 1964), 256; *AJYB,* XLI (1939), 380–381.

24. Ibid., 390; *FR, 1939,* II, 80; *Nation,* CXLIX (August 5, 1939), 138; *CJR,* II (March–April, 1939), 83, II (May–June, 1939), 91, II (September–October, 1939), 82.

25. *Congress Bulletin,* V (February 17, 1939), 1, 4, V (February 24, 1939), 1, 4, V (March 10, 1939), 6, V (March 24, 1939), 4, V (May 5, 1939), 3; Grossmann, "Refugees, DP's, and Migrants," 152; A. Leon Kubowitzki (ed.), *Unity in Dispersion: A History of the World Jewish Congress* (New York, 1948), 116; *National Jewish Monthly,* LIV (September, 1939), 3, 31; Arieh Tartakower and Kurt R. Grossmann, *The Jewish Refugee* (New York, 1944), 417–418.

26. Dorothy Thompson, "Escape in a Frozen World," *Survey Graphic,* XXVIII (February, 1939), 168; Dorothy Thompson, "Thanks for Anything," *New York Herald Tribune,* February 17, 1939, p. 21.

27. *CJR,* II (March–April, 1939), 83, II (May–June, 1939), 129; *FR, 1939,* II, 83, 96, 102–105.

28. Ibid., II, 83, 102–106, 108, 109–110, 123.

29. Ibid., II, 148, 149–150.

30. Erika Mann and Eric Estorick, "Private and Governmental Aid of Refugees," *Annals of the American Academy of Political and Social Science,* ccIII (May, 1939), 151–154; *FR, 1938,* I, 760, 787–788, 820–821, 829; James G. Vail to Clarence E. Pickett, March 6, 1939, Robert Balderston, "Re: Paris Conference of Liaison Committee," June 19, 1939, AFSC, GF.

31. Isaiah Bowman (ed.), *Limits of Land Settlement: A Report on Present-day Possibilities* (New York, 1937), 1, 23; *Science News Letter,* XXXIV (December 3, 1938), 358, 361; Popper, "International Aid to German Refugees," 195–196; A. Grenfell Price, "Refugee Settlement in the Tropics," *Foreign Affairs,* XVIII (July, 1940), 670; Bentwich, "The Evian Conference and After," 294; Myron C. Taylor, "The Problem of Political Refugees," Department of State, *Press Releases,* XIX (October 8, 1938), 249; *FR, 1939,* II, 120.

32. Ibid., II, 58–59, 65–69, 87–88, 90, 102, 107, 134, 143, 154; Clarence E. Pickett, note for Refugees' Proposals File, January 12, 1939, AFSC, GF†; Joseph C. Hyman to Pickett, March 24, 1939, AFSC, GF; Bernard M. Baruch, *Baruch: The Public Years* (New York, 1960), 274; T.C. Achilles to George S. Messersmith and Sumner Welles, February 25, 1939, NA, State Department Records, File 840.48 Refugees/1485; Achilles to Welles, April 27, 1939, April 28, 1939, NA, State Department Records, File 840.48 Refugees/1596; *FR, 1938,* I, 859–860; S. Ethelson, " 'It Is Good To Be An Orphan,' " *Jewish Workers' Voice,* IV (December, 1938), 22.

33. *NYT,* February 12, 1940, p. 3; *AJYB,* XLI (1939), 200–201; *CJR,* I (November, 1938), 75; *CR,* LXXXIII, Part 4, 75 Cong., 3 sess., 4228–4229, LXXXIII, Part 10, 75 Cong., 3 sess., A1207; telegram Christian Mobilizers, New York, to Franklin D. Roosevelt, October 18, 1939, FDR, OF 3186. Fifty-one senators and 194 members of the House signed the petition to the President.

34. *CJR,* II (November–December, 1939), 45–46; *AJYB,* XLII (1940), 445; *FR, 1939,* II, 156; Henry Field, *"M" Project for F.D.R.: Studies on Migration and Settlement* (Ann Arbor, 1962), 1–5, 328–329, 389.

35. Franklin D. Roosevelt to Isaiah Bowman, October 14, 1938, Bowman to Roosevelt, October 15, 1938, October 31, 1938, Roosevelt to Bowman, November 2, 1938, Bowman to Roosevelt, November 4, 1938, December 10, 1938, Roosevelt to Bowman, December 15, 1938, FDR, PPF 5575; Roosevelt to Aleš Hrdlička, Oc-

tober 29, 1942, Nelson A. Rockefeller to Roosevelt, December 21, 1942, Hrdlička to Roosevelt, December 23, 1942, Sumner Welles to Roosevelt, March 5, 1943, FDR, OF 133.

36. *Interpreter Releases*, xv (September 2, 1938), 309; *1940 Britannica Book of the Year* (Chicago, 1940), 576; George L. Warren, "The Prospect for New Settlers," *Survey Graphic*, xxx (March, 1941), 168; "Luncheon given by Myron C. Taylor in honor of The Right Honorable Earl Winterton, The Honorable Paul van Zeeland, The Honorable Sir Herbert Emerson," typescript, October 19, 1939, p. 22, photocopy in New York Public Library.

37. Sumner Welles to Franklin D. Roosevelt, January 11, 1939, FDR, OF 3186; Desmond Holdridge, "An Investigation of the Prospect for White Settlement in British Guiana," *Geographical Review*, xxix (October, 1939), 622–642; *AJYB*, xli (1939), 381–382; Simpson, *Refugees: A Review of the Situation*, 99–102; M.E. Tracy, "This Refugee Problem," *Current History*, xlix (January, 1939), 7; *CJR*, iii (May–June, 1940), 289; Bruno Lasker, "An Atlas of Hope," *Survey Graphic*, xxix (November, 1940), 589.

38. *FR, 1938*, i, 764–765, 773, 849; *FR, 1939*, ii, 70–71; *FR, 1940* (Washington, 1957), ii, 213; Lasker, "An Atlas of Hope," 590; Sumner Welles to Franklin D. Roosevelt, February 27, 1939, FDR, OF 3186; *CJR*, ii (September–October, 1939), 100.

39. Dominican Republic Settlement Association, Inc., *Concerning Refugee Settlement in the Dominican Republic: A Meeting at the Town Hall Club, New York City, February 15, 1940* (New York, 1940); Atherton Lee, *Agricultural Possibilities at Sosua Settlement* (New York [1940]), 1–2.

40. Earl P. Hanson, "New Citizens for Dominica," *Christian Science Monitor*, Weekly Magazine Section, August 10, 1940, p. 13; Joseph A. Rosen, "New Neighbors in Sosua," *Survey Graphic*, xxx (September, 1941), 474–478; Dominican Republic Settlement Association, Inc., *Sosua: Haven for Refugees in the Dominican Republic* (New York, 1941), 4, 6, 8–10, 16; *FR, 1941* (Washington, 1958), i, 438; *FR, 1942* (Washington, 1960), i, 451–452; *Refugee Settlement in the Dominican Republic: A Survey Conducted Under the Auspices of the Brookings Institution* (Washington, 1942), 285, 287, 327, 331, 332, 340; Holborn, *The International Refugee Organization*, 405.

41. *CJR*, ii (November–December, 1939), 45; *FR, 1939*, ii,

146; *Report of the Fourth Plenary Session of the Intergovernmental Committee on Refugees, August 15–17, 1944* (Washington [1944]), 24; Holborn, *The International Refugee Organization,* 9, 22–23.

## Chapter 4

1. *Nation,* cxlvii (December 10, 1938), 610.
2. *Interpreter Releases,* xv (April 18, 1938), 173; *NYT,* March 25, 1938, p. 8; Emanuel Celler to Cyrus Adler, April 5, 1938, ajc, Refugees, European Situation.
3. Mr. Schneiderman to Mr. Waldman, "Proposed imgn legisln," April 5, 1938, ajc, Immigration, 1939–; Harry Schneiderman to Dr. Cyrus Adler, April 7, 1938, Read Lewis to Samuel Dickstein, April 6, 1938, ajc, Refugees, European Situation; George S. Messersmith to Sumner Welles, April 7, 1938, na, State Department Records, File 150.01 Bills/34; *Interpreter Releases,* xv (April 18, 1938), 161.
4. Jewish People's Committee to Franklin D. Roosevelt, June 7, 1938, and January 31, 1939, fdr, of 3186. Proof of the Communist connections of this organization appeared in *Congress Bulletin,* vi (September 27, 1939), 1, and in Alexander S. Kohanski, "Communist Propaganda for Jews," *CJR,* iii (September–October, 1940), 473, 480–481. *Interpreter Releases,* xvi (January 23, 1939), 16; *NYT,* February 27, 1939, p. 4.
5. Robert R. Reynolds, "Aliens and the Unemployment Problem —It's High Time We Called a Halt!" *Vital Speeches of the Day,* iv (April 1, 1938), 363–365; *Junior American,* xv (August, 1940), 6; Alan Cranston, "Congress and the Alien," *CJR,* iii (May–June, 1940), 246, 248–250; *Interpreter Releases,* xvi (February 23, 1939), 55; "Informal Report on Immigration from Germany to the United States and Other Countries," mimeographed, November 21, 1939, p. 7, afsc, rs; *CJR,* iii (March–April, 1940), 141.
6. "Deportation of Aliens," *Hearings before a Subcommittee of the Committee on Immigration, United States Senate,* 76 Cong., 1 sess. (March 21, 22, and 23, 1939), 1–4.

7. Ibid., passim; unidentifiable writer to Dorothy Detzer, March 22, 1939, Swarthmore College Peace Collection, WILPF Correspondence, Refugees, 1939.

8. Dorothy Thompson, "Escape in a Frozen World," *Survey Graphic*, XXVIII (February, 1939), 168; Hertha Kraus to Anne Martin, November 25, 1938, AFSC, RS; James L. Houghteling to Franklin D. Roosevelt, January 5, 1940, FDR, OF 133.

9. *AJYB*, XLI (1939), 377–379; *CJR*, I (November, 1938), 56a; William L. Shirer, *The Rise and Fall of the Third Reich* (New York, 1960), 430.

10. Quentin Reynolds, "Unwanted," *Collier's*, CIII (February 11, 1939), 13; *Newsweek*, XII (November 21, 1938), 17; Shirer, *The Rise and Fall*, 431; *Parliamentary Debates*, CCCXLI, House of Commons (November 21, 1938), 1429–1430; *CJR*, II (January, 1939), 103, 107; *News Chronicle* (London), November 23, 1938, p. 1.

11. *CJR*, II (January, 1939), 42–43; Shirer, *The Rise and Fall*, 430–431.

12. *CJR*, I (November, 1938), 56c, II (January, 1939), 54–56, 64–65; Theodor H. Gaster, *A Digest of Nazi Legislation Against the Jews* (New York, 1940), 10. On the decrees eliminating Jews from German economic life, see above, p. 29.

13. Nevile Henderson, *Failure of a Mission: Berlin 1937–1939* (New York, 1940), 177; Lyman Cromwell White, *300,000 New Americans* (New York, 1957), 21–22; *AJYB*, XLI (1939), 384; *FR, 1938* (Washington, 1955), I, 821.

14. *Newsweek*, XII (November 28, 1938), 13–15, XII (December 5, 1938), 17–18; John Thomas Taylor to Franklin D. Roosevelt, November 25, 1938, FDR, OF 198; *NYT*, November 15, 1938, p. 1; *CJR*, I (November, 1938), 56d, 56g, 56h, II (January, 1939), 41–50.

15. *NYT*, November 16, 1938, p. 1; Hadley Cantril (ed.), *Public Opinion: 1935–1946* (Princeton, 1951), 382; Samuel I. Rosenman (ed.), *The Public Papers and Addresses of Franklin D. Roosevelt* (New York, 1941), VII, 598, 602–604; telegram James F. Byrnes to Franklin D. Roosevelt, November 16, 1938, Roosevelt to Byrnes, November 18, 1938, FDR, OF 3186.

16. *NYT*, December 9, 1938, p. 13; *Defender Magazine*, XIII (February, 1939), 3, 5, XIII (March, 1939), 18, XIV (July, 1939), 4; *Tablet*, XXIX (February 5, 1938), 11, XXX (March 26, 1938), 11,

xxx (May 14, 1938), 11, xxx (July 23, 1938), 7, xxx (October 15, 1938), 11, xxx (November 19, 1938), 1, 11, xxx (November 26, 1938), 1, 11, xxx (December 3, 1938), 1, 11, xxx (December 17, 1938), 1, 10, xxx (December 24, 1938), 1, 11; *Social Justice,* IIA (November 28, 1938), 7, 10–11, IIA (December 5, 1938), 7; George Maines to Marvin McIntyre, November 20, 1938, Malcolm Hatfield to McIntyre, December 6, 1938, FDR, OF 198-A.

17. *Commonweal,* XXIX (November 25, 1938), 113; *Catholic Worker,* VI (February, 1939), 2; *Collier's,* CII (December 31, 1938), 50; *Fellowship* (Fellowship of Reconciliation and Women's International League for Peace and Freedom), IV (December, 1938), 5, V (January, 1939), 14; *New Republic,* XCVII (November 23, 1938), 60; *Christian Century,* LV (November 30, 1938), 1456–1457.

18. Maurice R. Davie and Samuel Koenig, *The Refugees Are Now Americans,* Public Affairs Pamphlet No. 111 (New York, 1945), 17–18; "Excerpts from letters to the Children's Committee in Amsterdam," November 15, 1938, AFSC, RS; Quentin Reynolds, "Unwanted," 12, 28; John Hope Simpson, *Refugees: A Review of the Situation Since September 1938* (London, 1939), 27; "Admission of German Refugee Children," *Joint Hearings before a Subcommittee of the Committee on Immigration, United States Senate, and a Subcommittee of the Committee on Immigration and Naturalization, House of Representatives,* 76 Cong., 1 sess. (April 20, 21, 22, and 24, 1939), 16, 73.

19. William Rosenwald to Morris D. Waldman, "Re: Possibility of German Children Coming to the United States," December 2, 1938, AJC, Immigration, 1939–; *Nation,* CXLVII (December 10, 1938), 610; Marion E. Kenworthy to Clarence E. Pickett, January 7, 1939, AFSC, GF†; Kenworthy to Pickett, February 11, 1939, Minutes of a Meeting, March 16, 1940, pp. 7, 16, 22, AFSC, GF; "Admission of German Refugee Children," *Joint Hearings,* 121.

20. G.T. Furst to Clarence Pickett, January 6, 1939, Rufus Jones, "Night letter sent January 6th, 1939 to the attached list," Non-Sectarian Committee "News Letter," mimeographed, May 8, 1939, AFSC, GF; *CR,* LXXXIV, Part 2, 76 Cong., 1 sess., 1279; *NYT,* January 10, 1939, p. 9, February 9, 1939, p. 5; "German Refugee Children," radio address by Senator Robert F. Wagner from Washington, D.C., June 7, 1939, reprinted in *CR,* LXXXIV, Part 13, 76 Cong., 1 sess., A2473; "Admission of German Refugee Children," *Joint Hear-*

*ings,* 50; telegram Boris Shishkin to Robert F. Wagner, February 8, 1939, Robert F. Wagner Papers, Georgetown University. Actually, Representative John Dingell (D.) of Michigan introduced a bill identical to those of Senator Wagner and Mrs. Rogers one day before Mrs. Rogers submitted hers. However, in all the deliberations that followed, it was assumed that Mrs. Rogers was the author of the bill in the House.

21. "Admission of German Refugee Children," *Joint Hearings,* 15–16, 50, 53; Non-Sectarian Committee Press Release, March 2, 1939, Non-Sectarian Committee "News Letter," mimeographed, May 8, 1939, AFSC, GF.

22. Marion E. Kenworthy to Clarence E. Pickett, February 11, 1939, Non-Sectarian Committee Press Release, March 31, 1939, AFSC, GF; "Admission of German Refugee Children," *Joint Hearings,* 146.

23. "A Brief Statement Regarding the Wagner-Rogers Bill for Refugee Children," n.d., Winthrop Johnson to the mailing list of the California Division of the Non-Sectarian Committee, August 23, 1939, AFSC, GF; "Admission of German Refugee Children," *Joint Hearings,* 14, 16, 28, 44, 78, 81–82, 85–86, 124, 169, 171, 172, 175, 180, 201; *NYT,* February 9, 1939, p. 5; *CR,* LXXXIV, 76 Cong., 1 sess., 1458, 2338, 5200; *Congress Bulletin,* V (June 16, 1939), 1; Mabel Brown Ellis, *Refugees: December 1939* (New York, 1939), 2; *American Child,* XXI (April, 1939), 4; *Los Angeles Times,* August 4, 1939, clipping in Robert F. Wagner Papers, Georgetown University.

24. *CR,* LXXXIV, 76 Cong., 1 sess., 1457–1458, 2338–2341, 2805, 3865–3868, 4817–4819, and Appendix pages 641–642, 665–666, 835–836, 1073–1074, 1294, 1681–1682, 1886–1887, 2057–2059, 2792–2794, 3299; "Admission of German Refugee Children," *Joint Hearings,* 8, 45–49.

25. Ibid., 183, 205, 215, 224, 230; John Higham, *Strangers in the Land: Patterns of American Nativism 1860–1925* (New York, 1963), 319–321; John B. Trevor, "Humanitarian to Whom—American Children or Foreign Children?" mimeographed, February 20, 1939, copy in Robert F. Wagner Papers, Georgetown University; Minutes of a Meeting, March 16, 1940, p. 13, AFSC, GF; *CJR,* II (May–June, 1939), 95; *National Legionnaire,* V (May, 1939), 2.

26. *Official Proceedings of the Fifty-fifth Regular and Eighteenth*

Biennial Session of the National Council of the Junior Order United American Mechanics of the United States of North America (York, Pa., 1941), 114–116; Junior American, XIII (June, 1938), 1, XIII (July, 1938), 4; "Admission of German Refugee Children," Joint Hearings, 205, 206, 227, 236, 274–275.

27. Ibid., 183, 189, 190, 215, 229; "Admission of German Refugee Children," Hearings before the Committee on Immigration and Naturalization, House of Representatives, 76 Cong., 1 sess. (May 24, 25, 31, and June 1 [and 13], 1939), 134, 211, 213.

28. John Cecil, American Immigration Conference Board, Inc., New York City, "America's Children Are America's Problem! Refugee Children in Europe Are Europe's Problem!" n.d., AFSC, RS†; "Admission of German Refugee Children," Joint Hearings, 72, 79, 84, 111, 113, 144–145, 150, 163, 227–228; CR, LXXXIV, Part 14, 76 Cong., 1 sess., A3981; "Admission of German Refugee Children," Hearings before the Committee on Immigration and Naturalization, House of Representatives, 74; "Miamians Divided on Refuge for 20,000 German Children," Miami Herald, April 25, 1939, p. 1B. This newspaper article, a small survey of Miami, Florida, public opinion on the Wagner-Rogers Bill, showed that opponents of the proposal based their views on the "charity begins at home" theme.

29. Carbon copy of an extract from a letter with the penciled notation "type of criticism," n.d., AFSC, RS†; "Admission of German Refugee Children," Joint Hearings, 56–58, 61, 74, 131–132, 135, 138; Simpson, Refugees: A Review of the Situation, 30–31.

30. Right Reverend Monseigneur Michael J. Ready to Robert F. Wagner, April 6, 1939, Wagner to Msgr. Ready, April 17, 1939, Msgr. Ready to Wagner, May 3, 1939, Robert F. Wagner Papers, Georgetown University.

31. Most Reverend Joseph F. Rummel to Clarence E. Pickett, February 20, 1940, AFSC, GF†; "The Situation Which Justifies the Wagner-Rogers Bill," a statement by "a Jewish social worker recently returned from Germany," n.d., AFSC, GF.

32. Non-Sectarian Committee leaflets, form letters, press releases, news bulletins, and similar material are in AFSC, GF; Samuel Dickstein to Robert F. Wagner, April 4, 1939, Robert F. Wagner Papers, Georgetown University; "Admission of German Refugee Children," Joint Hearings, 216.

33. Clarence E. Pickett to Dear Friend [October, 1939], Winthrop

Johnson to Pickett, September 29, 1939, Winthrop Johnson to the mailing list of the California Division of the Non-Sectarian Committee, August 23, 1939, "News Letter—California Division," August 23, 1939, p. 2, AFSC, GF; Winthrop Johnson to Pickett, January 30, 1940, AFSC, GF†.

34. "Minutes of the Meeting of December 17, 1939," p. 1, "Congressional Poll, Subject: Refugee Immigration," March 24, 1939, AFSC, GF.

35. "Congressional Poll, Subject: Refugee Immigration," March 24, 1939, AFSC, GF.

36. Ibid.; "Digest of opinions on Increasing Quotas . . ." [May, 1938], p. 2, AJC, Immigration, 1939–; Jacob Billikopf to Minna L. Ruppert, April 24, 1939, Robert F. Wagner Papers, Georgetown University; telegram James F. Byrnes to Franklin D. Roosevelt, November 16, 1938, FDR, OF 3186; "Admission of German Refugee Children," *Joint Hearings*, 124–125; Winthrop Johnson to Betty Johnson, August 9, 1939, AFSC, GF†.

37. Clarence E. Pickett to Mrs. Dorothy Canfield Fisher, March 31, 1939, telegram Pickett to Mrs. Carl Rice, April 5, 1939, AFSC, GF; a list of notes on the attitudes of certain members of Congress regarding the Wagner-Rogers Bill, beginning "SENATE, 1. Austin, Vermont" [late March, 1939], AFSC, GF†.

38. The contents of this and the previous two paragraphs are supported by material scattered throughout "Admission of German Refugee Children," *Joint Hearings*. Most of the testimony of opponents of the Wagner-Rogers Bill appears in pages 183–280; that of the proponents in pages 49–182.

39. *Nation*, CXLIX (July 1, 1939), 3; "Admission of German Refugee Children," *Joint Hearings*, 184–186, 223, 225; *CJR*, II (May–June, 1939), 95.

40. "Admission of German Refugee Children," *Joint Hearings*, 6, 16, 65–66, 98; "Minutes of Meeting of June 27, 1939," of Non-Sectarian Committee, p. 27, AFSC, RS.

41. "Admission of German Refugee Children," *Joint Hearings*, 278; *Junior American*, XIV (May, 1939), 9; J.H. Patten, "Memorandum Re Wagner Resolution Propaganda," May 9, 1939, NA, Legislative Branch, File SEN 76A-E2.

42. "Minutes of Refugee Committee," April 28, 1939, AFSC, Minutes; *Commonweal*, XXX (June 23, 1939), 228; *Survey Midmonthly*, LXXV (May, 1939), 141.

43. "German Refugee Children," radio address by Senator Robert F. Wagner, June 7, 1939; "Report of the Joint Sub-Committee of the Committees on Immigration of the Senate and House of Representatives" [May 5, 1939], NA, Legislative Branch, File SEN 76A-E2; Robert F. Wagner to Anton Pros, May 12, 1939, Robert F. Wagner Papers, Georgetown University; Non-Sectarian Committee "News Letter," mimeographed, May 8, 1939, AFSC, GF; *New York Herald Tribune,* May 9, 1939, p. 24; Agnes Inglis to Clarence Pickett, May 8, 1939, AFSC, GF†; *National Legionnaire,* V (May, 1939), 1.

44. "Minutes of Meeting of May 22, 1939," of Non-Sectarian Committee, pp. 22–23, AFSC, GF.

45. "Admission of German Refugee Children," *Hearings before the Committee on Immigration and Naturalization, House of Representatives,* passim. Specific reference is to page 131. Hereafter this source will be referred to as "Admission of German Refugee Children," *House Hearings.*

46. Ibid., passim. Specific reference is to pages 31–32.

47. "Admission of German Refugee Children," *Joint Hearings,* 190–191, 206, 216, 218–219, 225, 232–233, 240–241, 247; "Admission of German Refugee Children," *House Hearings,* 7–13, 33, 48, 65–66, 209, 286, 294.

48. Ibid., 96, 164–165, 166, 292–293; *CR,* LXXXIV, Part 4, 76 Cong., 1 sess., 3671–3672.

49. "Admission of German Refugee Children," *House Hearings,* 165; *CR,* LXXXI, Part 6, 75 Cong., 1 sess., 6581–6583, LXXXIV, Part 4, 76 Cong., 1 sess., 3671–3672.

50. "Admission of German Refugee Children," *House Hearings,* 5, 12, 24–25, 81, 201–205, 231, 296, 302–303; Committee Print for H.J. Res. 168, June 1, 1939, NA, Legislative Branch, File HR 76A-D15 #15102; "News Letter—California Division," August 23, 1939, p. 2, AFSC, GF.

51. Clarence Pickett to Martha Balderston, May 31, 1939, AFSC, GF†; "Minutes of Refugee Committee," May 26, 1939, AFSC, Minutes.

52. "Admission of German Refugee Children," *House Hearings,* 203, 205; Avra M. Warren to George S. Messersmith, August 10, 1939, NA, State Department Records, File 150.01 Bills/151; "Minutes of Refugee Committee," June 16, 1939, AFSC, Minutes; Eleanor Slater to Harvey Perry, June 23, 1939, AFSC, GF†.

53. Report of the Senate Committee on Immigration on S.J. Res. 64, 5-page typescript [June 30, 1939], NA, Legislative Branch, File SEN 76A-E2; "Statement of Senator Robert F. Wagner of N.Y., on Senate Immigration Committee Action Concerning Wagner-Rogers Resolution," press release, July 3, 1939, Robert F. Wagner Papers, Georgetown University; *New York Herald Tribune*, July 3, 1939, p. 1.

54. "News Letter—California Division," August 23, 1939, p. 2, AFSC, GF.

55. Interview with Philip Levy of Washington, D.C., May 15, 1965. At the time that the Wagner-Rogers Bill was before Congress, Mr. Levy was Senator Wagner's Legislative Counsel.

56. Marion E. Kenworthy to Clarence E. Pickett, July 11, 1939, Pickett to Cecilia Razovsky, July 19, 1939, AFSC, GF; Margaret E. Jones to Mrs. Hull, Miss Balch, and others, July 14, 1939, Swarthmore College Peace Collection, WILPF Correspondence, Refugees, 1939; H.J. Res. 362, introduced by Charles Kramer (D.) of California, on July 14, 1939, copy in NA, Legislative Branch, File SEN 76A-E2.

57. *American Vindicator*, I (July, 1939), 1; *New York Herald Tribune*, July 3, 1939, p. 1; *Nation*, CXLIX (July 8, 1939), 29; Robert F. Wagner to Shelden D. Elliott, July 29, 1939, Robert F. Wagner Papers, Georgetown University; *NYT*, July 1, 1939, p. 3; "Temporary Prohibition of Immigration of Aliens," *Senate Report*, 76 Cong., 1 sess., No. 757 (July 11, 1939).

58. "News Letter—California Division," August 23, 1939, p. 1, Katherine C. Blackburn to Marion Kenworthy, September 10, 1939, AFSC, GF.

59. Clarence E. Pickett to John J.M. O'Shea, September 6, 1939, Katherine C. Blackburn to Marion Kenworthy, September 10, 1939, telegrams Pickett to Winthrop Johnson, September 5, 1939, and September 14, 1939, AFSC, GF; "Informal Report on Immigration from Germany to the United States and Other Countries," mimeographed, November 21, 1939, p. 7, AFSC, RS; "Minutes of Refugee Committee," November 17, 1939, December 14, 1939, AFSC, Minutes; *Newsweek*, XIV (July 10, 1939), 52.

60. Clarence E. Pickett to Winthrop Johnson, September 22, 1939, Justine Wise Polier to Pickett, August 19, 1939, "Memorandum on the Meeting, August 17, 1939," "Memorandum—Meeting

of August 25, 1939," Pickett to Marion R. Stern, November 11, 1939, "Minutes of the Meeting of November 20, 1939," pp. 7–8, 13, 16–20, "Minutes of the Meeting of December 10, 1939," pp. 5, 19, 21, "Minutes of the Meeting of December 17, 1939," pp. 7–8, Pickett to Members of the Foreign Service Section, July 18, 1939, Pickett to Most Rev. Abp. Joseph F. Rummel, November 20, 1939, Pickett to Msgr. Michael J. Ready, December 22, 1939, AFSC, GF; "Minutes of Refugee Committee," November 17, 1939, December 14, 1939, January 26, 1940, AFSC, Minutes.

61. "Memorandum on Proposed Plan to Aid Refugee Children," December 13, 1939, "Minutes of the Meeting of December 17, 1939," Minutes of a Meeting, March 16, 1940, Press Release of Non-Sectarian Foundation for Refugee Children, April 18, 1940, Owen R. Lovejoy to the Executive Committee, May 9, 1940, AFSC, GF; *CR*, LXXXVI, Part 15, 76 Cong., 3 sess., A2910.

62. Clarence E. Pickett to Clarence E. Pickett, sample of a form letter to members of the Non-Sectarian Foundation for Refugee Children, September 23, 1940, "Minutes of Special Meeting of Directors," Non-Sectarian Foundation, July 9, 1940, AFSC, GF.

63. Katharine F. Lenroot, chief of the United States Children's Bureau, stated that "ten thousand children 14 years of age or under represent three one hundredths of 1 percent of the total child population of the country under the age of 15 years according to the 1930 census." ("Admission of German Refugee Children," *House Hearings*, 76.) *Miami Herald*, April 25, 1939, p. 1B.

64. *CR*, LXXXIV, Part 14, 76 Cong., 1 sess., A3237.

65. Charles Herbert Stember and others, *Jews in the Mind of America* (New York, 1966), 149.

66. William Rosenwald to Morris D. Waldman, "Re: Possibility of German Children Coming to the United States," December 2, 1938, AJC, Immigration, 1939–; George S. Messersmith to Sumner Welles, December 15, 1938, NA, State Department Records, File 150.01/2617½; "Admission of German Refugee Children," *Joint Hearings*, 125; "Admission of German Refugee Children," *House Hearings*, 71; "Deportation of Aliens," *Hearings before a Subcommittee*, 24, 111.

67. Cordell Hull to Senator Richard B. Russell, Jr., March 31, 1939, NA, Legislative Branch, File SEN 76A-E2; T.C. Achilles to Sumner Welles, December 24, 1938, Achilles to George S. Messer-

smith, December 29, 1938, NA, State Department Records, File 840.48 Refugees/1224; Messersmith to Welles, December 27, 1938, NA, State Department Records, File 840.48 Refugees/1225.

68. George S. Messersmith to Hull, Welles, Moffat, Achilles, January 23, 1939, NA, State Department Records, File 150.01 Bills/99.

69. Interview with Philip Levy of Washington, D.C., May 15, 1965.

70. Clarence E. Pickett to Marion R. Stern, November 11, 1939, Minutes of a Meeting, March 16, 1940, p. 2, AFSC, GF.

71. "Admission of German Refugee Children," *House Hearings,* 71–72; telegram Eleanor Roosevelt to Franklin D. Roosevelt, February 22, 1939, telegram Franklin D. Roosevelt to Eleanor Roosevelt [February 22, 1939], FDR, OF 200–MMM; EMW [Edwin M. Watson] to Franklin D. Roosevelt, June 2, 1939, FDR, OF 3186.

72. Clarence E. Pickett to Marion E. Kenworthy, January 17, 1939, AFSC, GF†; Rufus M. Jones to Owen D. Young, February 7, 1939, AFSC, GF; "Admission of German Refugee Children," *Joint Hearings,* 17 (from Montgomery, Alabama, *Advertiser* of February 17, 1939); *NYT,* February 14, 1939, p. 12.

73. Gladys Bendit Skelton [John Presland, pseud.], *A Great Adventure: the Story of the Refugee Children's Movement* (London, 1944), 5; "Admission of German Refugee Children," *House Hearings,* 17; Stefan K. Schimanski, "Refugee Children in England," *CJR,* II (July–August, 1939), 23

## Chapter 5

1. Charles A. Buckley to Franklin D. Roosevelt, November 18, 1938, Sumner Welles to Roosevelt, December 7, 1938, Roosevelt to Buckley, December 8, 1938, FDR, OF 3186.

2. *NYT,* November 24, 1938, p. 8, August 16, 1939, p. 7; *The Problem of Alaskan Development* (Washington, 1939), 1–8, 11, 16–29. Pagination is that of the 46-page edition.

3. Ibid., 37–38.

4. Ibid., 38–41.

5. Ernest Gruening to Harold L. Ickes, October 28, 1939, Paul W. Gordon to E.K. Berlew, December 13, 1939, NA, Social and Economic Branch, Department of Interior File 9-1-2.

6. The Secretary of the Interior to the Director of the Division of Territories, November 10, 1939, NA, Social and Economic Branch, Department of Interior File 9-1-2.

7. Harold L. Ickes to Franklin D. Roosevelt, October 18, 1939, Roosevelt to Sumner Welles, October 19, 1939, Welles to Roosevelt, October 19, 1939, NA, Social and Economic Branch, Department of Interior File 9-1-2.

8. Harold L. Ickes, *The Secret Diary of Harold L. Ickes: Volume III: The Lowering Clouds, 1939–1941* (New York, 1954), 56–57, quotations by permission of the publisher, Simon and Schuster, Inc.

9. *Junior American,* XIV (November, 1939), 8; Department of Interior press release, February 11, 1940, NA, Social and Economic Branch, Department of Interior File 9-1-2.

10. *NYT,* August 18, 1939, p. 6; *CJR,* II (September–October, 1939), 83; Harold L. Ickes to Robert A. Taft, April 29, 1940, NA, Social and Economic Branch, Department of Interior File 9-1-2; Ickes, *Secret Diary,* III, 56, quotation by permission of the publisher, Simon and Schuster, Inc.

11. Luther Huston, "Alaska Weighed as a Refugee Haven," *NYT,* August 27, 1939, IV, p. 7; *American Vindicator,* I (November, 1939), 2.

12. Department of Interior press release, February 11, 1940, NA, Social and Economic Branch, Department of Interior File 9-1-2.

13. This and the preceding paragraph are based on the King-Havenner Bill itself (S. 3577; H.R. 8931). A copy appears in "Settlement and Development of Alaska," *Hearings before a Subcommittee of the Committee on Territories and Insular Affairs, United States Senate,* 76 Cong., 3 sess. (May 13, 15, 18, 1940), 1–5.

14. Interview with Clarence E. Pickett, December 14, 1964; Minutes of American Committee for Christian Refugees, mimeographed, May 3, 1940, AFSC, GF; Robert Marshall, "Should We Settle Alaska?" *New Republic,* CII (January 8, 1940), 49–50, and a letter in reply on page 54.

15. "Minutes of Refugee Committee," February 21, 1939, April 28, 1939, AFSC, Minutes; Harry Slattery to Robert K. Straus, August

22, 1939, NA, Social and Economic Branch, Department of Interior File 9-1-2.

16. Ibid.; "Statement of the National Committee for Alaskan Development" [October, 1939], Beatrice B. Schalet to Clarence E. Pickett, January 19, 1940, AFSC, GF†; "Organizations to Promote Development of Alaska," October 11, 1939, Erwin H. Klaus to Pickett, November 25, 1939, John F. Rich to Klaus, December 4, 1939, AFSC, GF.

17. "Memorandum on Proposed Alaskan Development Corporation Bill" [January, 1940], AFSC, GF†.

18. Roy Anderson to Vilhjalmur Stefansson, October 3, 1939, copy in AFSC, GF; editorial clipped from *Alaska Weekly*, May 24, 1940, NA, Legislative Branch, File SEN 76A-E1.

19. "Settlement and Development of Alaska," *Hearings before a Subcommittee*, 244–245, 248–249.

20. Ibid., passim. The quotations cited appear on pages 119, 170, 231.

21. Department of the Interior, General Land Office, "Statement of Materials for Hearings: Alaska Development Bill," mimeographed, May 6, 1940, NA, Legislative Branch, File SEN 76A-E1; "Settlement and Development of Alaska," *Hearings before a Subcommittee*, passim. The quotation appears on page 7.

22. Ibid., passim. Specific references and quotations can be found on pages 72, 92–94, 99, 131, 136–138.

23. Ibid., 85, 94, 128, 148, 150, 152, 229–230.

24. Ibid., 84, 85, 97–98, 128, 148, 150–152, 237.

25. Ibid., 151; *NYT,* December 10, 1940, p. 30.

26. Jack Underwood to Foster L. McGovern, May 15, 1940, Mrs. Paul Scharf to Millard E. Tydings, June 7, 1940, Tydings to Mrs. Scharf, June 14, 1940, NA, Legislative Branch, File SEN 76A-E1; Lex Green to C.H. Phillips, June 1, 1940, Green to J.J. Underwood, June 14, 1940, NA, Legislative Branch, File HR 76A-D37 #15469.

27. *NYT,* December 10, 1940, p. 30. Dickstein introduced his bill, H.R. 2791, on January 29, 1941. *CR,* LXXXVII, Part 10, 77 Cong., 1 sess., A419; Anthony J. Dimond to Samuel Dickstein, February 17, 1941, J.H. Kelly to James L. Wilmeth, March 4, 1941, Kelly to Felix Cohen, March 7, 1941, Alaska Senate Joint Memorial No. 12, March 19, 1941, NA, Legislative Branch, File HR 77A-D14 #15919; *Junior American,* XVI (February, 1941), 5.

28. Ickes, *Secret Diary,* III, 475; Vilhjalmur Stefansson, "Alaska," *Harper's Magazine,* CLXXXIII (June, 1941), 87–88, 90, 92; F.L. Kerzie to Harold L. Ickes, September 23, 1941, NA, Social and Economic Branch, Department of Interior File 9-1-2.

29. Nathan R. Margold to Harold L. Ickes, December 26, 1940, NA, Social and Economic Branch, Department of Interior File 9-0-12.

30. Cordell Hull to D.W. Bell, March 29, 1938, FDR, OF 133; Harold L. Ickes to Robert H. Jackson, March 21, 1940, appendix to memorandum from Frederic L. Kirgis to Ickes, August 9, 1940, Nathan R. Margold to Ickes, December 26, 1940, December 27, 1940, Frances Perkins to Ickes, February 3, 1940, NA, Social and Economic Branch, Department of Interior File 9-0-12. The clause authorizing the governor of the Virgin Islands to waive visa requirements for visiting aliens in emergency cases was repeated in Executive Order 8430 of June 5, 1940.

31. Appendix to memorandum from Frederic L. Kirgis to Harold L. Ickes, August 9, 1940, Robert H. Jackson to Ickes, October 23, 1939, Frances Perkins to Ickes, February 3, 1940, Cordell Hull to Ickes, December 15, 1939, Jackson to Ickes, March 29, 1940, NA, Social and Economic Branch, Department of Interior File 9-0-12.

32. Felix S. Cohen to Clarence Pickett, November 7, 1940, "Minutes of Meeting Held November 15, 1940, in the Department of the Interior . . . ," AFSC, GF; "Minutes of Meeting Held November 15, 1940, in Secretary's Conference Room, Department of the Interior . . . ," NA, Social and Economic Branch, Department of Interior File 9-11-26; *NYT,* December 10, 1940, p. 30; *New Republic,* CIII (December 2, 1940), 741; Nathan R. Margold to Harold L. Ickes, December 26, 1940, NA, Social and Economic Branch, Department of Interior File 9-0-12; American Jewish Committee, Committee on Peace Studies, "The Virgin Islands," mimeographed, November 14, 1940, pp. 7–10, copy in American Jewish Committee Library.

33. Ward M. Canaday to Marvin H. McIntyre, December 10, 1940, Canaday to Franklin D. Roosevelt, December 10, 1940, FDR, OF 6-Q.

34. Proposed Proclamation by the Governor of the Virgin Islands, under cover of "Opinion of the Legal Adviser, Department of State," December 16, 1940, FDR, OF 3186; BL Diary, 1940, pp. 204–205.

35. Nathan R. Margold to Harold L. Ickes, December 26, 1940,

NA, Social and Economic Branch, Department of Interior File 9-0-12; Max Gottschalk to Felix S. Cohen, November 20, 1940, AFSC, GF; Oscar L. Chapman to Gottschalk, November 29, 1940, Margold to Ickes, December 16, 1940, NA, Social and Economic Branch, Department of Interior File 9-11-26; "Opinion of the Legal Adviser, Department of State," December 16, 1940, Franklin D. Roosevelt to Ickes, December 18, 1940, FDR, OF 3186.

36. Nathan R. Margold to Harold L. Ickes, December 26, 1940, December 27, 1940, Ickes to Robert H. Jackson, February 21, 1941, Ickes to Cordell Hull, March 12, 1941, Hull to Ickes, April 3, 1941, Margold to Ickes, May 9, 1941, Ickes to Hull, June 3, 1941, NA, Social and Economic Branch, Department of Interior File 9-0-12.

37. Special arrangements made for political refugees are discussed in chapter 7.

38. BL Diary, 1940, p. 204. Fuller treatment of Breckinridge Long's response to the problem of possible subversive agents among refugees appears in chapters 7 through 9.

## Chapter 6

1. AJYB, XLIII (1941), 323; NYT, June 11, 1940, p. 10, June 15, 1940, p. 3, June 16, 1940, p. 32, June 23, 1940, IV, p. 8, November 8, 1940, p. 20; Morris C. Troper, "The Everlasting Mercy," address delivered on September 10, 1941, copy in AFSC, GF.

2. NYT, June 12, 1940, p. 25; Clarence E. Pickett to Dr. Bernard Sheil, June 14, 1940, AFSC, GF; Francis Biddle to Franklin D. Roosevelt, June 14, 1940, James H. Rowe to Roosevelt, June 15, 1940, FDR, OF 3186; Sumner Welles to Cordell Hull, June 17, 1940, NA, State Department Records, File 811.111 Refugees/118; Robert T. Pell to Julian F. Harrington, June 25, 1940, NA, State Department Records, File 840.48 Refugees/2175; "Minutes of Refugee Committee," June 20, 1940, AFSC, Minutes.

3. NYT, June 6, 1940, p. 1, June 8, 1940, p. 1, June 16, 1940, p. 1, June 19, 1940, p. 5, June 20, 1940, p. 1

4. Ibid., June 26, 1940, p. 12; *Time,* xxxvi (July 15, 1940), 10.

5. *NYT,* June 10, 1940, through September 3, 1940; *Life,* ix (July 22, 1940), 11–15; *Christian Century,* lvii (July 3, 1940), 846–847.

6. See above, p. 94; *NYT,* June 21, 1940, pp. 1, 13, June 22, 1940, p. 7, June 23, 1940, p. 28, July 4, 1940, p. 3, July 6, 1940, p. 2, July 11, 1940, p. 9; Kathryn Close, *Transplanted Children* (New York, 1953), 1–2; "Report on the Use of Volunteers in the United States Committee for the Care of European Children, Inc.," mimeographed, November 23, 1940, p. 2, afsc, gf.

7. Raymond Clapper, "Let's Save the Children," *Washington Daily News,* July 6, 1940, copy in fdr, of 3186; Franklin D. Roosevelt to Stephen T. Early, July 8, 1940, Early to Roosevelt, July 8, 1940, fdr, of 3186.

8. "The Press Conferences of President Franklin D. Roosevelt," xvi, Press Conference No. 659 (July 9, 1940), 29, Franklin D. Roosevelt Library; telegram Joseph P. Kennedy to Cordell Hull, July 10, 1940, na, State Department Records, File 811.111 Refugees/141; *NYT,* July 11, 1940, p. 9.

9. *Department of State Bulletin,* iii (July 13, 1940), 23; Harold L. Ickes, *The Secret Diary of Harold L. Ickes: Volume III: The Lowering Clouds, 1939–1941* (New York, 1954), 239, quotation by permission of the publisher, Simon and Schuster, Inc.

10. *Department of State Bulletin,* iii (July 20, 1940), 31–33.

11. Ibid.

12. Ibid.; *NYT,* September 25, 1940, p. 21.

13. Ibid., July 13, 1940, p. 11, July 17, 1940, p. 19, July 19, 1940, p. 19; *Parliamentary Debates,* ccclxiii, House of Commons (July 18, 1940), 394–395.

14. *NYT,* July 17, 1940, p. 13, July 18, 1940, p. 17, July 19, 1940, p. 19, July 23, 1940, p. 15, July 24, 1940, p. 12.

15. *CR,* lxxxvi, Part 9, 76 Cong., 3 sess., 10028; *NYT,* July 27, 1940, p. 1.

16. "Statement by Mrs. Harold D. Pulsifer—Co-Chairman American Women's Committee for the Release of Mercy Ships for Children," July 27, 1940, afsc, gf†; *NYT,* July 27, 1940, p. 12.

17. "The Press Conferences of President Franklin D. Roosevelt," xvi, Press Conferences Nos. 663 and 668 (July 26, 1940, and August 9, 1940), 68–70, 108, Franklin D. Roosevelt Library;

Franklin D. Roosevelt to Caroline O'Day, August 12, 1940, O'Day to Roosevelt, August 14, 1940, FDR, OF 3186; *NYT*, August 17, 1940, p. 7; Hadley Cantril (ed.), *Public Opinion: 1935–1946* (Princeton, 1951), 1150.

18. *NYT*, August 3, 1940, p. 17, August 6, 1940, p. 21, August 7, 1940, p. 10; *CR*, LXXXVI, Part 9, 76 Cong., 3 sess., 9861, 9872–9873, 9904, 10003–10033.

19. Ibid., 10006, 10007, 10020, 10032.

20. Ibid., 10028–10030, 10033.

21. Ibid., 10009–10010, 10020–10022.

22. Ibid., 10004, 10016, 10020, 10033; *NYT*, August 8, 1940, p. 1.

23. Ibid., August 9, 1940, p. 13, August 14, 1940, p. 11; "Permitting American Vessels to Assist in Evacuation of Refugee Children," *Senate Report*, 76 Cong., 3 sess., No. 2012 (August 16, 1940); *CR*, LXXXVI, Part 10, 76 Cong., 3 sess., 10471–10472.

24. Mrs. Harold T. Pulsifer to Clarence E. Pickett, August 24, 1940, Pickett to Mrs. Pulsifer, September 5, 1940, AFSC, GF; *NYT*, August 22, 1940, p. 21, August 27, 1940, p. 19, August 29, 1940, pp. 2, 18, August 30, 1940, p. 8.

25. Close, *Transplanted Children*, 5–7; *NYT*, September 2, 1940, p. 1, September 23, 1940, p. 1, September 27, 1940, p. 1, October 3, 1940, p. 3, October 10, 1940, p. 10, November 3, 1940, p. 17.

26. *Workmen's Circle Call*, VIII (August–September, 1940), 16; Francis R. Bellamy, "Campaign Memorandum," n.d., AFSC, GF; *NYT*, August 17, 1940, p. 5; *Christian Century*, LVII (August 21, 1940), 1019.

27. In the Preface it was stated that this study would confine itself to refugees who needed to emigrate to avoid Nazi persecution because of their political views or religious background.

28. *NYT*, July 6, 1940, p. 2.

29. Ibid., July 29, 1940, p. 12; New York *Daily News*, August 9, 1940, p. 21; *Collier's*, CVI (August 10, 1940), 54; "The Press Conferences of President Franklin D. Roosevelt," XVI, Press Conference No. 668 (August 9, 1940), 108, Franklin D. Roosevelt Library; Ray Atherton to Sumner Welles, August 8, 1940, August 9, 1940, NA, State Department Records, File 811.111 Refugees /282.

30. *NYT*, December 28, 1940, p. 4; *Community Service Release*

(National Refugee Service), No. 6 (January 31, 1941), 7; "Brief Memorandum on the Condition of Women and Children Interned in Southern France," May 26, 1941, AFSC, GF.

31. "To Provide a Temporary Haven from the Dangers or Effects of War for European Children Under the Age of Sixteen," *Hearings before the Committee on Immigration and Naturalization, House of Representatives,* 76 Cong., 3 sess. (August 8 and 9, 1940 [sic, actually the correct dates are August 7 and 8, 1940]), 2–6, 13, 15–22, 26–35.

32. Ibid., 23; "Providing a Temporary Haven from the Dangers or Effects of War for European Children Under the Age of 16 Years," *House Report,* 76 Cong., 3 sess., No. 2846 (August 12, 1940); *CR,* LXXXVI, Part 9, 76 Cong., 3 sess., 10031.

33. *NYT,* August 9, 1940, p. 1; E.E. Cox to J.H. Kelly, August 9, 1940, copy of H. Res. 571, introduced by Rudolph G. Tenerowicz, August 20, 1940, NA, Legislative Branch, File HR 76A-D15; Caroline O'Day to Franklin D. Roosevelt, August 14, 1940, FDR, OF 3186.

34. *Christian Register,* CXXII (November, 1943), 413; James Ford Lewis, "The Unitarian Service Committee," Ph.D. dissertation, University of California, June, 1952, p. 15, copy at offices of Unitarian Universalist Service Committee, Boston; United States Committee, "Report of the Executive Director to the Board of Directors," mimeographed, January, 1941, pp. 41–42, copy in AFSC, RS.

35. Howard L. Brooks, *Prisoners of Hope* (New York, 1942), 157, 160; *We Are Standing By: A Report of the United States Committee for the Care of European Children's Program, Accomplishments, and Present Status* (New York, 1941); memorandum from United States Committee to Howard Kershner, February 7, 1941, Louis S. Weiss to Members of the Board of Directors, United States Committee, mimeographed, February 22, 1941, AFSC, GF; Close, *Transplanted Children,* 26–27; Isaac Chomski, "Children in Exile," *CJR,* IV (October, 1941), 522–528.

36. *Newscast* (American Committee for Christian Refugees), II (October–November, 1942), 1; *CJR,* V (October, 1942), 526–527, V (December, 1942), 633–635; Donald A. Lowrie, *The Hunted Children* (New York, 1963), 218–219.

37. Close, *Transplanted Children,* 27; Francis Biddle to Franklin D. Roosevelt, September 11, 1942, FDR, OF 3186; Margaret Frawley to Burritt Hiatt, October 2, 1942, Frawley to James G. Vail, C. Reed

Cary, and others, October 8, 1942, "Statement by Mr. George L. Warren," September 14, 1942, AFSC, GF; Lowrie, *The Hunted Children,* 223–224; Philip A. Conard, "Human Tragedy of the European Refugee," under cover of letter Conard to Marjorie P. Schauffler, August 18, 1943, AFSC, RS; "Notes on the Present Situation of Refugee Children in Southern France," May 27, 1943, Universalist Historical Society Library, Tufts University, Unitarian Universalist Service Committee Records, France: Reports.

38. Close, *Transplanted Children,* 28, 35, 48; Margaret Frawley to Clarence E. Pickett and James G. Vail, December 8, 1942, AFSC, GF.

## Chapter 7

1. Simpson estimated that roughly ten percent of refugees who had emigrated from Germany by the end of 1937 were political fugitives. (John Hope Simpson, *The Refugee Problem: Report of a Survey* [London, 1939], 563.) With widespread terror against Jews beginning in 1938, it is reasonable to conclude that the refugee flow after 1937 was more heavily Jewish than before, causing the proportion of political refugees to fall well below ten percent. Davie reported that five percent of the refugees who reached the United States were political fugitives. (Maurice R. Davie, *Refugees in America* [New York, 1947], 43.) Varian Fry, *Surrender on Demand* (New York, 1945), ix–x; *NYT,* June 26, 1940, p. 4.

2. *Department of State Bulletin,* III (December 21, 1940), 563–564.

3. Telegram H.F. Armstrong to Marguerite Le Hand, June 18, 1940, Edwin M. Watson to Armstrong [late June, 1940], NA, State Department Records, File 840.48 Refugees/2183; telegram Armstrong to Franklin D. Roosevelt, June 19, 1940, FDR, OF 198-A; Watson to Armstrong, June 29, 1940, FDR, OF 3186; William Green to Breckinridge Long, July 3, 1940, NA, State Department Records, File 811.111 Refugees/127; Jewish Labor Committee, *American Labor to the Rescue* (New York, 1941); Jewish Labor Committee,

*The Jewish Labor Committee: What It Does and What It Stands For* (New York, 1942); "Rescue of the Jewish and Other Peoples in Nazi-Occupied Territory," *Extract from Hearings before the Committee on Foreign Affairs, House of Representatives,* 78 Cong., 1 sess. (November 26, 1943), 20; *FR, 1940* (Washington, 1957), II, 239; BL Diary, 1940, p. 154; *Congress Bulletin,* VII (November 29, 1940), 16.

4. *FR, 1940,* II, 232–233; "Meeting in the Office of the Acting Secretary," July 26, 1940, NA, State Department Records, File 811. 111 Refugees /348.

5. Ibid.; *FR, 1940,* II, 232–234, 238; James G. McDonald and George L. Warren to Sumner Welles and Robert H. Jackson, July 31, 1940, NA, State Department Records, File 811.111 Refugees /194; Breckinridge Long to McDonald, October 2, 1940, NA, State Department Records, File 840.48 Refugees/2276.

6. See above, chapter 3, especially pp. 47–48, 61; "Minutes, Third Meeting of the President's Advisory Committee on Political Refugees," June 2, 1938, NA, State Department Records, File 840.48 Refugees/340.

7. *Statutes at Large of the United States of America,* XLIII, Part 1, 154; "To Provide a Temporary Haven from the Dangers or Effects of War for European Children Under the Age of Sixteen," *Hearings before the Committee on Immigration and Naturalization, House of Representatives,* 76 Cong., 3 sess. (August 8 and 9, 1940), 36–37. The standards established by the Immigration Act of 1917 are summarized in a note to Appendix II.

8. *FR, 1940,* II, 234; *Department of State Bulletin,* III (December 21, 1940), 564; James G. McDonald and George L. Warren to Sumner Welles and Robert H. Jackson, July 31, 1940, NA, State Department Records, File 811.111 Refugees/194; Breckinridge Long to Adolf A. Berle, Jr., February 7, 1941, BL Papers, Box 211; Davie, *Refugees in America,* 31–32. The special arrangement under which aliens in the United States on visitors' visas were able to leave the country briefly and reenter as quota immigrants is explained in chapter 8, p. 181.

9. James G. McDonald and George L. Warren to Sumner Welles and Robert H. Jackson, July 31, 1940, NA, State Department Records, File 811.111 Refugees/194; Emergency Rescue Committee, "Documents Necessary for Application for Special Emergency Visa,"

mimeographed, n.d., copy in AFSC, RS; copy of affidavit form, August 9, 1940, files of the International Rescue Committee, Inc., New York City.

10. Congressional hostility toward refugee immigration was examined in chapter 4.

11. Fry, *Surrender on Demand*, x, xii, 7, 12, 18–19, 41–45, 92, 170, 189, 190, 226; *NYT*, August 15, 1940, p. 8; Lisa Lindbaek to American Friends Service Committee, May 21, 1941, AFSC, RS.

12. Karl Frank to Eleanor Roosevelt, August 30, 1940, Sumner Welles to Mrs. Roosevelt, September 12, 1940, NA, State Department Records, File 811.111 Refugees/322.

13. James G. McDonald and George L. Warren to Franklin D. Roosevelt, October 8, 1940, McDonald to Edwin M. Watson, October 10, 1940, FDR, OF 3186.

14. *FR, 1940,* II, 231, 236–237; Herbert C. Pell to Cordell Hull, September 6, 1940, NA, State Department Records, File 811.111 Refugees/260.

15. *FR, 1940,* II, 238–239.

16. Ibid., 239–240.

17. Ibid., 238–240.

18. Draft letter to James G. McDonald from Cordell Hull, under cover of letter Breckinridge Long to Franklin D. Roosevelt, September 18, 1940, McDonald and George L. Warren to Roosevelt, October 8, 1940, FDR, OF 3186; BL Diary, 1940, pp. 171, 175–176.

19. Ibid., pp. 176–177; telegram Cordell Hull to American Embassy, Moscow, September 26, 1940, NA, State Department Records, File 811.111 Refugees/424a; *CR*, LXXXVII, Part 5, 77 Cong., 1 sess., 4754–4755.

20. BL Diary, 1941, p. 145.

21. Telegram James G. McDonald to Edwin M. Watson, October 4, 1940, J.J[ackson] to Watson, October 9, 1940, FDR, OF 3186; interview with Henry M. Hart, Jr., April 12, 1965. In 1940 Mr. Hart was serving as a Special Assistant to the Attorney General.

22. BL Diary, 1940, p. 184.

23. Joseph Buttinger to Eleanor Roosevelt, November 15, 1940, FDR, OF 3186.

24. Breckinridge Long, "Report on a Conference, October 18, 1940," NA, State Department Records, File 811.111 Refugees/700; BL Diary, 1940, pp. 205, 209–210; Sumner Welles to Robert H.

Jackson, November 23, 1940, FDR, OF 3186; *Department of State Bulletin,* III (December 21, 1940), 565.

25. For example, *PM,* December 11–15, 1940, *Washington Post,* November 25, 1940, December 11, 1940; BL Diary, 1940, pp. 212, 217, 220, 221–222; *NYT,* December 19, 1940, p. 16; *Department of State Bulletin,* III (December 21, 1940), 563–565; *Nation,* CLI (December 28, 1940), 648–649.

26. "Explanation of New Regulations and Restrictions Affecting Immigration to the United States," mimeographed, July 23, 1941, p. 5, AFSC, RS; *Interpreter Releases,* XX (November 9, 1943), 362; report from Breckinridge Long to Cordell Hull, January 6, 1941, under cover of letter Hull to Franklin D. Roosevelt, January 6, 1941, FDR, OF 3186; Fry, *Surrender on Demand,* 235, 238.

27. Davie, *Refugees in America,* 32; Arieh Tartakower and Kurt R. Grossmann, *The Jewish Refugee* (New York, 1944), 91; *AJYB,* XLIII (1941), 337; *Daily Proceedings of the Third Constitutional Convention of the Congress of Industrial Organizations, November 18–22, 1940* (Washington, 1940), 261.

28. *CJR,* III (September–October, 1940), 536; Donald A. Lowrie, *The Hunted Children* (New York, 1963), 96–97; Fry, *Surrender on Demand,* 8–9, 14–15, 17, 98; *NYT,* December 15, 1940, p. 31; Centre Américain de Secours, "Administrative Report," September 3, 1941, p. 1, copy in personal files of Varian Fry, Ridgefield, Connecticut; Philip A. Conard, "Human Tragedy of the European Refugee," under cover of letter Conard to Marjorie P. Schauffler, August 18, 1943, "Reports of a consultation," under cover of letter Conard to James G. Vail, February 17, 1944, AFSC, RS; Elisabeth Anthony Dexter, "Last Port of Freedom," draft manuscript, 1942, chapter IV, pp. 13, 15, copy in personal files of Mrs. Robert C. Dexter, Belmont, Massachusetts.

29. *NYT,* December 15, 1940, p. 31; Joseph Buttinger to Eleanor Roosevelt, November 15, 1940, FDR, OF 3186; Fry, *Surrender on Demand,* 85–86, 94; Centre Américain de Secours, "Administrative Report," pp. 1–2; *FR, 1940,* II, 248.

30. Fry, *Surrender on Demand,* 170–171, 186–188; Centre Américain de Secours, "Administrative Report," p. 7; Marjorie P. Schauffler to James Vail, "Note re Urgent Need of Immediate Contacts in Madrid," January 10, 1941, AFSC, RS. Regarding the new American visa policy adopted in mid-1941, see chapter 9.

31. "Informal Report on Immigration from Germany to the United States and Other Countries," mimeographed, November 21, 1939, p. 1, AFSC, RS.

32. *CJR*, III (May–June, 1940), 299; Gerald Reitlinger, *The Final Solution: The Attempt to Exterminate the Jews of Europe 1939–1945* (New York, 1953), 28–29; Franklin D. Roosevelt to Harold L. Ickes, August 13, 1940, FDR, OF 3186; "Current News on Migration," mimeographed, No. 1, December 9, 1940, p. 9, AFSC, RS.

33. *NYT*, July 16, 1940, p. 9, July 26, 1940, p. 3; *Fortune*, XXIII (February, 1941), 157, quotation by courtesy of *Fortune*.

34. *Community Service Release* (National Refugee Service), No. 10 (March 17, 1941), 1, 4; Tartakower and Grossmann, *The Jewish Refugee*, 205; *NYT*, May 31, 1941, p. 2.

35. Telegram James G. McDonald and George L. Warren to Franklin D. Roosevelt, March 18, 1941, Breckinridge Long to McDonald, April 4, 1941, NA, State Department Records, File 840.48 Refugees/2486; Breckinridge Long, "Memorandum of a Conversation with Admiral Land," March 24, 1941, NA, State Department Records, File 840.48 Refugees/2535; Robert C. Dexter to Clarence E. Pickett, March 24, 1941, AFSC, GF; *CJR*, IV (June, 1941), 299.

## Chapter 8

1. *Department of State Bulletin*, III (December 21, 1940), 563.

2. "Report of Quaker Commissioners," July 1, 1939, AFSC, GF.

3. Gertrud Baer to Dorothy Detzer and Emily Greene Balch, April 12, 1938, Baer to Balch and Detzer, April 29, 1938, Detzer to Baer, May 13, 1938, Swarthmore College Peace Collection, WILPF Correspondence, Refugee Committee, 1938.

4. Dorothy Detzer, *Appointment on the Hill* (New York, 1948), 227–234; Dorothy Detzer to Gertrud Baer, January 12, 1940, Detzer to Baer, February 13, 1940, Swarthmore College Peace Collection, WILPF Correspondence, Gertrud Baer, 1940.

5. Detzer, *Appointment on the Hill*, 234; Dorothy Detzer to Gertrud Baer, February 13, 1940, Detzer to Baer, March 21, 1940, Swarthmore College Peace Collection, WILPF Correspondence, Gertrud Baer, 1940

6. Interview with Laura Z. Hobson, March 8, 1965; copy of affidavit of support, April, 1938, x to Vice Consul, Zurich, October 22, 1938, A.M. Warren to Laura Hobson, October 13, 1938. All documents cited in this and the following four notes are in the personal files of Laura Z. Hobson of New York City. Mrs. Hobson, author of *The Trespassers* (a novel about refugees), *Gentleman's Agreement,* and several other novels, very kindly made her papers available for this study. At the time she was involved in providing affidavits for refugees, Mrs. Hobson was director of promotion for Time, Incorporated. The letter x is substituted for the name of the Austrian refugee in order to keep his privacy intact.

7. Interview with Laura Z. Hobson, March 8, 1965; copy of affidavit of support, April, 1938, Agnes Crane to Laura Hobson, June 7, 1938, Hobson to x, June 14, 1938, Hobson to Avra M. Warren, October 6, 1938, Warren to Hobson, October 10, 1938, Warren to Hobson, October 13, 1938.

8. Cablegram Laura Hobson to American Consul, Zurich, October 17, 1938, A.C. Frost to Hobson, October 18, 1938, Hobson to American Consul General, Zurich, October 27, 1938, x to Hobson, October 20, 1938, x to Hobson, November 15, 1938, telegram Hobson to Avra M. Warren, October 29, 1938, Warren to Hobson, October 31, 1938.

9. A.C. Frost to x, November 2, 1938, x to American Consulate General, Zurich, November 5, 1938, A.M. Warren to Laura Hobson, November 2, 1938.

10. Cablegram x to Laura Hobson, November 24, 1938, x to Hobson, November 15, 1938, x to Hobson, January 5, 1939; interview with Laura Z. Hobson, March 8, 1965.

11. Margaret E. Jones to Mary Hoxie Jones, July 11, 1940, Margaret E. Jones to Clarence E. Pickett [early November, 1940], AFSC, GF; Miriam Treo to Charles R. Joy, November 3, 1941, personal files of Varian Fry, Ridgefield, Connecticut.

12. "Report of Quaker Commissioners," July 1, 1939, Robert W. Balderston to Clarence E. Pickett [June, 1939], "Conference with Mr. Avra Warren, Friday, February 2nd," 1940, "Committee Meeting of American Commission," May 20, 21, 22, 1939, James G. Vail to Pickett, April 1, 1939, Harvey and Julianna Perry to Pickett, June 23, 1939, AFSC, GF.

13. Harvey and Julianna Perry to Clarence E. Pickett, June 23, 1939, AFSC, GF.

14. Radiogram from 52 Austrian refugees in Luxemburg to Franklin D. Roosevelt, February 27, 1939, FDR, OF 3186; Henry J. Cadbury to Mary Rogers, August 14, 1939, AFSC, GF†.

15. Varian Fry, *Surrender on Demand* (New York, 1945), 215–216; Varian Fry, "Our Consuls at Work," *Nation*, CLIV (May 2, 1942), 507–508; James Ford Lewis, "The Unitarian Service Committee," Ph.D. dissertation, University of California, June, 1952, p. 46, copy at offices of Unitarian Universalist Service Committee, Boston; case history notes taken in France by Varian Fry in late 1940 and 1941, now in Fry's personal files.

16. Alfred Wagg, 3rd, "Washington's Stepchild: The Refugee," *New Republic*, CIV (April 28, 1941), 594; Marjorie P. Schauffler to Clarence E. Pickett, April 29, 1941, AFSC, GF†; *New Republic*, CIV (June 23, 1941), 843, CV (July 28, 1941), 106; *New Leader*, XXV (May 2, 1942), 4; Fry, "Our Consuls at Work," 508; "Vichy, Nov., 1940," draft chapter for a book [late 1941 or early 1942], personal files of Varian Fry.

17. Mary M. Rogers to James Vail, November 29, 1940, Marjorie P. Schauffler to Staff, March 1 to 3, 1941, AFSC, RS; Waitstill H. Sharp to Robert C. Dexter, August 16, 1940, Universalist Historical Society Library, Tufts University, Unitarian Universalist Service Committee Records; *Community Service Release* (National Refugee Service), No. 5 (November 29, 1940), 5.

18. Marjorie P. Schauffler to the author, January 29, 1968; Minutes Refugee Section Executive Committee, November 13, 1940, AFSC, Minutes; "Conference Regarding the Nature of the Work Marjorie P. Schauffler Should Endeavor to do in Lisbon & Spain," January 24, 1941, AFSC, GF; Schauffler to Staff, March 1 to 3, 1941, Schauffler to Staff, March 12, 1941, "Chief Points Regarding Services in Portugal and Spain Requiring Decision" [April, 1941], AFSC, RS.

19. Marjorie P. Schauffler to Staff, March 12, 1941, "Questions to Philip Conard via Henry Harvey," September 23, 1941, Letter No. 76 from Conard, October 4, 1941, AFSC, RS; Clarence E. Pickett to James Vail, September 13, 1941, AFSC, GF†.

20. "Conditions among the Spanish Refugees in North Africa" [February, 1941], "Committee Meeting of American Commission," May 20, 21, 22, 1939, James G. Vail to Clarence E. Pickett, March 6, 1939, AFSC, GF; Elisabeth Anthony Dexter, "Last Port of Freedom," draft manuscript, 1942, chapter II, pp. 5–6, chapter VI,

pp. 15–16, personal files of Mrs. Robert C. Dexter, Belmont, Massachusetts; *FR, 1938* (Washington, 1955), I, 847–849; *CJR*, III (July–August, 1940), 422; "Minutes of Refugee Committee," April 28, 1939, AFSC, Minutes; "Minutes of the Meeting of June 29, 1939" [of Non-Sectarian Committee for German Refugee Children], pp. 1, 14, AFSC, RS.

21. Centre Américain de Secours, "Administrative Report," September 3, 1941, pp. 7–9, copy in personal files of Varian Fry; Fry, *Surrender on Demand*, 10–12, 61, 66, 70, 80, 87–90, 215; interview with Varian Fry, May 17, 1965; Lewis, "The Unitarian Service Committee," p. 14; *Christian Register*, CXIX (November 1, 1940), 426; Lion Feuchtwanger, *The Devil in France* (New York, 1941), 257–261, 265.

22. See above, pp. 3–5.

23. See above, p. 73; Clarence E. Pickett to James G. Vail, February 14, 1939, Eleanor Slater to George A. Walton, March 6, 1939, AFSC, GF†; Clarence E. Pickett, *For More Than Bread* (Boston, 1953), 140–141.

24. *Interpreter Releases*, XVII (February 27, 1940), 83–86, XVIII (January 22, 1941), 11–13; "Informal Report on Immigration from Germany to the United States and Other Countries," mimeographed, November 21, 1939, p. 2, AFSC, RS.

25. Ibid., pp. 1–2; R.W. Balderston, "Report on A.M. Warren's conversation," January 24, 1940, AFSC, GF†; Clarence E. Pickett to Most Rev. Abp. Joseph F. Rummel, November 20, 1939, Minutes of a Meeting, March 16, 1940, pp. 2–3, "Minutes of the Meeting of December 17, 1939," pp. 4–5, AFSC, GF.

26. "Minutes of the Meeting of December 10, 1939," p. 4, AFSC, GF; "Informal Report on Immigration from Germany to the United States and Other Countries," mimeographed, November 21, 1939, pp. 1–2, AFSC, RS.

27. The statistics in this and the preceding paragraph are derived from the records of the Immigration and Naturalization Service. Convenient tables pertaining to "Hebrew" immigration appear in *AJYB*, XLII (1940), 615, XLIII (1941), 681, XLIV (1942), 436, XLV (1943), 589.

28. "Minutes of the Meeting of December 10, 1939," pp. 1–6, 17, "Minutes of the Meeting of December 17, 1939," pp. 4, 7, 8, AFSC, GF.

29. *AJYB,* XLIII (1941), 328, XLIV (1942), 296–297.

30. BL Diary, 1940, pp. 88, 96, 105–106, 110; Breckinridge Long to Sumner Welles, May 28, 1940, BL Papers, Box 211.

31. Breckinridge Long to Adolf A. Berle, Jr., and James C. Dunn, June 26, 1940, BL Papers, Box 211; see below, pp. 178–179, 194–195.

32. *FR, 1940* (Washington, 1957), II, 231–232; BL Diary, 1940, p. 140.

33. "Department of State Appropriation Bill for 1942," *Hearings before the Subcommittee of the Committee on Appropriations, House of Representatives,* 77 Cong., 1 sess. (February 3, 1941), 159–162; Herbert C. Pell to Cordell Hull, September 6, 1940, NA, State Department Records, File 811.111 Refugees/260; Margaret E. Jones to Clarence E. Pickett [early November, 1940], AFSC, GF.

34. Ibid.; K. Neumayer to Mary Hoxie Jones, August 31, 1940, Neumayer to Mary M. Rogers, September 26, 1940, Neumayer to Margaret E. Jones, October 4, 1940, AFSC, GF.

35. Laura Hobson to Avra M. Warren, April 19, 1940, X to Hobson [April, 1940], Warren to Hobson, May 10, 1940, X to Hobson, September 12, 1940, Eliot B. Coulter to Hobson [between September 20 and October 2, 1940], Y to Hobson, March 22, 1941, March 25, 1941, April 4, 1941. These documents are in the personal files of Laura Z. Hobson. The letter Y is substituted for the name of the son of the woman refugee discussed in this paragraph. The correspondent referred to as X is the same person cited as X in note 6 of this chapter.

36. Telegram Birch Ragaz to Women's International League, Washington, September 9, 1940, Swarthmore College Peace Collection, WILPF Correspondence, Gertrud Baer, 1940; Joseph Buttinger to Eleanor Roosevelt, November 15, 1940, FDR, OF 3186; "Current News on Migration," mimeographed, No. 1, December 9, 1940, p. 3, AFSC, RS; *Community Service Release* (National Refugee Service), No. 6 (January 31, 1941), 7; Marjorie P. Schauffler to Clarence E. Pickett, April 29, 1941, AFSC, GF†.

37. The statistics in this paragraph are derived from the records of the Immigration and Naturalization Service. Most numbers have been rounded off by the author. Convenient tables pertaining to "Hebrew" immigration appear in *AJYB,* XLIII (1941), 681, XLIV (1942), 436. A useful table on immigration from the Western Hemisphere is printed in Immigration and Naturalization Service, *Monthly Review,* I (April, 1944), 12–13. "Department of State Appropriation Bill for

1942," *Hearings before the Subcommittee,* 164; Y to Laura Hobson, March 22, 1941, March 25, 1941, Avra M. Warren to Hobson, April 2, 1941, personal files of Laura Z. Hobson. Regarding the use of the letter Y, see note 35 of this chapter.

38. *NYT,* July 17, 1940, p. 11; Karl Taussig to Clarence E. Pickett, September 27, 1940, Report on Dr. Haber's Meeting, September 17, 1940, Pickett to Mary Rogers and others, November 12, 1940, AFSC, GF; *Newscast* (American Committee for Christian Refugees), I (November 15, 1940), 1.

39. "10–21–40 Telephone conversation with Murray LeVine, HIAS," AFSC, GF; *NYT,* January 10, 1941, p. 11, June 24, 1941, p. 8; "Rescue of the Jewish and Other Peoples in Nazi-Occupied Territory," *Extract from Hearings before the Committee on Foreign Affairs, House of Representatives,* 78 Cong., 1 sess. (November 26, 1943), 33–34. HIAS was the term commonly used to designate the Hebrew Sheltering and Immigrant Aid Society.

40. Breckinridge Long to Sumner Welles, November 25, 1940, Charles B. Hosmer to Long, November 25, 1940, BL Papers, Box 211.

41. BL Diary, 1940, pp. 175, 215, 1941, p. 25; report from Breckinridge Long to Cordell Hull, January 6, 1941, under cover of letter Hull to Franklin D. Roosevelt, January 6, 1941, FDR, OF 3186; see below, pp. 194–195.

42. "Minutes of Meeting Held November 15, 1940, in Secretary's Conference Room, Department of the Interior . . . ," p. 21, NA, Social and Economic Branch, Department of Interior File 9-11-26; "Department of State Appropriation Bill for 1942," *Hearings before the Subcommittee,* 163; *Department of State Bulletin,* III (December 21, 1940), 564, IV (February 8, 1941), 162; "Current News on Migration: (2nd Edition)," mimeographed, January 15, 1941, p. 4, AFSC, RS.

43. Ibid.; *Community Service Release* (National Refugee Service), No. 10 (March 17, 1941), 1; *Interpreter Releases,* XIX (February 27, 1942), 83.

44. *Community Service Release* (National Refugee Service), No. 2 (October 11, 1940), 4, No. 5 (November 29, 1940), 3, No. 6 (January 31, 1941), 2, 5; *Newscast* (American Committee for Christian Refugees), I (May, 1941), 4; "Department of State Appropriation Bill for 1942," *Hearings before the Subcommittee,* 163.

45. "Our attempt to obtain ship's passage for emigrants in our

charge," anonymous memorandum, April 17, 1941, AFSC, RS; Margaret Jones to Clarence Pickett and Mary Rogers, May 9, 1941, AFSC, GF; *Interpreter Releases,* XIX (February 27, 1942), 83.

46. BL Diary, 1941, pp. 10, 14.

47. Ibid., 1940, p. 82; *NYT,* May 17, 1940, p. 10, May 27, 1940, p. 12; "The Press Conferences of President Franklin D. Roosevelt," XV, Press Conference No. 649-A (June 5, 1940), 496, Franklin D. Roosevelt Library; *FR, 1940,* II, 241–243.

## Chapter 9

1. *AJYB,* XLII (1940), 449–450, XLIII (1941), 139–141, XLIV (1942), 171; *CJR,* III (July–August, 1940), 417.

2. *Junior American,* XV (June, 1940), 1.

3. *American Vindicator,* I (October, 1939), 1; *CR,* LXXXVI, Part 1, 76 Cong., 3 sess., 680, Part 6, 6773; *Fortune,* XXII (July, 1940), insert. The Roper poll is quoted by courtesy of *Fortune.*

4. *American Magazine,* CXXX (August, 1940), 18 ff., CXXX (September, 1940), 44 ff., CXXX (November, 1940), 16 ff., CXXX (December, 1940), 24 ff., CXXXI (February, 1941), 35 ff., CXXXI (April, 1941), 14 ff.; *Reader's Digest,* XXXVII (October, 1940), 41–44, XXXVII (November, 1940), 46–48, XXXVII (December, 1940), 28–32; *Nation,* CLI (July 20, 1940, through December 28, 1940); *Fortune,* XXII (October, 1940), 46 ff., XXII (November, 1940), 85 ff.; *America,* LXIII (July 6, 1940), 345–346, LXIII (September 14, 1940), 623–624, LXIII (September 21, 1940), 651–652; J. Edgar Hoover, "Big Scare," *American Magazine,* CXXXII (August, 1941), 24 ff.

5. Harold L. Ickes, *The Secret Diary of Harold L. Ickes: Volume III: The Lowering Clouds, 1939–1941* (New York, 1954), 188, 211, quotations by permission of the publisher, Simon and Schuster, Inc.

6. "Nazi Agents in the U.S.," *Fortune,* XXII (October, 1940), 47, quoted by courtesy of *Fortune.*

7. Samuel I. Rosenman (ed.), *The Public Papers and Addresses of Franklin D. Roosevelt* (New York, 1941), IX, 223–229; "The Press Conferences of President Franklin D. Roosevelt," XV, Press Conference No. 645 (May 21, 1940), 352–353, Franklin D. Roosevelt Li-

brary; *NYT,* May 22, 1940, p. 1, May 23, 1940, pp. 14, 15, June 4, 1940, p. 12, June 15, 1940, p. 9; *Annual Report of the Attorney General of the United States for the Fiscal Year ended June 30, 1941* (Washington, 1942), 225.

8. *CR,* LXXXIV, Part 10, 76 Cong., 1 sess., 10455–10456, LXXXVI, Part 8, 76 Cong., 3 sess., 8347, 9036.

9. *NYT,* August 2, 1940, p. 1, August 19, 1940, p. 4; *Christian Century,* LVII (September 4, 1940), 1085.

10. *Nation,* CLI (August 31, 1940), 163–164; Heinz Pol, "Spies Among Refugees?" *Nation,* CLI (August 31, 1940), 167–168; *CJR,* IV (February, 1941), 90; William C. Bullitt, *Report to the American People* (Boston, 1940), 25; Michael Schapiro, "German Refugees in France," *CJR,* III (March–April, 1940), 140; Alfred Werner, "German Refugees in England," *CJR,* III (July–August, 1940), 386; *Newscast* (American Committee for Christian Refugees), I (October, 1941), 4.

11. A. Visson, " 'Fifth Column' Tricks and Treacheries," *New York Herald Tribune,* October 10, 1940, p. 24; Samuel Lubell, "War by Refugee," *Saturday Evening Post,* CCXIII (March 29, 1941), 12, 89; Donald E. Keyhoe and John Jay Daly, "Hitler's Slave Spies in America," *American Magazine,* CXXXI (April, 1941), 14, 120; *CR,* LXXXVII, Part 3, 77 Cong., 1 sess., 3069.

12. *NYT,* May 27, 1941, p. 11; "Investigation of Un-American Propaganda Activities in the United States," *Hearings before a Special Committee on Un-American Activities, House of Representatives,* 77 Cong., 1 sess. (May 26, 1941), XIV, 8481, 8489–8490.

13. *Nation,* CLII (June 7, 1941), 656; *NYT,* May 29, 1941, p. 40, June 1, 1941, p. 12.

14. *FR, 1940* (Washington, 1958), III, 234–235; *FR, 1941* (Washington, 1958), I, 598, 619.

15. Report from Breckinridge Long to Cordell Hull, January 6, 1941, under cover of letter Hull to Franklin D. Roosevelt, January 6, 1941, FDR, OF 3186; "Current News on Migration," mimeographed, No. 1, December 9, 1940, p. 5, AFSC, RS; *Community Service Release* (National Refugee Service), No. 10 (March 17, 1941), 2.

16. "Memorandum giving the gist of the telephone conversation between Assistant Secretary Breckinridge Long and Clarence Pickett," April 28, 1941, Long to Pickett, May 28, 1941, AFSC, GF.

17. Graham H. Stuart, "Wartime Visa-Control Procedure," *De-*

partment of State Bulletin, XI (September 10, 1944), 273; NYT, March 12, 1941, p. 5; "Additional Urgent Deficiency Appropriation Bill, Fiscal Year 1941," Hearings before the Subcommittee of the Committee on Appropriations, House of Representatives, 77 Cong., 1 sess. (May 1, 1941), XI, 137–146; see above, p. 148.

18. FR, 1941, I, 619–620; BL Diary, 1941, p. 82; Department of State Bulletin, IV (June 21, 1941), 748; NYT, June 18, 1941, p. 1.

19. Memorandum to Franklin D. Roosevelt, August 20, 1941, under cover of letter Breckinridge Long to Edwin M. Watson, August 20, 1941, FDR, OF 3186; see above, pp. 173–183, passim; "Minutes of fifth meeting, held December 3, 1940," of the Committee on Legislation of the Immigration and Naturalization Service, copy in personal files of Professor Henry M. Hart, Jr., Harvard University Law School; "Authorizing the Refusal of Visas to Undesirable Aliens," Senate Report, 77 Cong., 1 sess., No. 386 (June 5, 1941); CR, LXXXVII, Part 5, 77 Cong., 1 sess., 4757, 5048, 5133, 5386.

20. Ibid., 4757, 5133.

21. Ibid., 5047–5053, 5325–5326, 5385–5389; Department of State Bulletin, V (November 15, 1941), 381–382.

22. Ibid., IV (June 28, 1941), 764–765; "Explanation of New Regulations and Restrictions Affecting Immigration to the United States," mimeographed, July 23, 1941, pp. 1–4, AFSC, RS.

23. Centre Américain de Secours, "Administrative Report," September 3, 1941, p. 9, copy in personal files of Varian Fry, Ridgefield, Connecticut; Robert C. Dexter to Howard K. Travers, August 11, 1942, Universalist Historical Society Library, Tufts University, Unitarian Universalist Service Committee Records, State Department; interview with Mrs. Robert C. Dexter, March 3, 1965; Elisabeth Anthony Dexter, "Last Port of Freedom," draft manuscript, 1942, chapter II, pp. 11–12, chapter IV, pp. 10–12, copy in personal files of Mrs. Robert C. Dexter, Belmont, Massachusetts.

24. "Explanation of New Regulations and Restrictions Affecting Immigration to the United States," mimeographed, July 23, 1941, p. 2, AFSC, RS; NYT, July 20, 1941, p. 4; "Minutes of Mr. Abramson's Meeting Held on October 14th," October 23, 1941, AFSC, GF†; Newscast (American Committee for Christian Refugees), I (October, 1941), 2; Mary Rogers and Marjorie P. Schauffler, "Report on Visit to Washington," October 10, 1941, Marjorie P. Schauffler, "Notes on recent conversations and meetings in New York," December 1, 1941, AFSC, GF

25. *NYT,* June 17, 1941, p. 1, June 20, 1941, p. 5, June 24, 1941, p. 8; "Explanation of New Regulations and Restrictions Affecting Immigration to the United States," mimeographed, July 23, 1941, pp. 3, 4, AFSC, RS.

26. *Congress Weekly,* VIII (June 27, 1941), 3; *Jewish Frontier,* VIII (July, 1941), 5; *Opinion,* XI (July, 1941), 4; *Workmen's Circle Call,* IX (October, 1941), 4; *National Jewish Monthly,* LVI (December, 1941), 113.

27. Albert Einstein to Eleanor Roosevelt, July 26, 1941, FDR, PPF 7177; *NYT,* July 14, 1941, p. 4.

28. *New Republic,* CIV (June 30, 1941), 873; Freda Kirchwey, "A Scandal in the State Department," *Nation,* CLIII (July 19, 1941), 45.

29. *FR, 1941,* I, 619–620; *Department of State Bulletin,* IV (June 21, 1941), 748; telegram Clarence E. Pickett to Frank Kingdon, July 10, 1941, AFSC, GF†; *Federal Register,* VI (November 22, 1941), 5916.

30. Telegram James G. McDonald and others to Franklin D. Roosevelt, August 8, 1941, E.M.W[atson] to Sumner Welles, August 18, 1941, memorandum to Roosevelt, August 20, 1941, under cover of letter Breckinridge Long to Edwin M. Watson, August 20, 1941, Cordell Hull to Roosevelt, August 25, 1941, FDR, OF 3186; BL Diary, 1941, pp. 100, 105.

31. Telegram James G. McDonald to Edwin M. Watson, September 2, 1941, President's Advisory Committee (by McDonald) to Franklin D. Roosevelt, September 4, 1941, FDR, OF 3186.

32. BL Diary, 1941, p. 110.

33. Ibid., pp. 125, 127, 136, 144; Marjorie P. Schauffler, "Notes on recent conversations and meetings in New York," December 1, 1941, AFSC, GF.

34. *Federal Register,* VI (November 22, 1941), 5917–5918; *Department of State Bulletin,* V (December 20, 1941), 566.

35. Marjorie P. Schauffler, "Notes on recent conversations and meetings in New York," December 1, 1941, Clarence E. Pickett to George L. Warren, May 27, 1942, Pickett to Annelise Thieman, June 2, 1942, Mary M. Rogers to Warren, June 4, 1942, AFSC, GF; Stuart, "Wartime Visa-Control Procedure," 276.

36. Ibid., 276, 277; Robert J. Bulkley, Frederick P. Keppel, and F.D.G. Ribble, *Report to the President: Board of Appeals on Visa Cases: November 9, 1942* (n.p., 1942), 4–5, 12–13, 19.

37. Harry Greenstein, Summary of Invitation Conference, New York, October 18–19, 1941, AFSC, GF; Bulkley, Keppel, and Ribble, *Report to the President,* 14.

38. Immigration statistics in this paragraph came from the records of the Immigration and Naturalization Service and appeared in *Interpreter Releases,* XIX (February 27, 1942), 83. Most of the numbers have been rounded off by the author. "Department of State Appropriation Bill for 1943," *Hearings before the Subcommittee of the Committee on Appropriations, House of Representatives,* 77 Cong., 2 sess. (January 21, 1942), XI, 94.

39. *NYT,* September 3, 1941, p. 18; Philip A. Conard, "Brief Report . . . May to August 1941," August 23, 1941, Conard to American Friends Service Committee, September 22, 1941, AFSC, RS.

40. *Newscast* (American Committee for Christian Refugees), I (December, 1941), 4; Gerald Reitlinger, *The Final Solution: The Attempt to Exterminate the Jews of Europe 1939–1945* (New York, 1953), 28; *AJYB,* XLIV (1942), 297.


# Conclusion


1. See Appendix I; Malcolm J. Proudfoot, *European Refugees: 1939–52* (Evanston, Illinois, 1956), 27, 68; Maurice R. Davie, *Refugees in America* (New York, 1947), 14, 24; Arieh Tartakower and Kurt R. Grossmann, *The Jewish Refugee* (New York, 1944), 346.

2. Ibid., 344; Jacques Vernant, *The Refugee in the Post-War World* (London, 1953), 60.

3. These estimates are based on Maurice Davie's method as explained in Appendix I; on data from Davie, *Refugees in America,* 24; and on statistics of the Immigration and Naturalization Service.

4. Charles Herbert Stember and others, *Jews in the Mind of America* (New York, 1966), 148–149; *Fortune,* XIX (April, 1939), 102. The Roper poll is quoted by courtesy of *Forutne.*

5. Note 3 of this chapter gives the basis for this estimate and for the figure of 120,000 in the preceding paragraph.

6. See above, pp. 144, 194, 203–204.

# Appendix I

1. Cordell Hull, *The Memoirs of Cordell Hull* (New York, 1948), II, 1538; "Rescue of the Jewish and Other Peoples in Nazi-Occupied Territory," *Extract from Hearings before the Committee on Foreign Affairs, House of Representatives,* 78 Cong., 1 sess. (November 26, 1943), 23. On the basis of statistics of the Immigration and Naturalization Service, the inaccuracy of Long's estimate was pointed out by the American Jewish Conference, the World Jewish Congress, the *Nation,* the Yiddish Scientific Institute, and other groups. ("Statement by the Commission on Rescue of the American Jewish Conference," mimeographed, December 27, 1943, copy in AJC, Immigration, Refugees, Rescue of, 1943–47; *Congress Weekly,* X [December 24, 1943], 14–17; *Nation,* CLVII [December 25, 1943], 748; *NYT,* December 31, 1943, p. 14.)

2. Sophia M. Robison, *Refugees at Work* (New York, 1942), 2, 12–14.

3. Maurice R. Davie, *Refugees in America* (New York, 1947), 23–24, 27.

4. Ibid., 25–27; *Annual Report of the Immigration and Naturalization Service* (Philadelphia, 1944), 71, table 15a.

5. Davie, *Refugees in America,* 37.

# Appendix II

1. The Immigration Act of 1917 excludes aliens with dangerous diseases, those with mental defects or a history of insanity, polygamists, prostitutes, paupers, criminals, anarchists, those believing in violent overthrow of the United States government, people likely to become public charges, contract laborers, and aliens whose passage is paid by an organized group. Children under 16 who are neither with a parent nor on the way to a parent may be admitted only with the approval of the Secretary of Labor. This Act also excludes illiterates, but exempts from the literacy test fugitives from religious persecution.

2. In fiscal 1939, 32,759 quota immigrants came with German quota numbers. This apparent oversubscription of 5,389 consisted of people who had been granted visas under the 1938 quota late in that fiscal year and who did not arrive in the United States until fiscal 1939. A quota visa was generally valid for a four-month period. A more accurate picture is had by adding the 5,389 to the 1938 total. If this is done, the 1938 quota is seen to have been 85 percent filled.

# Bibliography

# Primary Sources

Four archival collections contributed most significantly to the development of this book. Four other depositories provided important though less extensive sources. In addition, two sets of personal papers were invaluable.

The American Friends Service Committee Archives, stored in the Haverford College Library, yielded the material which forms the backbone of this volume. The American Friends Service Committee (AFSC), with central offices in Philadelphia, was not a large organization and refugee work comprised only one of its many areas of activity. Yet the AFSC occupied a strategic position in the American refugee aid effort. Of major importance was the high regard in which the executive secretary, Clarence E. Pickett, was held in both governmental and nongovernmental quarters. In addition, the Quaker reputation for political neutrality and disinterested service opened doors to contacts and cooperation in many circles, foreign as well as domestic. (For instance, child feeding programs in Germany in the aftermath of World War I earned the Friends and their work a continuing welcome in that country. Again, because it pioneered in refugee aid on both sides of the lines in the Spanish Civil War, the AFSC brought a record of impartial service to the refugee crisis of the later 1930's and 1940's.) As a result, memoranda, correspondence, reports, minutes of meetings, pamphlets and leaflets, accounts of interviews with government officials, and other types of information flowed into the AFSC files from its own workers and from all the most involved groups, Jewish, Christian, and governmental, both in the United States and overseas. Research scholars have hardly tapped these files. The wealth of refugee information in them points to the probability that the AFSC Archives contain similarly useful sources for the several areas of social concern, in the United States and abroad, in which the American Friends Service Committee has worked since its establishment in 1917.

The American Jewish Committee Archives, located in the committee's offices in New York City, provided valuable insight into the efforts made on behalf of refugees by this major organization for defense of Jewish rights. These records, as they relate to refugee matters, are composed mainly of correspondence, memoranda, and reports. The American Jewish Committee's Blaustein Library, which specializes in intergroup relations and other problems affecting the Jewish community, contains what is probably the most complete collection available of modern American anti-Semitic literature. Here the Pelleys, Winrods, Coughlins, and a host of other hate-peddlers of not very long ago can, if one wishes to behold them, be resurrected from the pages of their periodicals and pamphlets.

The Franklin D. Roosevelt Papers, housed in the Franklin D. Roosevelt Library at Hyde Park, New York, offered a comprehensive range of material on the governmental side of the refugee issue. Intra-Administration memoranda, especially to and from the State Department, were particularly helpful. These records also show the role Eleanor Roosevelt played as an advocate of refugees.

The fourth major source of documentary material was the National Archives in Washington, D.C. Of the collections held there, the Records of the Department of State proved the most valuable. These papers include reports on meetings, memoranda of conversations, cablegrams to and from foreign service officials, intradepartmental communications, correspondence, and other materials. The Legislative Branch of the National Archives provided some crucial documents. The Department of the Interior files in the Social and Economic Branch of the National Archives supplied basic sources on efforts to open Alaska and the Virgin Islands to refugees.

Additional important information came from the Breckinridge Long Papers in the Manuscript Division, Library of Congress; the Robert F. Wagner Papers at Georgetown University; the correspondence of the Women's International League for Peace and Freedom, deposited in the Swarthmore College Peace Collection; and the Unitarian Universalist Service Committee Records, stored at Tufts University. The Breckinridge Long collection, especially Long's comprehensive office diary, threw a good deal of light on State Department policy-making procedures regarding the refugee issue. The Wagner Papers were vitally important to the study of the Wagner-Rogers Bill. The Women's International League files provided further insight into the Roosevelt Administration's refugee policy. The records of the earliest years of the Unitarian Service Committee, established in 1940, are mostly missing, though one hopes not permanently. The remnants were useful.

Finally, Mrs. Laura Z. Hobson of New York City and Varian Fry of Ridgefield, Connecticut, by opening their personal files, have made possible clearer and fuller development of important aspects of the American response to the refugee crisis. The relevant papers in Mrs. Hobson's collection are mostly correspondence. Mr. Fry's records include correspondence, a file on which he based a book, and some notes taken on refugee cases in which Fry was involved as an emigration worker in Vichy France. Mrs. Robert C. Dexter of Belmont, Massachusetts, made available a manuscript entitled "Last Port of Freedom" which she wrote in 1942 on the basis of her experience as a Unitarian Service Committee staff member in Lisbon in 1941.

### INTERVIEWS

Several individuals who were involved in refugee affairs of the period shared their experiences and insights with the author. Among those who helped in this way were Mrs. Dorothy Detzer Denny, Philip Levy, and George L. Warren, all of Washington, D.C.; Kurt R. Grossmann of New York City; Clarence E. Pickett, since deceased, of Philadelphia; Professor Henry M. Hart, Jr., of Cambridge, Massachusetts; Mrs. Marjorie Page Schauffler of Downingtown, Pennsylvania; Mrs. Robert C. Dexter; Mrs. Laura Z. Hobson; and Varian Fry.

### PUBLIC DOCUMENTS

The most convenient references for Federal legislative enactments and executive actions were the *Statutes at Large of the United States of America* and the *Federal Register*. The *Congressional Record,* while it seldom exposed more than surface events, provided a starting point for examination of the legislative situation. Hearings held by Congressional committees, though not deeply penetrating, at times revealed important information about congressmen, witnesses, and the organizations the witnesses represented. The two sets of hearings on the Wagner-Rogers Bill yielded nearly 600 pages of reportage, some of it very valuable. Testimony in the usually arid area of appropriations occasionally uncovered steps in the development of State Department policy because new plans often necessitated requests for new funds. Less helpful were the House and Senate *Reports* summarizing committee conclusions and recommendations on specific pieces of legislation.

The State Department included information pertinent to the refugee problem in its *Press Releases,* a weekly publication replaced in July 1939 by the more comprehensive *Department of State Bulletin.* Of major importance to this study was the *Foreign Relations of the United States* series, the State Department's well-selected and remarkably thorough collection of diplomatic papers. "The Press Conferences of President Franklin D. Roosevelt," in typescript at the Franklin D. Roosevelt Library and on microfilm elsewhere, shed some light on President Roosevelt's attitudes.

The annual reports of the Immigration and Naturalization Service, especially valuable for statistical material, appeared in the following sequence of documents.

*Twenty-Seventh Annual Report of the Secretary of Labor, for the Fiscal Year ended June 30, 1939.* Washington, 1939.

*Twenty-Eighth Annual Report of the Secretary of Labor, for the Fiscal Year ended June 30, 1940.* Washington, 1940.

*Annual Report of the Attorney General of the United States for the Fiscal Year ended June 30, 1941.* Washington, 1942.

"Annual Report of Lemuel B. Schofield, Special Assistant to the Attorney General in charge of the Immigration and Naturalization Service, Year ended June 30, 1942." N.p., n.d. (Mimeographed).

*Annual Reports of the Immigration and Naturalization Service.* Philadelphia, 1943, 1944, 1945.

In 1943 the Immigration and Naturalization Service expanded its information efforts by commencing publication of a *Monthly Review.*

The following list includes the most important Public Documents used in this study other than those specifically named above.

"Additional Urgent Deficiency Appropriation Bill, Fiscal Year 1941," *Hearings before the Subcommittee of the Committee on Appropriations, House of Representatives,* 77 Cong., 1 sess. (May 1, 1941).

"Admission of German Refugee Children," *Hearings before the Committee on Immigration and Naturalization, House of Representatives,* 76 Cong., 1 sess. (May 24, 25, 31, and June 1, 1939).

"Admission of German Refugee Children," *Joint Hearings before a Subcommittee of the Committee on Immigration, United States*

Senate, and a Subcommittee of the Committee on Immigration and Naturalization, House of Representatives, 76 Cong., 1 sess. (April 20, 21, 22, and 24, 1939).

BULKLEY, ROBERT J., FREDERICK P. KEPPEL, and F.D.G. RIBBLE. *Report to the President: Board of Appeals on Visa Cases: November 9, 1942.* N.p. [1942].

"Department of State Appropriation Bill for 1942," *Hearings before the Subcommittee of the Committee on Appropriations, House of Representatives,* 77 Cong., 1 sess. (February 3, 1941).

"Department of State Appropriation Bill for 1943," *Hearings before the Subcommittee of the Committee on Appropriations, House of Representatives,* 77 Cong., 2 sess. (January 21, 1942).

"Deportation of Aliens," *Hearings before a Subcommittee of the Committee on Immigration, United States Senate,* 76 Cong., 1 sess. (March 21, 22, and 23, 1939).

*Documents on British Foreign Policy, 1919–1939,* 3d series, III. London, 1950.

*Documents on German Foreign Policy, 1918–1945,* series D, IV, V. Washington, 1951, 1953.

MC DONALD, JAMES G. *Letter of Resignation: Addressed to the Secretary General of the League of Nations: With an Annex.* London, 1935.

*The Problem of Alaskan Development.* Washington, 1939. Also, rev. ed., 1940.

*Proceedings of the Intergovernmental Committee, Evian, July 6th to 15th, 1938, Verbatim Record of the Plenary Meetings of the Committee.* N.p., 1938.

"Rescue of the Jewish and Other Peoples in Nazi-Occupied Territory," *Extract from Hearings before the Committee on Foreign Affairs, House of Representatives,* 78 Cong., 1 sess. (November 26, 1943).

"Second Deficiency Appropriation Bill for 1938," *Hearings before a Subcommittee of the Committee on Appropriations, House of Representatives,* 75 Cong., 3 sess. (May 25, 1938).

"Settlement and Development of Alaska," *Hearings before a Subcommittee of the Committee on Territories and Insular Affairs, United States Senate,* 76 Cong., 3 sess. (May 13, 15, 18, 1940).

"To Provide a Temporary Haven from the Dangers or Effects of War for European Children Under the Age of Sixteen," *Hearings before the Committee on Immigration and Naturalization, House of Representatives,* 76 Cong., 3 sess. (August 8 and 9, 1940).

BOOKS

Memoirs helped to clarify many problems, filled several small gaps, and supplied numerous hints for further archival investigation. The most useful of these books were Dorothy Detzer's *Appointment on the Hill* (New York, 1948), a report on her career as a peace lobbyist for the Women's International League for Peace and Freedom; Varian Fry's *Surrender on Demand* (New York, 1945), describing his work for the Emergency Rescue Committee in unoccupied France; *The Secret Diary of Harold L. Ickes: Volume III: The Lowering Clouds, 1939–1941* (New York, 1954); and Clarence E. Pickett's *For More Than Bread* (Boston, 1953), an account of his 22 years as executive secretary of the American Friends Service Committee. *The Memoirs of Cordell Hull,* volume II (New York, 1948), includes a brief section on refugee problems. Volumes VIII and IX of *The Public Papers and Addresses of Franklin D. Roosevelt,* edited by Samuel I. Rosenman (New York, 1941), contain materials relevant to refugee policy along with comments on the documents made in retrospect by the President.

Other books important as primary sources appear in the following list.

BROOKS, HOWARD L. *Prisoners of Hope.* New York, 1942.

DEROUNIAN, ARTHUR [JOHN ROY CARLSON, pseud.]. *Under Cover: My Four Years in the Nazi Underworld of America.* Philadelphia, 1943.

[GINSBOURG, ANNA]. *Jewish Refugees in Shanghai.* Shanghai, 1940.

LAUGHLIN, HARRY H. *Conquest by Immigration.* New York, 1939.

*Refugee Settlement in the Dominican Republic: A Survey Conducted Under the Auspices of the Brookings Institution.* Washington, 1942.

SCHACHT, HJALMAR H. G. *Confessions of "The Old Wizard."* Boston, 1956.

THOMPSON, DOROTHY. *Refugees: Anarchy or Organization?* New York, 1938.

WELLES, SUMNER. *Where Are We Heading?* New York, 1946.

A sizeable pamphlet literature developed around the question of refugee immigration. Representative of extremist opposition were J. H. Patten's *The "Immigration Crew" on the New Deal "Railroad"* ([Chicago], 1935), an indictment of the Roosevelt Administration's alleged softness toward aliens; the German-American Bund's *Free America!: Six Addresses on the Aims and Purposes of the German-American Bund* (New York, 1939), which demanded a "Jew-free America," cessation of the refugee influx, and return to the foreign policies of George Washington; and William Dudley Pelley's warning that Jews controlled the Federal government in *What Every Congressman Should Know* (Asheville, N.C. [1938]). Reasoned statements for continued or moderately increased refugee immigration appeared in Louis Adamic's *America and the Refugees* (New York, 1939) and Bruce Bliven's *The Jewish Refugee Problem* (New York, 1939).

Several groups issued pamphlets defending refugees and emphasizing the positive contributions the newcomers could make to American society. The National Board of the YWCA sponsored *Meet the Refugees* (New York, 1940), *Refugees* (New York, 1938), and *Refugees: December 1939* (New York, 1939), the latter two written by Mabel Brown Ellis. The American Friends Service Committee and the American Jewish Committee collaborated in producing *Refugee Facts* (Philadelphia, 1939). The National Refugee Service stressed the favorable economic impact of refugee immigration in *Dividends from New Americans* (New York, 1941) and *They Can Aid America* (New York, 1943).

The following entries are typical of reports published by organizations active in refugee rescue.

DOMINICAN REPUBLIC SETTLEMENT ASSOCIATION, INC. *Concerning Refugee Settlement in the Dominican Republic.* New York, 1940. A series of three pamphlets.

————. *Sosua: Haven for Refugees in the Dominican Republic.* New York, 1941.

JEWISH LABOR COMMITTEE. *American Labor to the Rescue.* New York, 1941.

————. *The Jewish Labor Committee: What It Does and What It Stands For.* New York, 1942.

LEE, ATHERTON. *Agricultural Possibilities at Sosua Settlement.* New York [1940].

*Report of the Committee for Catholic Refugees from Germany for January 1, 1937 to September 30, 1938.* New York [1938].

*Report: The Committee for Catholic Refugees from Germany from January 1, 1937 to September 30, 1939.* New York, 1939.

*We Are Standing By: A Report of the United States Committee for the Care of European Children's Program, Accomplishments, and Present Status.* New York, 1941.

Many refugee agencies distributed serialized news bulletins in addition to their annual reports and other pamphlets. The most useful of these bulletins were *Community Service Release,* issued by the National Refugee Service, and *Newscast,* published by the American Committee for Christian Refugees.

### PERIODICALS AND NEWSPAPERS

The periodical press in the late 1930's and early 1940's offered extensive coverage of the refugee problem and related issues. Research in a wide range of periodicals proved exceedingly helpful in the effort to learn about attitudes, policies, and actions of important segments of the American public.

Most consistently critical of American policy from a liberal, pro-refugee stance were the *New Republic* and the *Nation,* joined occasionally by *PM* in New York and Drew Pearson and Robert S. Allen in their syndicated "Washington Merry-Go-Round" column.

Restrictionist opinion was voiced in the *American Legion Magazine,* the *National Legionnaire,* and the Junior Order United American Mechanics' *Junior American.*

Among Catholic periodicals examined were *America,* the National Catholic Welfare Conference's *Catholic Action,* the *Catholic World,* the *Commonweal,* and the Brooklyn diocese's *Tablet.* The most vocal of these periodicals on the refugee issue were the *Commonweal,* which spoke constantly for a more generous refugee policy, and the *Tablet,* which was, to say the least, negative toward Jewish immigration.

Protestant publications consulted included the *Christian Century,* the *Christian Register* (Unitarian), the *Churchman* (Episcopal), the *Friends Intelligencer,* and the *Methodist Woman.*

The effort to obtain a sufficiently comprehensive, yet manageable, cross section of the vast variety of opinion to be found in the Jewish periodical press led to research in *Congress Bulletin,* changed to *Congress Weekly* in 1941 (American Jewish Congress); the *Contemporary Jewish Record* (American Jewish Committee); *Jewish Frontier* (labor Zionist); the *National Jewish Monthly* (B'nai B'rith); *Opinion;* and *Workmen's Circle Call.*

Among several social work journals interested in the refugee problem were the *Social Service Review, Social Work Today,* and especially the *Survey Graphic.*

Extreme nativism filled North Carolina Senator Robert R. Reynolds' *American Vindicator.* Vitriolic anti-Semitism joined antirefugee writing in the Rev. Gerald Winrod's *Defender Magazine,* Fr. Charles E. Coughlin's *Social Justice,* William Dudley Pelley's *Liberation,* James B. True's *Industrial Control Reports,* and many lesser hate sheets.

Reports and editorials on the refugee situation and allied topics appeared in such popular magazines as *Collier's, Fortune, Liberty, Life, Newsweek, Saturday Evening Post,* and *Time.* Through the courtesy of *Fortune,* lengthy quotation was permitted from material copyrighted by that magazine.

The *New York Times,* helpful throughout, was especially valuable as a guide in tracing the overall trend of events in a largely uncharted area of study. Also useful were the *New York Herald Tribune,* the *Christian Science Monitor,* and, to a lesser extent, several other newspapers.

CONTEMPORARY ARTICLES

The following articles appeared in the *Annals of the American Academy of Political and Social Science,* CCIII (May, 1939), a special issue devoted to the refugee problem.

ESTORICK, ERIC. "The Evian Conference and the Intergovernmental Committee."
HOLBORN, LOUISE W. "The League of Nations and the Refugee Problem."
LEVMORE, BERNARD W. "A Stimulus for American Industry: Nonprofessional Refugees."

LEWIS, READ, and MARIAN SCHIBSBY. "Status of the Refugee Under American Immigration Laws."

MANN, ERIKA, and ERIC ESTORICK. "Private and Governmental Aid of Refugees."

OSTROLENK, BERNHARD. "The Economics of an Imprisoned World— A Brief for the Removal of Immigration Restrictions."

A selection of other contemporary articles used in this study appears in the following list.

BELTH, NORTON. "Problems of Anti-Semitism in the United States," *Contemporary Jewish Record,* II (May–June, 1939), 6–19.

BENTWICH, NORMAN. "The Evian Conference and After," *Fortnightly,* CL (September, 1938), 287–295.

———. "The International Problem of Refugees," *Foreign Policy Reports,* XI (February 12, 1936), 306–316.

" 'Christian American' Jew Baiting," *Christian Social Action,* IV (September, 1939), 101–115.

COHEN, FELIX S. "Exclusionary Immigration Laws—Their Social and Economic Consequences," *Contemporary Jewish Record,* III (March-April, 1940), 141–155.

COUNTESS WALDECK. "The Great New Migration," *Foreign Affairs,* XV (April, 1937), 537–546.

CRANSTON, ALAN. "Congress and the Alien," *Contemporary Jewish Record,* III (May–June, 1940), 245–252.

FORD, COREY, and ALASTAIR MACBAIN. "Uncle Sam's Icebox," *Collier's,* CVII (January 4, 1941), 28–30, 40.

FRY, VARIAN. "Our Consuls at Work," *Nation,* CLIV (May 2, 1942), 507–509.

GOTTSCHALK, MAX. "The Jewish Emigrant—1941," *Contemporary Jewish Record,* IV (June, 1941), 261–268.

HIGH, STANLEY. "Star-Spangled Fascists," *Saturday Evening Post,* CCXI (May 27, 1939), 5–7, 70–73.

HOLDRIDGE, DESMOND. "An Investigation of the Prospect for White Settlement in British Guiana," *Geographical Review,* XXIX (October, 1939), 622–642.

IRWIN, THEODORE. "Inside the 'Christian Front,' " *Forum,* CIII (March, 1940), 102–108.

KEYHOE, DONALD E., and JOHN JAY DALY. "Hitler's Slave Spies in America," *American Magazine,* CXXXI (April, 1941), 14–15, 120–121.

KRAMER, DALE. "The American Fascists," *Harper's Magazine,* CLXXXI (September, 1940), 380–393.

LASKER, BRUNO. "An Atlas of Hope," *Survey Graphic,* XXIX (November, 1940), 583–590.

LAVINE, HAROLD. "Fifth Column 'Literature,'" *Saturday Review of Literature,* XXII (September 14, 1940), 3–4, 14, 16.

LEIPER, HENRY SMITH. "Those German Refugees," *Current History,* L (May, 1939), 19–22ff.

LUBELL, SAMUEL. "War by Refugee," *Saturday Evening Post,* CCXIII (March 29, 1941), 12–13, 88–90, 92.

LUNDBERG, ISABEL. "Who Are These Refugees?" *Harper's Magazine,* CLXXXII (January, 1941), 164–172.

"Nazi Agents in the U.S.," *Fortune,* XXII (October, 1940), 46–51ff.

POPPER, DAVID H. "International Aid to German Refugees," *Foreign Policy Reports,* XIV (November 1, 1938), 186–196.

PRICE, A. GRENFELL. "Refugee Settlement in the Tropics," *Foreign Affairs,* XVIII (July, 1940), 659–670.

REYNOLDS, QUENTIN. "Unwanted," *Collier's,* CIII (February 11, 1939), 12–13, 28, 30.

RITCHIE, FRANK. "America Needs Them," *Forum,* CI (June, 1939), 319–320.

ROSEN, JOSEPH A. "New Neighbors in Sosua," *Survey Graphic,* XXX (September, 1941), 474–478.

SHUSTER, GEORGE N. "The Conflict Among Catholics," *American Scholar,* X (Winter, 1940–41), 5–16.

STEWART, MAXWELL S. "The Immigrant as a Worker," *Social Work Today,* VII (December, 1939), 39, 44.

STUART, GRAHAM H. "Wartime Visa-Control Procedure," *Department of State Bulletin,* XI (September 10, 1944), 271–278.

THOMPSON, DOROTHY. "Escape in a Frozen World," *Survey Graphic,* XXVIII (February, 1939), 93–96, 168–169.

———. "Refugees, A World Problem," *Foreign Affairs,* XVI (April, 1938), 375–387.

"Voices of Defeat: Dissident Groups Sow Lies and Hate within U.S.," *Life,* XII (April 13, 1942), 86ff.

WAGG, ALFRED, III. "Washington's Stepchild: The Refugee," *New Republic,* CIV (April 28, 1941), 592–594.

Three serial publications, absolutely essential to a study of American refugee policy in the 1930's and early 1940's, yielded both primary and secondary material. The *Contemporary Jewish Record,* published by the American Jewish Committee from 1938 through June 1945, was a bimonthly compendium of significant articles and responsible reporting of events of importance to Jews and others. The *American Jewish Year Book,* also sponsored by the American Jewish Committee, annually brought together important factual information, useful reports and articles, and a comprehensive and penetrating "Review of the Year." Issued approximately weekly by the Foreign Language Information Service (after June 1940, the Common Council for American Unity), *Interpreter Releases* provided indispensable immigration information, including statistics, reports on legislation before Congress, and explanations of administrative procedures. The sponsoring organization, based in New York City, worked in the interest of the foreign born and of cultural pluralism.

## STATISTICS

Statistics used in this study have been drawn mainly from the annual reports of the Immigration and Naturalization Service, the *Monthly Review* of the same agency, *Interpreter Releases,* and the *American Jewish Year Book.* The Immigration and Naturalization Service also kindly supplied some statistics not otherwise available.

# Secondary Sources

### BOOKS AND PAMPHLETS ON THE REFUGEE ISSUE

No attempt will be made to list here the mountainous literature on the Jewish holocaust. The reader seeking a starting place might choose Raul Hilberg, *The Destruction of the European Jews* (Chicago, 1961), or Leon Poliakov, *Harvest of Hate: The Nazi Program for the Destruction of the Jews of Europe* (Philadelphia, 1954), or

Gerald Reitlinger, *The Final Solution: The Attempt to Exterminate the Jews of Europe 1939–1945* (New York, 1953).

Displacement of vast numbers of people and international efforts to cope with the continuing problem since World War I have called forth several works. Sir John Hope Simpson, *The Refugee Problem: Report of a Survey* (London, 1939) is a classic study for the period from World War I into late 1938. Simpson's *Refugees: Preliminary Report of a Survey* (New York, 1938) and *Refugees: A Review of the Situation Since September 1938* (London, 1939) are useful supplements, as is his later pamphlet *The Refugee Question* (2d ed., London, 1940). Malcolm J. Proudfoot carries the story through 1952 in *European Refugees: 1939–52* (Evanston, Ill., 1956). Jacques Vernant, *The Refugee in the Post-War World* (London, 1953) is basically a detailed analysis, country by country, of the refugee situation in the early 1950's. John G. Stoessinger, *The Refugee and the World Community* (Minneapolis, 1956) focuses on the development of international organization in response to the refugee problem from World War I into the mid-1950's. Louise W. Holborn has written the history of *The International Refugee Organization* (London, 1956).

A general study of Jewish population movement is Mark Wischnitzer, *To Dwell in Safety: The Story of Jewish Migration since 1800* (Philadelphia, 1949). Very helpful on the topic of Jewish fugitives from Nazism is Arieh Tartakower and Kurt R. Grossmann, *The Jewish Refugee* (New York, 1944).

Old, but by no means out of date, is Maurice R. Davie, *Refugees in America* (New York, 1947), an account of refugees from Nazism and their adjustment to the United States. Donald P. Kent has contributed *The Refugee Intellectual: The Americanization of the Immigrants of 1933–1941* (New York, 1953). Sophia M. Robison, *Refugees at Work* (New York, 1942) reports briefly on a 1941 survey of occupational patterns of refugees, mostly in the New York City area. A very recent book on American policy toward Jewish refugees from Nazism is Arthur D. Morse, *While Six Million Died: A Chronicle of American Apathy* (New York, 1968).

STUDIES OF REFUGEE AID AGENCIES

Thirty-five to 40 American agencies worked on behalf of refugees. An annotated list of many of these organizations appeared in *Survey*

*Graphic*, XXIX (November, 1940). Much more complete information is available for several agencies. Herbert Agar, *The Saving Remnant: An Account of Jewish Survival since 1914* (London, 1960) tells about the American Jewish Joint Distribution Committee. Kathryn Close has sketched the work of the United States Committee for the Care of European Children in *Transplanted Children* (New York, 1953). Donald A. Lowrie, *The Hunted Children* (New York, 1963) traces rescue efforts of several agencies in Vichy France. Lyman C. White's *300,000 New Americans* (New York, 1957), a history of United Service for New Americans, provides coverage of that organization's predecessor, the National Refugee Service. Other accounts are A. Leon Kubowitzki (ed.), *Unity in Dispersion: A History of the World Jewish Congress* (New York, 1948); James F. Lewis, "The Unitarian Service Committee" (Ph.D. dissertation, University of California, 1952); and Mark Wischnitzer, *Visas to Freedom: The History of HIAS* (Cleveland and New York, 1956).

OTHER BOOKS

BOWMAN, ISAIAH (ed.). *Limits of Land Settlement: A Report on Present-day Possibilities.* New York, 1937.

CANTRIL, HADLEY (ed.). *Public Opinion: 1935–1946.* Princeton, 1951.

DIVINE, ROBERT A. *American Immigration Policy, 1924–1952.* New Haven, 1957.

FIELD, HENRY. *"M" Project for F.D.R.: Studies on Migration and Settlement.* Ann Arbor, 1962.

GROSSMANN, KURT R. *Ten Years: American Federation of Jews from Central Europe, Inc., 1941–1951.* New York, 1952.

HIGHAM, JOHN. *Strangers in the Land: Patterns of American Nativism 1860–1925.* New Brunswick, N.J., 1955; New York, 1963.

ISRAEL, FRED L. (ed.). *The War Diary of Breckinridge Long.* Lincoln, Nebr., 1966.

LAVINE, HAROLD. *Fifth Column in America.* New York, 1940.

LEE, ALFRED M. and ELIZABETH B. LEE (eds.). *The Fine Art of Propaganda.* New York, 1939.

SAENGER, GERHART. *Today's Refugees, Tomorrow's Citizens.* New York, 1941.

SHIRER, WILLIAM L. *The Rise and Fall of the Third Reich.* New York, 1960.

STEMBER, CHARLES HERBERT, and others. *Jews in the Mind of America.* New York, 1966.

STRONG, DONALD S. *Organized Anti-Semitism in America: The Rise of Group Prejudice During the Decade 1930–1940.* Washington, 1941.

WHALEN, RICHARD J. *The Founding Father: The Story of Joseph P. Kennedy.* New York, 1964.


OTHER PAMPHLETS

DAVIE, MAURICE R., and SAMUEL KOENIG. *The Refugees Are Now Americans.* Public Affairs Pamphlet. New York, 1945.

GASTER, THEODOR H. *A Digest of Nazi Legislation Against the Jews.* New York, 1940.

GENERAL JEWISH COUNCIL. *Father Coughlin: His "Facts" and Arguments.* [New York], 1939.

GINZBERG, ELI. *Report to American Jews.* New York, 1942.


ARTICLES

BETTELHEIM, BRUNO. "Freedom from Ghetto Thinking," *Midstream,* VIII (Spring, 1962), 16–25.

BRODY, DAVID. "American Jewry, the Refugees and Immigration Restriction (1932–1942)," *Publications of the American Jewish Historical Society,* XLV (June, 1956), 219–247.

ESH, SHAUL. "Between Discrimination and Extermination," *Yad Washem Studies,* II, 79–93. Jerusalem, 1958.

GROSSMANN, KURT R. "Refugees, DP's, and Migrants," in Institute of Jewish Affairs, *The Institute Anniversary Volume,* 118–154. New York, 1962.

"The Jewish Catastrophe and Its Aftermath," in Institute of Jewish Affairs, *The Institute Anniversary Volume,* 49–84. New York, 1962.

PRINZ, ARTHUR. "The Role of the Gestapo in Obstructing and Promoting Jewish Emigration," *Yad Washem Studies,* II, 205–218. Jerusalem, 1958.

TENENBAUM, JOSEPH. "The Crucial Year 1938," *Yad Washem Studies,* II, 49–77. Jerusalem, 1958.

# Index

The following abbreviations are used in the Index:

| | |
|---|---|
| FDR | *Franklin D. Roosevelt* |
| ICR | *Intergovernmental Committee on Refugees* |
| INS | *Immigration and Naturalization Service* |
| LPC | *"likely to become a public charge"* |
| PAC | *President's Advisory Committee on Political Refugees* |
| USC | *United States Committee for the Care of European Children* |

Dunn, Matthew A., 124
Early, Stephen, 119
Einstein, Albert, 25, 94, 198
Emergency Rescue Committee, 141–42, 147, 149, 163, 167–68
Emergency visa program for political and intellectual refugees. *See* Political refugees
Emerson, Sir Herbert, 32, 33, 55
Emerson, Ralph, 12
Emigration from Germany. *See* Germany, emigration from
Espionage. *See* Fifth column; Nazi subversion tactics
European-Jewish Children's Aid, 132
Evian Conference: significance of US initiative in calling, vii; definition of refugee, viii, ix; origins and purposes, 32–33, 43–45; FDR's motivation in calling, 44–45; international response to call for, 45; US reaction to call for, 45–46, 68; US preparations for, 47–48; sessions, 48–50; Jewish disunity at, 49; established ICR, 50; American evaluation of, 51; mentioned, 57, 61, 68, 73, 134, 169
Fairbanks, Alaska, Chamber of Commerce, 106
Fascism: tendencies toward in US, 14–21
Federal Bureau of Investigation (FBI): and Christian Front, 19; and subversion, 187; and screening of refugees, 194, 200, 201; mentioned, 198
Federal Council of Churches, 20, 45, 48, 78, 105
Feuchtwanger, Lion, 168
Field, Henry, 59
Field, Marshall, III, 77, 118, 198
Fifth column: described, 184; and US periodical press, 185–86; linked with refugee immigration, 185, 188–91; seriousness of threat, 203, 212
——— anxiety about: and question of refugee immigration, 107, 211; and State Department action to exclude subversives, 114, 115, 173–79 passim, 192–94, 195–96; and emergency program for political refugees, 141, 143–44, 148; effects in US consulates, 162; and legislation to exclude subversives, 173, 178–79, 194–95, 211; a cause of tightened visa policies, 174, 177, 181–83, 191–93, 194; in US, 184–87, 188–91; and closing of German consulates in US, 197
Fisher, Dorothy Canfield, 83
Foreign Language Information Service, 24, 87
*Fortune*, 47, 185, 186, 187
Fosdick, Reverend Harry Emerson, 77

France: as a refugee receiver, 33, 34, 37; at Evian, 49; and ICR, 52; response to Night of Broken Glass, 72; and admission of child refugees, 97
French refugee camps, 129–30, 132
Friends, Society of. *See* American Friends Service Committee
Frost, Arthur C., 158
Fry, Varian, 142, 163
German-American Bund, 14–15, 18, 21, 187
German American Congress for Democracy, 191
German children: conditions of, 74–75, 80
German Foreign Ministry, 35–36
German Jews: Nazi definition of, viii; descriptive data, 27; persecution of, 27–29; numbers, 27, 37, 232n*l*, 234n*l7*; emigration encouraged by Nazis into 1941, 35–36, 172; extermination plans, 35–36, 205; Bettelheim's comments on, 36, 39; causes for failure to leave Germany, 36–39; efforts to leave Germany, 37–39. *See also* Germany, emigration from; Night of Broken Glass
Germany, emigration from: numbers and destinations, 28, 29, 33–34, 37–38; removal of capital problem, 28, 34, 36, 50, 53–54; to Poland, 33; and world resistance to immigration, 34, 36, 37–39, 57; Nazi pressure on Jews to leave, 35–36, 172; halted in 1941, 36, 205; refugee ships problem, 38–39; in response to Night of Broken Glass, 72, 74–75; by political refugees, 137, 258n*l*. *See also* German Jews; Immigration into US
Gestapo: pressure on Jews to emigrate, 35, 38; and political refugees, 137, 138, 150, 151; and espionage in US, 190–91; mentioned, 198, 203
Glass, Carter, 122
Goebbels, Paul Joseph, 18, 72
Goering, Hermann, 54, 56
Goold, Herbert S., 166
Gordon, Paul W., 101
GPU (Russian secret police), 138, 192
Graham, Frank Porter, 77, 89
Great Britain: as a refugee receiver, 33, 37; at Evian, 49; and ICR, 52; response to Night of Broken Glass, 72; and admission of child refugees, 97; US support for, 115, 117; and evacuation of children, 117, 118–19, 121–22, 126. *See also* Children in Great Britain; Palestine
Green, Lex, 110
Green, William, 45, 72–73, 138, 149
Gruening, Ernest, 101

and institution of 4th visa policy, 192–95, 196; and PAC-FDR conference, 200–201; as administrator of refugee affairs, 212

Luxemburg: evacuation of royal family to US, 153; US mission and refugees in, 167

McDonald, James G.: as High Commissioner for Refugees, 31; resignation from High Commission, 31–32; reaction to Nuremberg Laws, 31–32; predicted major refugee crisis, 32, 34; chairman of PAC, 48; and emergency program for political refugees, 139, 145, 146–47, 149; conferences with FDR, 146–47, 200

Maciejewski, Anton, 82
McIntyre, Marvin, 74
McWilliams, Joseph E., 14
Malcolm, Sir Neill, 32, 50
Manning, Helen Taft, 77
Margold, Nathan R., 114
Maritime Commission, US, 153
*Meet the Refugees*, 23
Mercy ships: origins of movement for, 122; enactment of legislation permitting, 122–26; opinion poll on, 123; public response to contrasted with responses to Wagner-Rogers and Schulte bills, 127–28, 131–32; mentioned, 134
Messersmith, George S., 44, 96, 157, 169
*Miami Herald*, 95, 245n28
Military Intelligence Division. *See* War Department
Moley, Raymond, 93
Moseley, George Van Horn, 21
"M" Project for FDR, 59
Mundelein, George Cardinal, 19, 76
Munich Conference, 30, 52, 219
Nansen, Fridtjof, 30–31
Nansen Office for Refugees, 30–31, 32
"Nansen passport," 30–31
*Nation:* denounced Schacht Plan, 54; opposed Rublee Plan, 54; on Congress and immigration, 67; for child refugee legislation, 76; on Wagner-Rogers Bill, 85, 92; silent on Alaska Bill, 104; on fifth column, 186; rejoinder to Bullitt, 189; challenged Krebs's testimony, 191; criticism of 4th visa policy, 198–99
National Association for the Advancement of Colored People, 45
National Catholic Welfare Conference, 19, 80–81
National Child Labor Committee, 78
National Committee for Alaskan Development, 105
*National Jewish Monthly*, 6, 24, 198
National Origins Immigration Act. *See* Immigration Act of 1924

National Refugee Service: survey of refugee businesses in US, 8; resettlement of refugees, 26; and 3rd visa policy, 176, 177; mentioned, 105

Nativism: and US response to refugee crisis, 3, 10–14, 210; bases of, 10–13; in Congress, 10, 12, 13, 211; and suspicion of "internationalists," 11–12; and suspicion of Labor Department and INS, 12; and failure of Wagner-Rogers Bill, 94–95; and failure of Alaska Bill, 111–12; and fifth column fears, 185. *See also* Restrictionists

Naval Intelligence, Office of, 148, 194, 200, 201

Nazi agents. *See* Fifth column
Nazi persecution of Jews. *See* Jews
Nazi subversion tactics: use of refugees in, 182–83; British and French precautions against, 184; described by Krebs, 190–91; and closing of German consulates in US, 197

Neilson, William A., 77, 149
Netherlands: as a refugee receiver, 33, 37; at Evian, 49; and ICR, 52; response to Night of Broken Glass, 72; and admission of child refugees, 97

Neutrality Act of 1939, 122–26, 152
*New Palestine*, 55
*New Republic:* and the *St. Louis*, 38; denounced Schacht Plan, 54; favored increased refugee immigration, 74; and Alaska settlement plans, 104; accused State Department of anti-Semitism, 163, 198–99; criticism of 4th visa policy, 198–99; mentioned, 24

*Newsweek*, 44, 50, 93
New York *Daily News*, 129
*New York Herald Tribune*, 88, 189–90
New York State Chamber of Commerce, 11
New York State Senate, 78
*New York Times:* on Alaskan reaction to refugee settlement plans, 103; on evacuation of British children, 118, 123, 126, 127; early reports on 4th visa policy, 193, 194

Niebuhr, Reinhold, 198
Night of Broken Glass: Coughlin's reaction to, 18; further persecution in wake of, 29, 72; indicative of shift in Nazi Jewish policy, 36; effect on ICR negotiations, 52; summary of events, 71–72; world reaction, 72; US reaction, 72–74; effect on German children, 74–75; mentioned 34, 95, 97, 99, 167, 169, 209, 210

Non-Aryans, viii, 27, 28
Non-Sectarian Committee for German Refugee Children: origins and forma-

tion, 76–77; efforts for child refugee legislation, 76–77, 81–82, 83–84, 88–93 passim; care plan for child refugees, 77; state branches, 82; and Wagner-Rogers Bill hearings, 83–84, 86, 88–89, 90; accused of conspiracy, 86–87; dropped Wagner-Rogers Bill, 93, 96; shifted basis of child aid plans, 93–94; and Alaska Bill, 104; mentioned, 87, 91

Non-Sectarian Foundation for Refugee Children, 94, 97

Nuremberg Laws, 28–29, 31–32

O'Day, Caroline, 97, 123, 131

Office of Naval Intelligence, 148, 194, 200, 201

O'Neill, Mrs. Arthur J., 85–86

*Opinion,* 24–25, 198

Opinion polls. *See* Public opinion polls

Orinoco River valley: suggested for refugee settlement, 59–60

Ostrolenk, Bernhard, 8

Oswego, N.Y., refugee camp, 218

Otto, Archduke of Austria, 138

Pace, Stephen, 69

Palestine: as a refugee haven, 33, 37, 209; attempts at illegal entry into, 37, 38; discussion of excluded from Evian Conference, 49

—— British immigration policy regarding: criticized by Jewish press in US, 24–25; from 1933–1937, 34, 233–234n13; White Paper of 1939, 34, 37; and the *Struma,* 38–39

Patriotic Order Sons of America, 78

Patriotic orders, 78–79, 84, 128

Patten, J. H., 12–13, 86–87

Pell, Herbert, 143–44, 145

Pell, Robert, 56

Pelley, William Dudley, 14, 15–17, 21

Perkins, Frances: distrusted by restrictionists, 12–13, 47; alleged Jewishness, 16; favored child refugee legislation, 76, 95; mentioned, 68, 86, 187

Philadelphia *Evening Bulletin,* 6

Phillips, William, 58

Pickett, Clarence E.: executive director of Non-Sectarian Committee, 77; on plight of German children, 80, 81, 86; on status of Wagner-Rogers Bill, 87, 90; and Alaska Bill, 108; and offer to help staff US consulates, 169; and rabbinical students in Japan, 192

Pioneers of Alaska, 106

*PM* (New York City), 24

Poage, William R., 90, 92

Pogroms of November 1938. *See* Night of Broken Glass

Pol, Heinz, 189

Polish refugee children, 129–30

Political refugees: persecution by Nazis, 27, 137; US government and, 115, 137–41, 142–50, 151, 212; numbers, 137, 258n1; inclusion of intellectuals in program for, 137–38; US private groups and, 137–39, 141–42, 146; PAC and, 138–40 passim, 143–48 passim; statistics on emergency program for, 143, 144–45, 148–49; screening procedures for, 148, 193–94; and difficulty in reaching Lisbon, 150–51; and transportation problems, 151–54; and alleged involuntary spying, 190–91

Polls of public opinion. *See* Public opinion polls

Portugal: refugees in, 129, 130, 134, 150–51; and transit of refugees bound overseas, 150–51

Pre-examination system for immigration, 181

President's Advisory Committee on Political Refugees (PAC): formation and original duties of, 47–48; work with ICR, 55; and Dominican Republic project, 61, 139; and child refugee legislation, 96; and Virgin Islands refugee plan, 114; and Continental European refugee children, 133; and emergency program for political and intellectual refugees, 138–40 passim, 143–48 passim; financing of, 139; friction with State Department, 142–43, 145–48 passim, 200–201; and refugee transportation problems, 153–54; efforts to modify 4th visa policy, 199–201; mentioned, 81, 137, 144, 149, 192

Press, Jewish, 24–25, 197–98

Press, US: on issue of refugees as job competitors, 6, 9; and debarkation of refugees, 23; on Evian Conference, 45, 51; and colonization plans, 58; and Night of Broken Glass, 72–73; on Wagner-Rogers Bill, 78, 82; and Alaskan settlement plans, 102–103, 106; and evacuation of British children, 118; criticism of State Department, 148. *See also, Miami Herald; Newsweek;* New York *Daily News; New York Herald Tribune; New York Times; Time; Washington Daily News*

Press Conferences of FDR. *See* Roosevelt, Franklin D.

*Problem of Alaskan Development, The,* 99–103, 105, 106, 110

*Protocols of the Elders of Zion,* 17–18, 19–20

Public opinion polls: on Coughlin's broadcasts, 17; on American attitudes toward Jews, 22–23, 225n3; on refugee immigration, 47, 210; on withdrawal of

US ambassador from Germany, 73; on Nazi persecution, 73; on legislation for German refugee children, 95, 210; on evacuation of English and French children, 117–18; on mercy ships, 123; on fifth column in US, 185
Pulsifer, Mrs. Harold T., 125
Quakers. *See* American Friends Service Committee
Quotas. *See* Immigration Act of 1924
Rainey, Homer P., 89
Rankin, John, 10, 14
*Reader's Digest*, 186
Ready, Monseigneur Michael J., 80–81
Red Cross, 122, 129
Rees, Edward H., 89–90
Refugee aid organizations: quietism regarding US refugee policy, 23–24; quietism regarding immigration legislation, 67–68, 70–71, 210; causes for quietism, 67–69, 70–71, 210
*Refugee Facts*, 9, 23, 26
Refugee havens, 57–62
*Refugee Immigration—Facts and Figures*, 25
Refugee ships tragedy, 38–39
Refugees, intellectual. *See* Political refugees
Refugees, political. *See* Political refugees
*Refugees at Work*, 217
Reorganization Act of 1939, 188
Resettlement of refugees, 57–62
Restrictionists: and FDR's refugee policy, 5, 45, 46–47, 67–68; linked refugees with unemployment, 5–8, 9; and estimates of refugee influx, 13, 70, 217; strength of feared by pro-refugee groups, 67–69, 70–71; and antialien legislation, 69, 70; attacked Labor Department, 70; fought Wagner-Rogers Bill, 78, 79–80, 84, 88; in Senate, 82–83; feared erosion of quota system, 85, 88; and mercy ships, 128. *See also* Nativism
Review procedures in refugee immigration cases, 201–203
Reynolds, Quentin, 75
Reynolds, Robert Rice: on refugee job competition, 6; nativism of, 10; quoted Coughlin on refugees, 13; and antialien bills of 1939, 69–70, 92; fought Wagner-Rogers Bill, 87, 92; opposed Alaska refugee plans, 103, 108–109; on fifth column threat, 185, 190
Reynolds antialien bills of 1939, 69–70, 92
Ribble, F.D.G., 202–204
Rivesaltes, France, detention camp, 130, 132
Robsion, John M., 124, 125

Rogers, Edith Nourse, 75, 76, 78, 81
Roland German American Democratic Society, 105
Roosevelt, Eleanor: a sponsor of Non-Sectarian Foundation, 94; and formation of USC, 94, 118; and Wagner-Rogers Bill, 97; and evacuation of European children, 117, 118; and political refugees, 142, 145, 147, 149; and Zurich consulate, 157; mentioned, 198
Roosevelt, Franklin D. (FDR): and Evian Conference, vii, 33, 43–45, 51; continued, but eased, Hoover LPC policy, 4–5, 168; opened quotas to full use, 5, 43, 168; response of German-American Bund to, 15; alleged Jewish ancestry, 16; reactions to *Anschluss*, 43–44; press conferences of, 43, 119, 123, 129, 182, 187; criticized for pro-refugee policies, 45–47, 68, 74; and formation of PAC, 47–48; no support for government funds for refugee relocation, 48; no support for widening quotas, 48, 73; and refugee colonization plans, 58, 59–60, 61–62; protested Night of Broken Glass, 73; extended visitors' visas for refugees, 73, 169, 211; inaction on Wagner-Rogers Bill, 96–97; and Alaska as a refugee haven, 99, 101–102; and Virgin Islands refugee plan, 114; and refugee relief supplies, 116; and aid to Britain, 117; and evacuation of Continental European children, 117, 129; and evacuation of British children, 119, 120, 123; and emergency program for political refugees, 145, 146–47, 150; and 1st and 2nd visa policies, 168–70; and fear of fifth column, 173, 182–83, 187–88; and 3rd visa policy, 174, 177, 212; and 4th visa policy, 200–201; summary of refugee policy of, 211; ambiguity of refugee policy of, 212–13; mentioned, passim
Rosenberg, James N., 61
Rublee, George: named director of ICR, 51–52; resigned from ICR, 55; on world resistance to refugee immigration, 57; member of Non-Sectarian Committee, 77; sponsor of Non-Sectarian Foundation, 94. *See also* Intergovernmental Committee on Refugees; Rublee Plan
Rublee Plan, 54–56
Rummel, Most Reverend Joseph F., 48, 81
Russell, Richard B., 83, 179, 195
Ryan, Monseigneur John A., 19
*St. Louis* (steamship), 38
*Saturday Evening Post*, 190
Schacht, Hjalmar H.G., 53–54
Schacht Plan, 53–54, 55

for questioned, 80–81; and question of dividing families, 80, 81, 84–85; development of pressure for, 81–82, 83–84, 92–93; polls in Congress on, 82–83, 91; hearings on, 84–87, 88–91; and anti-Semitism, 85–86; proposed changes in, 90, 92; amended, 91–92; efforts to salvage, 92–93; abandoned, 93; public opinion surveys on, 95; and Labor Department, 95–96; opposed by State Department, 96; and FDR, 96–97; and Eleanor Roosevelt, 97; reception of contrasted with that of mercy ships plan, 127–28

Waller, George P., 167

War Department: and British Guiana refugee project, 60; screening of refugees by Military Intelligence Division of, 148, 194, 200, 201; reported spies in Canal Zone, 188–89

Warren, Avra M.: and Zurich consulate, 156–57, 158–60; tried to increase US consular staffs in Europe, 169; and legislation to exclude subversives, 173; and 3rd visa policy, 173–74, 175–76; and "unblocking" of quotas, 180; mentioned, 177, 183, 204. See also Visa Division

Warren, George L., 139, 145, 146–47

Washington Daily News, 119

Watson, Edwin M., 147

Welles, Sumner: and origins of Evian Conference, 44; and formation of PAC,

48; on failure of ICR, 51; and Alaska as a refugee haven, 101–102; and problem of French exit permits, 142; visit to Zurich, 158; on opening of quotas to full use, 236n1; mentioned, 97, 145, 147

Whelchel, B. Frank, 69

White, William Allen, 77, 83, 198

White Paper of May 1939, 34, 37

Whitney, Alexander F., 77

Wilbur, Ray Lyman, 82

Willkie, Wendell, 119

Wilmeth, James L., 88

Wilson, Hugh R., 73

Winchell, Walter, 25

Winrod, Reverend Gerald B., 10–11, 19–20, 21, 73

Wise, Mrs. Stephen S., 77

Wise, Rabbi Stephen S., 55

Wohlthat, Helmuth, 54, 56

Women's Committee for Mercy Ships. See American Women's Committee for the Release of Mercy Ships for Children

Women's International League for Peace and Freedom, 87, 156–57

Workmen's Circle, 127, 198

Workmen's Circle Call, 198

Works Progress Administration, 89–90

World Service, 20

Worrell, Margaret Hopkins, 85

Young Women's Christian Association, 23, 24, 45, 78